The Walton Gang

WINNING
BASKETBALL'S
OSCAR HAS
BECOME HABIT
(9 OF THE LAST 10)
FOR JOHN
WOODEN
BUT HE ADMITS
THIS ONE WAS
THE BEST
OF ALL...

1973
NCAA
CHAMPS

BEST
PERFORMANCE
BILL WALTON
21 OF 22 SHOTS,
RECORD 44 POINTS

The
Walton
Gang

by Bill Libby

Coward,
McCann
& Geoghegan

New York

SBN: 698-10565-6

Library of Congress Catalog Card Number: 73-78769

Printed in the United States of America

To Allyson's "Poppy," her father; Ron Adler, a graduate of UCLA; his wife, Elaine; their son, Jeremy; Ron's mother and father, Vera and Herbert Adler, Allyson's "Omi" and "Opi"; and Ron's brother, Frankie. In friendship in the most civilized of worlds. And with hope for their happy life.

Acknowledgments

The author is most deeply grateful to all who contributed in one way or another to this book, including Matt Merola and Paul Goetz of Mattgo Enterprises; Peggy Brooks of Coward, McCann and Geoghegan, publishers; Athletic Director J. D. Morgan, Coach John Wooden and his assistant coaches and UCLA players, past and present; Vic Kelley and Frank Stewart of the UCLA Athletic Information Department; Stan Troutman and Norm Schindler of the UCLA Campus Studio Photography Department; photographer James Roark and artist Karl Hubenthal of the *Los Angeles Herald-Examiner;* writer Rich Roberts of the *Long Beach Independent-Press-Telegram,* writer Mitch Chortkoff of the *San Diego Tribune and Union;* artist-writer Murray Olderman of *Newspaper Enterprise Association;* Ben Olan of the Associated Press in New York; Jerry Miles, National Collegiate Athletic Association Director of Public Relations and many others.

Front jacket photo by Norm Schindler. All inside photos identified as from UCLA by Norm Schindler or Stan Troutman and the UCLA Campus Studio Photography Department and from them or from the UCLA Athletic Department.

Many other photos, so identified, by James Roark of the *Los Angeles Herald-Examiner.*

Title page cartoon by Karl Hubenthal of the *Los Angeles Herald-Examiner.*

The Walton Gang

1

They kept saying it wasn't all that important, but, of course, it was. This, more than anything else in their lives at this time was what they were doing, and it was important to them to do it right. They kept saying it was the championship, which would come at the end of the season, which was the most important thing this season and every season, and this other thing, this record winning streak, was just something else, a token, a matter of arithmetic which didn't matter, but they must have known better. They already had captured the championship, their school had captured more championships than any other school, but they didn't have the record, another school had it, and they wanted it so much they did not dare admit it.

Everyone who was interested in sports knew who held college basketball's all-time longest winning streak, but before UCLA began to dominate basketball on the college level in the early 1960s and made it easy by winning every year or almost every year, few could tell you who won the championship a year before or a few years before. There is a champion crowned every year, but a team comes along to threaten the all-time record winning streak only once every five or ten or twenty years, and they could tell all the little white lies about it they wanted, you knew better, anyone who knew players and coaches and teams and games knew better.

It was a way of trying to ease the tension, of relieving the pressure for John Robert Wooden, the coach, to say, "We'd like to get the record, but it isn't what counts; it's the championship that counts, that's what we really want," or for William Theodore Walton, the star player, to say, "These are just two more games in the middle of the season, and it's only the games at the end of the season that really mean anything." But it was just talk, what they thought were the right things to say, it was only words without real meaning.

They also said these two teams they had to play and beat to get the record were good teams who could beat them, but everyone knew better about this, too, everyone knew this was just talk, too, because there was no way these teams, Loyola of Chicago and Notre Dame, could beat UCLA if UCLA did not beat themselves; they may have been good, but they weren't good enough, and the Bruins, nicknamed "The Walton Gang," were great, maybe the greatest team ever to play college basketball, and if they worried at all about losing, it was because it would be almost a disgrace for a team this good to be defeated by one of those other two teams and not take exclusive possession of the only laurel that had eluded them.

In John Wooden's twenty-fifth year as UCLA basketball coach, his Bruins were well on their way to the school's ninth National Collegiate Athletic Association championship in 10 years. He had been coaching for 28 years and had been coach at UCLA for 15 years before his team had won a championship and then he had lost only once in 10 years. And now his teams' domination of this sport was so complete it threatened to destroy interest in it, to wreck the enthusiasm of other schools that played in it and those who followed it.

His greatest team, The Walton Gang, was halfway through its second straight undeafeated season, an accomplishment never before achieved in college basketball, coming on, almost coasting, toward a second straight coveted crown, and on the way they had to finish up a job started a few years earlier by another of the several UCLA teams that had dominated the decade.

Wooden's earlier great teams had been led by other great players, by Walt Hazzard and Gail Goodrich and Keith Erickson and Lew Alcindor and Lucius Allen and Sidney Wicks and Curtis Rowe, but no team had been better than this team and no player better than Bill Walton who led this team, which might go on to stretch this staggering streak of victories to more than 100, and which had only to match the three straight titles of Alcindor's Army to establish beyond argument its claims of superiority.

You could say these were just college kids and just games they played, but they were the best group of college basketball players ever put together; they were tough, skilled kids, young men, really, some of whom were worth a lot of money to the professionals, at least one of whom, Walton, was worth millions, and they can serve as a marvelous example of the raw stock of the big business that is college basketball today, and professional basketball, too, of course, for they are polished by men like Wooden as amateurs and then signed up to take their places in the major leagues, if not by design for that specific purpose, inevitably pointed toward it.

For some, studies count for more. For many who will not be able to make professional basketball, other professions beckon. For some, if they cannot make it, there is nothing else of value. For almost all those who can make it, this is a stepping-stone toward it. Who turns it down who is offered it? No one. Not Rhodes scholars. Not those who will be doctors or lawyers or big businessmen, themselves, later. No one. The gold glitters too brightly.

Bill Walton hates it when his team is called The Walton Gang, a nickname hung on it by the media, a nickname stemming from the cowboy bunch who shot down all who stood in the way of what it wanted in Wild West days, and he will hate it as the title of this book. He is a private person who will give up very little of himself to the press or public, a modest young man who detests the spotlight, an unselfish fellow who wants no more than a share of the success he and his teammates have managed. But he is ignoring reality when he says he is just another player on his team, that his team would win without him. It is nonsense and he must know it. He has his pride and he is no fool.

He is the greatest player on the greatest team, probably the greatest player in the history of college basketball, possibly, potentially, the greatest player in the history of basketball. Only his sore and weak knees, stretched dangerously by his rapid growth, could prevent him from becoming the best if he wants it enough, which he may not. No one says you have to be the best at something even if you can be. Maybe you want to be something else. Bill Walton suggests he wants to be the best, but he may want to be something else, too, a lawyer, perhaps, or a hermit, maybe, with the wild woods as his only companion. But at 6-11, the gangling redhead was a better combination scorer, defender, shot blocker, rebounder, and passer, a more complete college player, than any who had come before him, he dominated games as no college player ever had, and so his team was bound to be called something like the Walton Gang.

The forwards were Keith Wilkes, a minister's son from Santa Barbara, and Larry Farmer from Denver, flashy off the court, subdued on it. The guards were Larry Hollyfield from the ghetto, flashy on the court and an operator off it, and Greg Lee, a coach's son from the San Fernando Valley, but a freethinker, subbing for ailing Tommy Curtis, a cocky, likable character from Florida. When Curtis started, Walton was the only white starter. Until this time, Walton thought of himself as a brother to his black teammates. Shortly, however, a national magazine story broke suggesting Walton preferred to see his buddy, Lee, also white, start, and there was formed for the first time a subtle racial division on this team.

The extra forward was Dave Meyers. The spare center, 6-11 Swen Nater, who might have been the second-best center in the country, seldom played. Seven-foot Ralph Drollinger seldom played. The other subs—Vince Carson, Pete Trgovich, Gary Franklin, Casey Corliss, and Bob Webb—seldom played. One who should have been with them, Andre McCarter, did not even suit up, having dropped out for the season before the season even began. Two years earlier, he had been the best high-school player in Pennsylvania. Two years earlier, Pete Trgovich had been the best high-school player in Indiana, which has as many of the best high-school players annually as almost any other state. Now, they could have been starring for any other college club in the country. But they had come here because they thought they were the best and could beat out the best and now they suffered resentments in the shadows.

It was Wooden who kept them together as a team—the star and the supporting cast. Except for Walton they were not the most talented group he had gathered. With Walton, they were the most effective. There was not a great outside shooter in the bunch, but when they got their good shots and they always got their good shots, they were all good shooters. They were all athletes who had marvelous moves, awesome agility, and complete control of their bodies, even in the air. Even Walton could take a high pass up near the basket, twist in the air any way he had to, and get it in the basket smoothly, as Alcindor and other centers could not.

They could all do things on the move, passing, taking passes, and shooting, slashing through the air, as their foes could not. And they passed unselfishly to give each other their best shots. Except for Walton, they were not a big team. But with Walton blocking shots, rebounding missed shots, and passing out fast to get the fast break running, they did not need a lot of size. With Walton backing them up, they all played deadly defense. They played Wooden's pressing zone defense which destroyed their foes' offensive systems. They played Wooden's system unselfishly. If they did not, they did not play. They played his way, not their way. As long as they were there, his way became their way. And they won that way.

In the middle fifties, Bill Russell's University of San Francisco teams had won two consecutive NCAA titles and put together a winning streak which reached 60 straight games before it was snapped. Now Bill Walton's second UCLA team, on its way to its second consecutive NCAA title, was flying from the Far West to the Midwest to Chicago in quest of its record-tying sixtieth straight triumph in a game against Loyola. That taken care of, it would move on to Indiana to take on Notre Dame in a bid for a sixty-first straight victory and a new record. They had won 14 straight this season, and none had come hard.

The record-tying Loyola game would complete the first half of the season, if you count four playoff games at the end of the season, for the team which got that far, and UCLA could count on those because it was the one team which could count on getting that far. "We count on the championship," one UCLA player said. "As far as we're concerned, the other clubs can send in their games. Why take the trouble to play them? They'll just lose them. They know it and we know it. Coach wouldn't like to hear us say that, but he knows it, too. He would never say it, but he knows it. He doesn't always say what he means. He says what he feels he's supposed to say. I tell it as it is.

"It's so easy for us to win, it's not any fun for us anymore. There's no competition, no challenge. It's just something we're committed to do, like a job. We're workmen, doing piecework. We take 'em to pieces. We take 'em apart one at a time. We laugh at them. That's the only fun we get. That and things like the playoffs and setting the record. We need something special to stir us up. The record is special, so these games coming up are special. We'll laugh through them, but at least they mean something, so they'll be fun to play. Winning isn't fun anymore. Because we never lose. And we ain't gonna lose these games, either."

But Walton insisted, "We can lose. We'll lose sooner or later. No one wins every time." Wooden insisted, "The time comes when you're going to get beat. You're going to play a bad game or the other team is going to play a better game. On a cold night, you're going to catch a hot team. Our streak, any streak, cannot last forever."

Floodlights made the TWA plane seem a Hollywood set before the flight departed. Then the cameramen and interviewers got off and the flight got going. Two blue and gold UCLA pennants dressed up the front of the 747's cabin, and the pretty stewardesses, wearing UCLA T-shirts, brought the eggs benedict and the toasted banana bread to the first-class section, and coach Wooden switched seats so he could better carry on a conversation with a reporter. He was wearing a conservative business suit and conducting himself in a formal manner which is his way.

He is 62 and his close-cut brown hair is flecked with gray and his skin is seamed. He wears horn-rimmed glasses, has a narrow, sharp nose and a pinched expression as though he has just tasted something sour. He smiles frequently, but it is a short smile and sometimes sarcastic. He is a very straight person, who does not smoke or drink or use profanity, but he is a cat who, cornered, could tear you apart. He is scholarly, like a teacher, and he is a teacher, and if you do not do by him as he feels you should, he can with an expression, with a smile, with words without profanity, tear you apart, put you down, put you in your place beneath him.

He has his pride. He deserves to be proud. He has cut his way through a jungle to the top, put himself beyond reach, and he knows it, and his manner, which sometimes seems haughty, sometimes shows it, which is all right, because he is all right, he is brilliant and he has beaten back and beaten down all his rivals without breaking any rules, without once swearing, without asking for any favors, without compromising his principles.

He was saying, "Almost any team we play is capable of beating us on the right night, but I think we have the best team and I think we could beat any team in any series of games, best two out of three, best three out of five, whatever. I am not sure any college team could beat us twice. I am not sure any will beat us once. But, it could happen, especially if we do not play our game, if we do not play as the best team should, and I can only hope our young men know it. We are going into the enemy's lair, but we don't worry about that, about the other teams or the road, we take care of ourselves, and if we do that the rest will take care of itself."

He does not even bother to scout other teams or prepare his teams with special tactics to use on other teams; he prepares his own team to play its game and lets other teams figure out special tactics to try on his teams. He says there are no special tactics that will work on his teams. He says a slowdown style won't work on his teams. He says it over and over again and keeps saying it. Perhaps because slowdowns do work against his teams. They have almost beaten his teams several times and have beaten them a few times in the last ten years. He has been threatened and he has been beaten by other tactics in this time, too, but not as often. He has been beaten only seven times in nine of these 10 years. He has not been beaten at all in four of these years. He has had winning streaks of 41 and 47 games, and now his latest streak is 59 and he was going for the record with the Walton Gang.

Chicago Stadium is an ancient arena not far from The Loop in distance, but a million miles in manner. It sits at the end of the longest skid row around, and as a team buses to the ballpark, it sees out the windows panhandlers and prostitutes on the street and winos, lying in the doorways of splintered tenements. The stadium, itself, is surrounded by a ghetto, its pavements prowled by toughs and strays. The players from sunny southern California, from a school nestling in a wealthy and grassy sector, got off the bus, hit the pavement, and moved into the old building, where George Mikan began as a basketball star and where his modern-era successor, Bill Walton was set to strut his stuff.

"We can give them one hell of a game. We're not afraid of them. After all, we've already played Minnesota and Marquette," said Loyola coach George Ireland.

"I'm not worried at all about this game. UCLA is great, but it doesn't bother us. Bill Walton is good, but he doesn't bother me. He's just a ballplayer," said Loyola center Paul Cohen.

"We like pressure," UCLA center Bill Walton said. "I know I thrive on it. And I like hostile crowds. They make me want to play better."

Wooden said, "I believe we are ready to play. We try to hold an even emotional level, so I have not tried to stir the team. We are worried about the game, but no more than any other game we play. I do not believe the pressure of the streak has gotten to the players. If we lose this weekend, I don't think it will be because we're tight or tense, but because Loyola or Notre Dame play a great enough game to beat us.

"Anybody who doesn't put pressure on himself isn't worth much. But if we permitted outside pressure to influence us very much, we wouldn't be worth much, either. Might we be looking past Loyola to Notre Dame? There always is that danger, but we have an intelligent team and our players can count and I believe they know they cannot win number 61 until they win number 60."

He was conservatively splendid in blue suit, tie and shirt. He seemed as always calm, so calm he appeared to be chewing gum. He said, "Now that we've gotten this close, I definitely want the record. But not so much for myself. I have won so much, while people tend to forget that while UCLA teams have won a great deal, this particular team has not yet won that much. I've gotten so much out of basketball that to be denied something now wouldn't hurt me too much, but these players have worked hard for this and I know they'd be disappointed if it eluded them and I'd like to see them get it."

He smiled one of those spare smiles of his. He said, "I mean this sincerely. I'm not trying to be modest about it. I think false modesty is as bad as having no modesty at all. This is how I honestly believe." At the risk of being immodest, did Wooden believe the Bruins would win these two games? "I believe so," he said.

As so often, the games themselves were almost anticlimactic to the buildup that came before them. UCLA's latest basketball team was just too good to be beaten. The crowd of more than 18,000 fans in Chicago Stadium seemed to sense this; it was strangely quiet from the start, as if expecting the worst.

Loyola gave UCLA as good a game as it could. Getting good outside shooting from its guards, the Ramblers stole an early lead, fell behind by 11 points, fought back with 10 straight points to close within one shortly before intermission, but then faded finally and were put away in the last 10 minutes.

The Bruins were relaxed to the point of carelessness, turning the ball over 27 times. But Cohen could not handle Walton inside. At the start of the Loyola rally, Walton was called for dunking the ball illegally at the offensive end and for goal-tending illegally at the defensive end. He was called for goal-tending six times in the contest.

It bothered him. He shook his head each time in annoyance, smiling that smile of his which says someone must be kidding him, but it didn't bother him as much as a year ago when he was younger and less composed. He just kept moving around and doing all the things he does well and he led his side to a 14-point triumph.

As usual, he played with energy and animation. Aside from the roughhousing with his opposing pivot, he seems to enjoy the game. He works harder than other big men. He jumps up and down and claps his hands at the good plays. He congratulates his teammates expansively for their play. His face expresses his many moods every game. Then the game ends and his face becomes expressionless and he gets away from everyone as fast as he can.

With the last play of this game, tying the record, Walton and his teammates rushed into their dressing room, where reporters almost always are barred. But someone neglected to close the door for a while, and the curious crowded around the doorway to see what they could see, which made the UCLA players, unused to invasions of their privacy, feel like animals in the zoo.

The players stared back. There was no sign of celebration. Walton went to hide in the shower room. Hollyfield opened a can of soda pop and toasted the public. Then someone shut the door. Someone outside asked, "What is this, a museum?" Curry Kirkpatrick of *Sports Illustrated* said, "It was only UCLA Taking It In Stride," all capitalized, of course.

Behind the doors, Hollyfield said, "That's 60. Saturday is 61. Then 62, 63, 64, and we won't have to think about it anymore." Walton and Lee, under orders not to answer interviewers, interviewed each other sarcastically. Asked Walton, "How was it winning number 60? The Ultimate? The Pinnacle?"

"No," Lee answered.

As the bus rolled past the flat farmlands of Indiana, where he was born and reared, toward South Bend where he coached high-school ball and where his son was born, Wooden, wife Nellie by his side, reminisced. "I was born near Indiana University, but played for Purdue University. Notre Dame was the last team to defeat us. It seems somehow appropriate that I should be taking my team to a record game here."

The players were loose and laughing. The acid rock of

Mick Jagger was blasting from Walton's tape deck. "You like this kind of music, don't you, coach?" kidded Walton from the back of the bus.

"I wouldn't turn him on. But he doesn't bug me," said John, who says he will not impose his taste in music, dress, or hairstyle on his young men in this modern era any more than he deems necessary. He says, "These are changing times and I have changed with the times."

Athletic director J. D. Morgan and he have been criticized for scheduling weak teams and playing most of them at home. He lost his temper about this the year before at a press party, critical of a critical article. Morgan condemns such criticism. Both point out schedules are drawn up far in advance when weak teams may seem strong. Both point out they have won their championships on neutral courts.

Now, Wooden seemed pleased he had his team going for the record on the road. He had said, "We aren't the ones on a crusade. Everybody gets passionately up for us. Oh, my, will there be some screaming!" Possibly he was disappointed by the lack of partisan screaming at his side in Chicago. But now he knew it would be different at Notre Dame, where the game had been sold out for two months.

At UCLA, the Bruins had beaten Notre Dame by 26 points earlier in the season, but the Fighting Irish players and their supporters hoped the home court advantage, the challenging chance presented them, and the pressure on their foe would somehow turn things around. As the drums rolled and the cheerleaders led the Irish students in cheers saluting their players, stirring them up, at a pregame rally on campus, the Bruins rested and waited with confidence in their hotel rooms.

Larry Farmer said, "We're here now. We have to think about the record." Larry Hollyfield said, "Sometimes we do save ourselves. These are the kind of games we play great in." Bill Walton said, "We hope to win." John Wooden said, "Walton has the flame in his eyes." Indeed, the big youngster, usually loose before games, seemed to be turning on emotionally before this game.

As he took the court and the more than 11,000 fans packed into the small Irish Convocation Center started to scream at him, booing him, sparks seemed to issue from his eyes.

Notre Dame coach Digger Phelps had said, "It will take a perfect game to beat UCLA, but I think we can do it." Center John Shumate said, "We can beat UCLA. They can only put five men on the court at a time."

But they were five good men who played as a team and one of them was Walton, who played better than anyone else. Notre Dame took it to him physically, but he gave it back. So did Hollyfield, who flailed out with an elbow, laying open the nose of Pete Crotty, a roughhouser called "Karate" by his teammates. Hollyfield just laughed at the lot of them. Walton shouted at them.

All was madness, with the Notre Dame students standing and screaming throughout and throwing coins on court and singing their famed fight song to stir up their side, and the Irish stayed close for a while, but then they started to slip further and further back with Walton taking high passes at the hoop from Lee and twisting whatever way was necessary in the air to drop the ball in and with Wilkes and Farmer firing from short range.

The Irish were so rough, Wooden, losing his usual composure, went over to Phelps even as play was proceeding, and complained about Shumate's tactics against Walton, and threatening to substitute tough Swen Nater to teach Shumate a lesson. "If he doesn't knock it off, I'll send Nater in, and you know what he'll do," threatened Wooden.

"It's a two-way street," responded the startled Phelps.

Later, he laughed it off, saying, "Wooden just asked me if I'd read his book." But, still later, he reported what Wooden really had said, and he admitted anger. Four days later, Wooden sent a note to Phelps, which started, "I owe you and John Shumate an apology and hope you will accept it in the spirit it is offered. . . ."

The incident was of little importance except to betray the tensions that stirred beneath the surface of the coach's composure. In that madhouse of a place, he worried away the record triumph until it was assured him. When it was, and it was by the wide margin of 19 points, he relaxed and removed his regulars from the game.

Walton and his teammates slapped palms and smiled and Big Bill turned to add insult to injury to the Irish rooting section, which responded en masse, "Shut up, Walton." He shut up, retreating to the dressing room for his postgame ritual of icing his sore knees.

Wooden stood out at center court for the ceremony of receiving the ball used in his side's record-setting triumph, with the television cameras sending it all across the nation and he said, "This isn't the greatest thing that's happened on this day. It's my granddaughter's birthday." He smiled. "But the most important thing is that this was cease-fire day in Vietnam. That's much more important than this."

Nevertheless, it was important enough for Wooden to let the reporters into the dressing room to talk to his players, a concession that staggered some. Unsure of themselves, they wandered into these strange surroundings. Hesitantly, they began to ask questions. Wilkes insisted, "Our goal this season wasn't to break the record, but we broke it and I'm proud we did."

The writers went to Walton, who was smiling, which surprised them. His hair was mussed. Sweat was drying on his pale skin. He refused personal credit. "It was an accomplishment for the team," he said. He did not seem excited. No one there, except the reporters, seemed excited. The players, as these players always are, were subdued, smiling, but without the laughter of treasured triumph.

Walton was asked, "Will you remember this game for a long time? More than the others?"

Walton looked at the reporter a moment. Then he said, "No. The game I'll remember most is the game UCLA loses."

Kirkpatrick used it to conclude his *Sports Illustrated* story. It was as good a way as any to sum up the sentiments of The Walton Gang.

2

On court, Bill Walton plays with excesses of energy, animation, and ability.

The young center towers tall at 6 feet, 11 inches in height and may have grown past seven feet by now. He began at UCLA skinny at 210 pounds, but has matured and beefed up and may have passed 230 pounds by now. These are guesses. He does not permit himself to be measured publicly. These are just some of the secrets he keeps. Nor are any such statistics passed on to the press ever reliable. Suffice to say he is one of basketball's taller players and is becoming one of its huskier and stronger performers.

He also is rapidly becoming as good as the best centers, such as the older and more experienced professional centers—Wilt Chamberlain, Nate Thurmond, Willis Reed, Dave Cowens, Elvin Hayes, and Kareem Abdul-Jabbar, whose original name was Lew Alcindor and who shall be called by that name herein because he was known by it when he played at UCLA as Walton's predecessor.

Chamberlain is the biggest all around at 7-1 and 275 pounds and, though in his late thirties seriously slowed down and no longer a scorer, remains the most powerful player in the game, a great rebounder and effective defender and shot blocker. At 6-11 and 225 pounds, the slender, thirtyish Thurmond is frail and often injured, but a deadly defender and unselfish team player. Listed at 7-2, the 230-pound Alcindor/Jabbar may actually be an inch or two taller, and he is the best all-around shot maker among the giants, though in his middle twenties he has not developed into the rebounder, shot blocker, defender, and dominator he had been expected to be.

At 6-10 and 240 pounds, Reed, in his early thirties, is a powerful player, though restricted by continuing problems with his legs. At 6-9 and 230 pounds, Cowens and Hayes are small as centers go, but in their middle twenties, healthy and agile. Hayes is a sharpshooter and strong rebounder, but his statistics surpass his effectiveness as a team player, and he often is played in a corner instead of at center. Cowens does not have enormous natural skills, but he is the best runner among the centers and a team man and he makes the most of himself. Both he and Reed are complete players.

Walton plays more like them than he does the taller players, but he is tall and can do the things tall men can do. He can jump better than most tall men, adding to his reach. As he learns the angles, he may become as good a rebounder as Wilt has been and as the retired Bill Russell was. He can make the fast pass to start the fast break as few others ever could. He cannot yet or does not yet set picks for his shooters as Wilt can. But he handles the ball and dribbles it and passes it as Wilt never could, as few his size ever could. He has tremendous timing and control of his body in the air and he is by far the best shot blocker since the retired Russell. And he is a strong defender.

Walton is not as powerful inside offensively as was Wilt in his prime, and never will be, but he is a better shooter, and while not as versatile a shooter as Alcindor/Jabbar or as good an outside shooter as Hayes or Reed, he could become similar as a scorer, certainly superior to Thurmond or Russell. There is not a player who ever played center who could have taken the high passes from Greg Lee and converted them into baskets as did Walton in the 1973 NCAA championship game. They were wonderful passes, but they were not all on target and some were hard to convert and Walton made them look easy by twisting in the air whichever way necessary to lay them in softly, not permitted to dunk them home, as can pros, some of whom cannot score any other way. With these perfectly timed, twisting-in-the-air soft shots, Walton hit most of the 21 shots he scored with in 22 attempts.

Basketball is a badly constructed game. It was designed as a no-contact game, but with big men going for position on a small court, it has become a contest of continual contact. The big men who can reach the basket easily, beat it easy, and big Bill Walton has not only been beating it, he has been battering it. Only Alcindor dominated it on the college level as Walton has done, and he had help beyond what Walton has had; he had a superior supporting cast because Lucius Allen and Mike Warren and Sidney Wicks and Curtis Rowe were greater than the good players who surround Walton. Walton is as unselfish a team player as Alcindor was. Usually he does not go for the high pass and the easy basket. Usually he does not go for the shot. Usually he scores by rebounding and putting in his team-mates' missed shots.

He is resisting reality when he says, as he has said, "I'm just starting in sports and already I'm being called a superstar and it's just not right. I don't go out on the court to impress anyone. I just try to play my game and help us win. I'm sorry I stand out. It hurts when people talk as if I'm the only player on the team. I wish sportswriters wouldn't ask me anything personal at all. I'd prefer they got the whole team together to talk. I don't like to be singled out as an individual because I don't play as an individual. We play as a team and the team would win without me or any other player, but we could not have done what we have done without any of the other players. This is a team game, and I'm just one of the guys on the team. The big center is important, but we have big centers we could win with playing behind me. One-on-one is the most overrated part of this game. Centers playing against other centers do not decide the games. The five on the floor and those who come off the bench to replace them decide games. The coach who gets them to play as a team decides the games."

Others do not agree, except that he is a team player. John Wooden admits, "Bill has made a good team into a great team. He is an outstanding individual player who plays team ball to bring out the best in his teammates. He accepts coaching as well as any player I've had, and this spirit has made his the most coachable team I've had. He practices and plays with spirit, and this spirit is contagious and has made the team spirited. He is outstanding, but he plays unselfishly, and this has helped the others to be unselfish." Teammate Greg Lee says, "You would have to be a real student of the game to appreciate him. We look to him. He's at the center of everything we do." Teammate Tommy Curtis says, "He's our one indispensable man. We would not be nearly what we are without him. We can all play. Some of us are great players. He's better than that."

USC's Bob Boyd, who has coached against Walton without success, who is one of the few coaches who has had some success against other UCLA teams during the decade of dynasty, has said, "Put Walton on any team in the country, and that team would quite likely be the national champion. He's unreal. He's virtually unstoppable. He has it all. He may be the best ever to play this game."

"Ever?" he was asked.

"Ever," he replied flatly.

"You are taking in a lot of people, like Chamberlain and Jabbar."

"I intend to take in a lot of people, like Chamberlain and Jabbar, for instance."

Shelby Metcalfe of Bradley said, "I thought the Lord divided things up evenly, but he gave it all to Walton." Fred Schaus, coach of Purdue, formerly of the Lakers, said, "He's the best young player I've seen. Maybe Alcindor scored more and Russell was better on defense, but neither at a similar stage did so many things as well as Walton at both ends of the court." Dick Harter, coach of Oregon, said, "Walton's the best big man I've ever seen." Marv Harshman, coach of Washington State, said, "I'm not so sure I'm glad Alcindor graduated. Walton never lets up on you. At least, at times, Alcindor did."

Walton would deny reality when he denies he can be compared to Alcindor. He has said, "It's ridiculous to compare me to him. Players like him come along once in twenty years. He's the best there's been. Comparing me to him means nothing to me or to anyone who really understands the game of basketball." But no one ever dominated a big game the way Bill dominated the NCAA final game against Memphis State in 1973, not even Alcindor. Boyd says, "He's better than Alcindor was because he has more control of the outcome of his games." Jerry Tarkanian, formerly of Cal State at Long Beach, says, "He's better than Alcindor because he plays with more enthusiasm." Harshman says, "His greatest asset is his enthusiasm." Walton does play with enthusiasm; it is a great asset, and it is what gives him a chance to be more effective than Alcindor or Chamberlain, who are moody men, who are erratic emotionally, who often have seemed simply to be going through the motions.

Walton is as animated as an actor on court. With a long face and a long jaw, with a lot of red hair falling all over a freckled face, he looks like some elongated Huckleberry Finn. He walks and runs as if he was all loose joints flopping all over the place, like a farmboy, bandages binding his bad knees that are so obvious you wonder if he will not come apart when they are undone. Apart from the rough treatment he gets from his foes, and which he gives back to them in turn—shoving, pushing, slashing with sharp elbows—aside from the pain produced in his knees, he seems to enjoy the game.

He plays better without the ball on offense than any other center. He is always in motion, moving to get in position to get the ball, literally running back and forth across the court at times. He keeps his hands up and he waves them distractingly at his opponents and he shouts at them. He argues with them when they roughhouse him, and he complains to the officials over almost every call that goes against him, and often he smiles that smile which says the decision was silliness, and he shrugs a short shrug as if to say there's not much he can do about such nonsense, but it sure is too bad and don't all you out there agree?

In his sophomore season, he complained about calls so constantly—calls that were made against him or calls that weren't made for him—that he came to be called "a crybaby" by several of his opponents. He resented this. He said, "I felt because of my position and the attention directed at me the officials seemed to feel it was all right if I got beat up, but it wasn't all right if I retaliated. Well, I felt I had cause for complaints. And I just can't stifle my emotions." Wooden said, "His worst weakness is he lets his emotions get the best of him at times."

Walton admitted, "If things aren't going right, I get upset. But when I start playing without complete control, this aggravates the situation, and I hope I'm outgrowing it." He seems to be. In his junior year, 1972–73, he complained a lot less, and less expressively, he seemed to be getting himself under control, and he wasn't called a crybaby very often, though he still smiled that smile of his a lot. Wooden said, "I've talked to him about keeping himself in control and he's listened. He's improving even faster than I thought he would, mainly because he seems to be maturing emotionally."

He is a collegian comparable to the best pros, much better than any other collegians. When both were high-school seniors, Tom McMillen from Pennsylvania was much more publicized and pursued than Walton, possibly because he was an Easterner and got the benefit of the massive Eastern press, but Wooden was content to corral Walton, and he suggested, with one of those smiles *he* has that says I know something you don't know, but you will

come to know I am right in time, that time would deter-
mine which was better. And it has. Swiftly Walton is seen
to be far superior to McMillen, who was landed by Lefty
Dreisell to help make Maryland "the UCLA of the East,"
but has been unable to do anything like that, who has been
able to be only just another good player, while Walton is a
great one. Probably, Walton was the best in his high-school
time, too. He always has been ahead of his years.

He has abilities beyond his height and is better than
others of comparable height. As a boy, Bill grew fast and
soon began to play with bigger and older kids. By the time
he got to Helix High in San Diego, he was coveted by most
major colleges in the country. He helped his school win 49
straight games, capped by a 33-0 senior season in which he
averaged 29 points and 22 rebounds a game. As a freshman
at UCLA, he led his team to 20 straight victories without a
defeat. Joining the varsity as a sophomore, he led the
Bruins to another 30-0 season, averaging 21 points and 15
rebounds per contest. As a junior, his side went 30-0 again
and he averaged 20 points and 16 rebounds.

Statistics reflect his consistency, but not his performance. John Wooden says, "Bill does a great many things
which do not show up in the box score. His defense, for
example; his blocked shots, the way he intimidates our
rivals out of their normal pattern and shooting habits. He
is an exceptional passer and probably is among the nation's
leaders in assists. He draws defenders to him, freeing his
teammates for shots. His presence near the basket frees his
teammates to gamble on defense. He makes every one of
our players a better player with his presence."

Walton has said, "I know I'm good. I'm not that modest.
I know I can play. I also know I can be better. I'm tall, of
course, but I'd like to be taller. That would make me a
better player all by itself. And it would help me in pro ball
where a lot more teams have seven-foot centers than in
college ball. And, of course, they're a lot better than they
are in college ball. They're not only older and more

experienced, but heavier and stronger. I've run into college centers who could move me around and I'm sure big strong men like Chamberlain and Reed could shove me around some in pro ball. I'd have to rely on my quickness and agility to combat this. But I'm also maturing and I eat a lot and I'm getting heavier and stronger. I'd like to be bigger.

"I'd like to be quicker. I'd like to be smarter, too. I'd like to be a lot of things. Mainly I'd like to make the most of what I am. I never thought about what makes me better than other players my size. I have thought about my limitations. I know what they are, and if they're something I can work on, I want to work on them.

"I try to do in games the things I do well. I get roughed up and I have to fight back for survival, but I don't really play a physical game. I have to fight to get and hold position, but I don't push people around or try to run right over them. My game depends on movement. When I stand around, I don't play as well. So I stay on the move. I may move well, but not as well as I could if my knees were better. I don't want to make excuses, but sometimes I could do things better if my knees would let me. I'm not as agile as I might be with better knees.

"I get tired carrying my 225 pounds around, but I get doubly tired when I carry someone else's 225 pounds around on my back. Most of the teams we play try to rough me up. I think they think because I'm big and tall I don't feel pain. I know I'm singled out and have to get used to it, but I get sick and tired of it. That's not the game. I get double-teamed and triple-teamed a lot and I don't like it. It frees my teammates, so I pass to them, but it doesn't free me to play the game the way it should be played. That's one reason why I look forward to playing with the pros. They're the best, for one thing. And it's man-to-man. Some may concentrate on stopping me, but I doubt they'll double-team me and triple-team me the way they do in college. They have too many good players to play against me in the pros."

The retired pro immortal Elgin Baylor says, "No one has more talent than Jabbar, but Walton is a little more aggressive. Jabbar is not muscular, but he has found ways to avoid having guys like Chamberlain push him around, and I'm sure Walton will, too. The first time around the league, Walton would learn a few things. But he'd hold his own, I'll guarantee you that. And he'd get better and better. Most of the big stars in the league today are black, but I don't like to think black and white. Being white might help him at the box office, but if a basketball player has talent, he should be recognized, whether he is black or white, and Bill Walton definitely has talent. He really is a terrific player. He plays like a veteran. The only real question mark about him is his knees."

Walton says, "It's funny, but one good part of my game and one that will help me in pro ball—the ability to take down a rebound and get off the fast outlet pass to start a fast-break—developed when I first injured a knee in high school. I had an operation, and, while I recovered from it, I couldn't run well when I first started to play again, so there was no way I could stay with everybody in our fast break. So, all I did was get the rebound, make the quick pass, and watch everyone go. I couldn't help but get good at it because I did it so much. I sort of enjoyed just standing back there watching our guys destroy everybody at the other end.

"Now, I have to get down there to rebound any missed shots. While we shoot with confidence, because we try to take only our best shots, coach has taught us to react as if every shot will be missed, to keep our arms up and to go after the rebound instead of waiting to see if the shot will go in or not. But I am always thinking fast break when I rebound off the defensive board, I make a point of knowing where everyone is, I look to make the fast-break pass first, and when I'm trailing the play and see everything materialize in front of me—wow! That pleases me the most."

He sighed and said, "One reason I don't look forward to playing pro is the long season. I've been playing 30 games a season, and in pro ball I'll have to play 80 to 100. That's a lot more running. And pro ball is rough and I don't know if my knees will hold up. I don't say the guys go after my knees, but they don't do me any favors, either. And just playing on my knees, twisting, turning, landing awkwardly sometimes hurts them."

At the age of 14, between his freshman and sophomore terms in high school, Walton twisted a knee and tore cartilage in it. He had surgery to have it repaired, endured countless hours of painful therapy to strengthen it, and appeared to recover completely. But, he shot up six inches during his junior year, at the age of 15, and as a senior he started to be troubled in both knees with weakness and pain, which has been diagnosed by doctors as inflammation in the tendons of the joints—a condition called "tendonitis," often caused by accelerated growth. Many say as his growth slows and stops and his joints settle and mature, the problem will disappear, he simply will outgrow it, and many do. But as Bill points out, "No one can make me any promises. It may be something which will just go away and it may be something which will stay. I may just have to live with it, but I'm not sure how long or how much I can play basketball with it."

He applies heat pads to his knees for a half hour before every game and ices them for a half hour after every game and is excused from some practices between games. In games, he runs and moves with grace, speed, and agility, until suddenly he will collapse in a pile of pain, rubbing his sore knees. In action, he will be running, and then, at time-outs, he will limp off, expressing pain in agonized expressions. Then the game will resume and he will resume as though nothing was troubling him. One minute he is all smooth, swift, free motion, the next he is struggling slowly with each step, seemingly imprisoned in pain. The transformations come so swiftly and so completely they are difficult to accept. One coach says, "He is a hell of an actor. There is no way he could do what he does most of the time if his knees were as bad as he makes them seem some of the time."

Another says, "The way he plays, no way his knees can be really bad. He may be the greatest actor of our time." A rival player says, "He's a con artist, putting us on, seeking sympathy." Even a teammate smiles and says, "He seems sometimes to be really suffering, but he may have begun to baby himself a bit and I suspect he leans to the dramatic." However, coach Wooden insists, "His problems with his knees are real and he endures pain and overcomes it."

After his sophomore season, Walton said, "I don't care what some people say, my problem *is* real and it is not easy to overcome. I can't describe the pain. As a freshman I had pain 24 hours a day, which made my life misery. It wasn't comfortable doing anything. It really was no fun to play basketball because my knees hurt so bad. Then the pain began to lessen. At least it wasn't continuous. Sometimes I can do anything and it won't hurt; sometimes it hurts even when I'm sitting down. In January when we played a game on Friday night and then another on Saturday afternoon, the pain really got to me. I need at least 15 hours between games to be ready to play again.

"The pain didn't go away for a long time that time. Then I got some trouble with my toes. The tendons were torn from jumping. It was so painful that at first I had to take cortisone shots. I also started taking medicine to reduce inflammation. It was supposed to be for my toes, but it helped my knees, too. There were times the knees hurt so bad I honestly thought of quitting. If I hadn't been part of a team that was finishing a schedule and going for a championship, I would have quit. With the pain, it wasn't pleasant to play. If it was for fun, I wouldn't have done it. Unfortunately, it is not for fun. I can't just play when I feel like playing."

He looked down at his empty hands. Lost in thought, he

started to massage his knees with his large hands and long fingers, but gently, wincing a little with his expression. He said, "It comes and it goes. When I twist it some way, it's a quick jolt of pain and it feels like I've broken something and I can't help limping and maybe making a face, but then it eases up right away and I can go again. It always hurts some, but when I'm playing I forget about it. Most of the time I just try not to think about it. I don't worry about it. If I get hurt, I get hurt. If I wake up one morning and find I can't play anymore, I'll just have to find something else to do. I just wouldn't want to wake up some morning without being able to walk.

"I could quit. I do other things besides play basketball. I'm more interested in some things than I am in basketball. I'm not all that interested in money, but I know I could make a lot of money playing pro basketball and someday there may be some good use I've found for money. It's something I can do well, so it's hard for me to give it up. It's a lot of fun. It's not the most important thing in the world. I like other things. But I also like basketball. It's a game and I really like it. I enjoy basketball. It's a game, isn't it? That's what it's called. And everyone likes to play games. Games are to have fun. But it's not always fun. When some people act like we have no right to win, it's no fun. When my bad knees are acting up, it's no fun. If it wasn't fun most of the time, I wouldn't put up with the pain and the problems.

"It bothers me when the other teams don't play basketball against us, when they hold the ball or stall or rough me up, when they rough all of us up. To me, these things aren't basketball. To me, basketball is running and fast breaking. If I wasn't playing in college, I'd be out on the pavements or in a schoolyard or a gym, playing somewhere. I'd like that more, I think. I like the thought of playing pickup games where if you have a bad game or lose a game, it's not like it would be the end of the world. I like the idea of playing when I want. I like to play the game, but I get enough of it half the year. I don't know if I'd like playing 50 or 60 or 70 more games every year like they do in the pros. I don't go looking for pickup games on the pavements or in the schoolyards or gyms the other six months of the year. I don't miss it.

"I know it means more to some of the guys. It's hard for some of the guys as great as they are not to get the recognition they deserve. Because I'm the big center, I get all the attention even though I don't want it. Also, because I'm white. I'm the great white hope in a game that has come to be dominated by blacks. Most of the writers and broadcasters who control the publicity are white. Most of the fans who can afford to buy tickets to games are white. But it's not right that I should be made more of than I am because I'm white. The way it should be is either I'm a good basketball player or I'm not. Color shouldn't matter. But it does. If I was black, I'd be just another good big man and I wouldn't get nearly as much publicity. Most of my teammates are black. Most of my teammates were high-school all-Americans. Most of them could star on any other team in the country. I don't enjoy being a star shining over them. I think they realize that, anyway, I hope they do."

He sat back, silent for a few seconds. To a great extent, he was right of course. There has not been a white player good enough to be drafted first out of college by the pros since Rick Barry in 1965. Most of the top pros are black. The players voted blacks Most Valuable Player in the National Basketball Association 13 straight seasons until Dave Cowens won in 1973, although Jerry West had some seasons he should have won in that time. It is only natural a white star should attract attention when a Walton comes along. Sports uses a star system.

"I really like playing with the guys on my team," Walton said. "They are very intelligent. They are smart players. They play as a team. They sacrifice for the team. They accept being overshadowed by me. They never complain. It doesn't affect their personalities. They treat me well.

They play unselfishly. I don't consciously play unselfishly. I don't say to myself, 'Hey, I better pass up this shot because I've had too many shots.' If I have my shot, I shoot it. If I don't, I pass off. I don't care who scores as long as we score. It's just the way I've always played.

"I like to play well. It's not a matter of winning and losing. It's if we feel good after the game. I like to do things that make me feel good. I don't mean I don't try to win every game I play. It's that I don't like it when instead of us playing to win, I find us playing not to lose. I want to win. But I don't enjoy winning when I don't play well, when we don't play well. I wouldn't want to lose because we played bad. I wouldn't mind losing if someone else played better. I just don't want to make more of it than there is. If others take the game too seriously, that's their problem. I wouldn't want it to be mine."

He stood in the sunshine, towering, attracting attention, others turning to stare at him. He pretended not to notice. He was thinking out what he wanted to say. He said, "I believe in doing the best you can at what you do. My freshman year in college was a total waste of time for me athletically and academically. One of the biggest reasons was that there were no goals, nothing to play for, nothing I was set on studying for. After that, it got better. I'm still not set in what I want to major in, but I've found courses of study that interest me. Joining the varsity, I went on a team that wanted to have the best possible season and wanted to win the championships at the end of every season. There was incentive.

"I don't think much of winning streaks. When people talk of our streak reaching 105 games before I leave, they're being ridiculous. You see, we know we're going to lose. You can't win all the time. That's not real. We just hope that when we do lose it's to a better team and we don't beat ourselves. If the other team wins, they'll be just as happy as we would have been if we'd won. That'd be cool. But we don't show extra emotion when we win and I don't anticipate we will when we lose," he said.

How would he know? you wondered. It is not true that his teams never have lost, as some have written, but from his senior year in high school through his freshman year in college to the end of his junior year, his teams have won 129 consecutive times. He has not lost for four years and may have forgotten what it feels like. Though he and his teammates have earned everything they have won, he is spoiled by success.

It is easy to say you will lose and you will be gracious when you lose, when you do not lose and do not expect to lose. When they came close to losing unexpectedly in the 1972 NCAA championship contest against Florida State, he complained his team had not played as well as it should have, had not won by as many points as it should have, and he said he did not feel as if his team had won. And walked away in anger.

Well, he was only 19 and not yet in complete control of his emotions, and he was used to winning. When you are just about the best and have been told you are the best for a couple of years and may or may not think you are the best, but would never want to admit it, when you are a modest young man and always want to seem as modest as possible, when you have been winning every game for years and winning easily and then you almost let a big one, a championship game get away from you, when you are put into a position of enormous pressure, which might cave in the sides of some men's skulls, when you are put in a position where immortality is deemed imminent and you suddenly seem mortal, well, it is hard to handle.

He stood scuffing his toe in a patch of earth, tired of talking in this rare interview, but wanting to wrap it up right. His reddish hair fell over his freckled face. He shook it back, squinting into the sunny skies. He said, "The thing is, UCLA's teams before us had won all those championships.

When we started we were a young and inexperienced team and I don't think we were expected to win everything, but we didn't want to be the first team to blow a big one, so no one would remember that you had a good season, that you weren't 30 and 0, but, say, 29 and 1, which is tremendous, but not tremendous enough because you didn't win everything, the championship and everything. UCLA's teams have been winning everything for so many years now that we didn't want to get to the title game and lose it, we didn't want to be the team to spoil the record."

3

John Wooden may not have had a losing season at UCLA, but in his first 15 seasons as coach of the Bruins he had five seasons in which his team lost 10, 11, or 12 games, and he was in his seventh season before it lost less than seven. In this span, his teams won five divisional crowns, but lost three conference championship playoffs. In his first 15 seasons, his Bruins won only three conference crowns, and the third came in the tenth year of a long drought. And they not only did not win any NCAA championships, but lost their first five tournament efforts, nine of 12, and won only two that meant anything.

After this, things turned around dramatically and completely. Wooden had help in this. His star player from the fifties, Jerry Norman, who had been coaching at West Covina (California) High School, where the principal was Wooden's brother, Maurice (Cat) Wooden, had joined John as freshman coach for the 1957–58 season and moved up as his assistant before the 1962–63 season. An aggressive, imaginative young man, he became a brilliant recruiter and an alert tactician who argued with Wooden over strategy and won some arguments.

J. D. Morgan, an Oklahoman and former UCLA tennis player, longtime tennis coach and business manager, took over as the school's athletic director in the summer of 1963 from Wilbur Jones, the man Wooden had succeeded as basketball coach in 1948. Morgan has presided over a great growth in the school's sports program, including the construction of a new basketball arena and track stadium on campus. A titanic, tough sort, it cannot be considered mere coincidence that the school's dynasty in basketball began his first season. Under his control, UCLA has won more national titles in other sports than it has in basketball, and he talked Wooden into the softer schedule that has helped the basketball team win its titles. He took away the business and other details from him, gave him a free hand with scholarships and full-time assistants.

Norman talked Wooden into returning to an all-out running offensive and adopting an all-court pressing defense for the 1962–63 season, and, when the latter was not entirely effective that season, helped him devise the pressing zone defense which worked wonders and has ever since. Wooden is The Wizard of Westwood and it is the system he devised and taught that has worked so well and with refinements began to work wonders in the 1963–64 season, but he had help, he was willing to consider an aide's advice, he was not alone in leading his school's surge to unsurpassed success in a college sport. The right players helped, of course.

From Philadelphia came Walt Hazzard, the cornerstone of the school's first championship basketball team, nick-named The Nigger in Charge. From North Hollywood's Poly High in the Valley came Gail Goodrich, known as Baby Gail. The forwards on the 1963–64 team were Keith Erickson (Beach Bum) from El Segundo High School and Jack Hirsch (Jew Boy) who had been L.A. Player of the Year at Van Nuys High School.

The center was "Fat Fred" Slaughter, who still packed 230 pounds on his 6-5 frame and seemed as wide as he was tall. Slaughter came from Kansas. The sixth man was Kenny Washington, who came out of Beaufort, South Carolina, affectionately nicknamed Nigger Boy.

Wooden believes it is best to divide playing time among seven or eight players at the most, and that year he went almost all the time with six, and this was the team on which he was able to build a dynasty. From The Nigger in Charge through Fat Freddie, Baby Gail, Beach Bum and Jew Boy to Nigger Boy, they were a wonder. Wooden says he prefers to recruit in southern California, but they came from Pennsylvania and South Carolina and Kentucky and Kansas also. He says he seldom selects talent out of junior colleges, but Hazzard and Erickson came from junior colleges. He says he prefers good students, but some could hardly get into his school, and Hazzard and Hirsch and Goodrich and Washington admit the books bored them.

The dynamic little team kept going, game after game, running and pressing its opponents ragged. Not that it was easy. In one of its games with USC, UCLA missed 17 out of 18 shots until it led by a mere five late in the last half before it recovered its composure and its shooting touch to win. The largest nontournament college crowd in L.A. history—13,575 fans—filled the Sports Arena and saw Stanford's contenders within three points with a fourth of the game to go before sixth man Washington went in to ignite a blitz of 13 straight points that settled it.

UCLA got through the season without a loss and by capturing the conference crown won its way into the NCAA tourney. The regionals were held at Corvallis, Oregon, where so many UCLA clubs had collapsed in past years. And both foes it drew proved difficult.

Still, they won both, and this took them to Kansas City where they drew Kansas State in the tournament semifinals. The two teams were tied many times most of the game, and Kansas State led by six midway in the last half, but the Bruins went on a brief tear to pass their foe and to win by six.

This brought the Bruins to the final against Duke, which had Jeff Mullins, Jack Marin, and a couple of big men. Wooden's pregame pep talk was short: "Who can remember which team finished second in this tournament two years ago?" Goodrich says, "No one knew. We knew we had to win." Washington went in to spark a string of 16 straight points in less than three minutes that blew the game wide open before the first half was finished. Goodrich scored 27 points and Washington 26. Washington took down 12 rebounds and Kentuckian Doug McIntosh, replacing a struggling Slaughter, 11. UCLA won, 98-83, going away, to complete a perfect 30-0 campaign, but as they were whooping and hollering in celebration of their first championship, Wooden cautioned, "Now you are champions and you must act like champions."

Years later, sitting sweaty in a dressing room after a pro game, a fading veteran Walt Hazzard, now the Muslim Mahdi Abdul-Rahman, recalled those marvelous moments: "It was a very exciting team and it excited those of us that played on it. Wooden had clubs which had come close to reaching the top before, and this time he got together a team which played as a team and fit his system perfectly. We lacked a big man, but didn't need one. We beat teams with big men. We were quicker than our foes. We were in better shape than they were. Sooner or later, we'd explode on them."

Of course, Wooden's first two title teams did have better players than people realized. Three players from these teams—Hazzard, Goodrich, and Erickson—became top pros. Others played pro, if only briefly. When Hazzard, Hirsch, and Slaughter left, Freddie Goss (who passed up the 1963–64 season to concentrate on his studies) returned and two talented sophomores—Edgar Lacey and Mike Lynn—moved in to join Goodrich, Erickson,Washington, and McIntosh for the 1964–65 season. At 6-7, Lacey now was the tallest player on the team, but he was placed in a corner opposite Erickson, with McIntosh moving in as the starting center. Goss joined Goodrich at guard. Washington stayed the super sub. Lynn became the seventh man. Wooden went mainly with seven men.

Balance remained a blessing. No one took most of the shots, no one scored 30 points a game. Goodrich took more shots than anyone else, but the season after Hazzard left and Gail emerged from his shadow and became the team leader, he took less shots than the year before. He led the team in scoring for the second straight season, but his average per game went up only four points from 21 to 25. No one else had more than 12, but for the second straight year four starters averaged in double figures. Hazzard had not been the best defensive player ever and the team seemed tougher defensively. Wooden altered the zone defense slightly to stress the play as a point man of Erickson, who directed defense on the floor. The team lacked Hazzard's sensational passing, but Goodrich became a good field general and matured into unselfishness.

Many teams have won one championship. Few have taken two. Only Oklahoma A&M and Kentucky in the 1940s and San Francisco and Cincinnati in the 1950s had won two in a row. It was the second in a row that really marked the Bruins as the big team in college competition in the 1960s. It helped bring them Lew Alcindor, with whom they would become the first team to win three in a row. The Goodrich group which successfully defended the school's first college crown was not as good as the one that had preceded it. The replacements were not as good as Hazzard and Hirsch. And the club still lacked a top pivot. This team lost a couple of games. But, it won the national title again, which established Wooden's system as outstanding and brought top talent to the school.

But, they just couldn't get there the next season. Anyway, they had won a second straight, even if they couldn't make it three in a row. Washington was back, but Goodrich wasn't, and there was no way to replace him. And everything seemed to turn sour for Lacey, who stopped laughing. But they got a big, beautiful building, Pauley Pavilion, to play in, and a big, beautiful new player, Lew Alcindor, was waiting in the wings about to help them win the big games, and the dynasty that was due was only to be delayed a little.

Lew Alcindor was the nation's most widely sought

schoolboy basketball star of the 1960s. He was 6-8 when he began and 7-1 when he graduated from Power Memorial Academy, a private Catholic high school in New York City, and he was far more graceful and agile than the average player his height, a more complete player than most and more unselfish on the court. He was black, but he had been brought up in better than ghetto conditions, he had been in no personal trouble, and he was a good student.

Everyone wanted him. UCLA got him. The Bruins had won two straight national titles and were the most attractive team at the time. The school had the reputation of being one of the best for blacks and Dr. Ralph Bunche, the noted educator and a UCLA basketball player of the 1920s, wrote Lew a letter, Jackie Robinson, a UCLA football, baseball, and basketball star of the 1930s, wrote him, too, and Willie Naulls, UCLA basketball star of the 1950s spoke to him personally, all encouraging him to attend this splendid school in splendid southern California.

Jerry Norman recruited him and brought him to campus to see the facilities, including the newly finished $5,000,000 Pauley Pavilion, a splendid place in which his splendid teams would play. John Wooden spoke to him, more about his studies than his basketball, which impressed him. Edgar Lacey and Mike Warren, black stars on the team, befriended him and escorted him around, but did not party him with beautiful dates, which UCLA does not do, which many schools do, which is a risk, since it turns off a few straight and suspicious prospects, such as Alcindor was. The soft sell sold Lew.

Alcindor was a moody young man who often was bored by basketball. He played without expression, without traces of emotion, often without interest, often loafing and lagging behind the play. He lived alone in an apartment off campus at first, then in a bungalow, without a telephone, often without a woman or close friends. He was a loner and often seemed lonely. He had some friends who were black with whom he discussed the situation of the blacks in this country and in the world. He was sensitive to the persecutions, segregations, slurs, and slanders inflicted on blacks, which was understandable, certainly, but he was less sympathetic to sympathetic whites than are many blacks.

In his first few months at UCLA, Lew simply was homesick for the totally different atmosphere of New York City. Soon, however, he also became disenchanted with southern California. He felt its reputation for being the best place for blacks in this country was all out front, for show, and without substance, and suggested he would prefer the open and at least honest bigotry shown his people in some other sections of the country. He felt he was accepted and even exalted as a person only because he was a super player and called his fellow students "crackers," as blacks call whites down south.

He always was uncomfortable with his height and sat down and slouched in public as though to reduce it. He sometimes seemed relaxed only when alone with his teammates, who were tall and used to taller people and understood the pressures of having to play almost perfectly. He hated the attention his height attracted in public as he moved through life, assuming he was considered a freak. He knew he was accepted because he used his height to become the best basketball player around and wondered what would be thought of him if he didn't play basketball. He had been protected from the press at Power Memorial by his coach, Jack Donohue, and he asked athletic director Morgan, coach Wooden, and publicist Vic Kelley at UCLA to provide similar protection, which they did.

They decided the easiest way was to shut off the entire team from the press. The dressing room was denied them. All interviews had to be arranged, all requests were screened, and Lew permitted few, though his teammates, denied the publicity they deserved, and needed more than did Alcindor, were less exclusive.

Alcindor's career at UCLA began with a bang. Pauley Pavilion was opened for play with a full house to see the freshmen take on the varsity, the defending national champions, in a preseason contest, and it was no contest as the freshmen took apart the varsity by 15 points with Alcindor scoring 31 points. He had help. His was the finest freshman team ever, including also Lucius Allen from Kansas, Kent Taylor from Houston, who later transferred to school there, and California's Lynn Shackelford and Kenny Heitz. It almost certainly was the best team in the country and everyone around UCLA was waiting for them to become eligible to prove it on the varsity level. That may have been the varsity's trouble. Everyone was waiting for these freshmen, who won 21 straight games, some by such scores as 152-49 and 142-63 and 133-51.

Wooden still insists that varsity also could have won the national title, which would have made it 10 in a row in 1973, but they were overshadowed and overawed by the freshmen waiting in the wings, they had physical and psychological problems, and then became the only Bruin basketball team of the decade which failed to maintain national domination. While everyone was saying "Alcindor's Army" would win 90 in a row the next three seasons, this team won only 18 of 26 this season, although it did win all its games at its new home palace.

The Alcindor team was something else. Given to grand debuts, Lew scored a school record 56 points as UCLA ripped USC by 15 in the opener the next season at Pauley in the fall of 1966. Boyd's Trojans played him man-to-man, but that was one of the last times anyone tried that. The next game, Duke triple-teamed him. Lew didn't even get a shot until the eighth minute of the game, so he passed off. He scored only 19, but his freed mates won by 34. The next night Duke put only two men on him, and Lew scored 38 and the Bruins won by 30. The other teams the remainder of Lew's college career tried almost every kind of defense imaginable on him, but they could not contain him, for if they slowed his scoring, his passes produced increased scoring by others.

Whatever Alcindor was and is, he always has been an unselfish team player. Later in his first season he raised his school scoring record to 61 points in one game against Washington State, but he did not in the next two years top that, he never averaged as many as 30 points a game, in fact his seasonal averages went down every year from 29 to 26 to 24 as he shot less every year and passed off more, and he consistently held his average rebounds to around 15 a game. He was so devastating in close he forced the NCAA to outlaw "stuff shots." He is one of the few players who has forced a revolution in his sport's rules. He dominated his foes defensively and blocked uncounted numbers of shots.

He was imperfect as a player and remains so. He is a tremendous talent, enormously effective, but he is not the defender or shot blocker he had been expected to become, and he does not dominate pro centers. He may be the best, but he may not be.

Distressed by predictions of success assured his side, Wooden insisted, "With such a young team it is hardly likely we will go undefeated." But they did, through 30 straight games, though the 90 some expected escaped them; they won only 88 of these. That first season they had only a couple of close calls—in slowdown games they won from USC, 40-35, and from Oregon, 34-25. The other teams were driven to desperate tactics to try to stop the Bruins, but even these did not work. However, when USC ran with UCLA, the Trojans lost games by 24 and 28 points. When Oregon ran with UCLA, the Ducks lost by 34 points. Notre Dame and Santa Barbara lost by 44 points each, and Portland by 65. The Bruins won by such scores as 122-57, 120-82, and 119-75.

Everyone really expected they would win 90 in a row. They came close. They won 47 in a row, but there was one team which could win from them when they did not play well. That was Houston with Elvin Hayes, whose ego was such he did not believe Alcindor to be better and who fired up his side for a rare "home game" in the awesome Astrodome, which drew a record college crowd of 52, 693 to see a basketball game, although most were so far away in this indoor baseball stadium they could not see much of the game. Alcindor couldn't see either. A finger had been stuck in his eye in a game eight days earlier. For two days he lay in a darkened room. When he returned, he was unable to practice. He said later, "Not only was my vision blurred, but I was out of shape. After five minutes, the coach should have taken me out. He should have seen the team would have been better off without me."

Hayes had hit 17 of 25 shots and collected 15 rebounds. Alcindor had hit four of 18 shots and collected 12 rebounds. As a team, Houston outshot and outrebounded UCLA. Years later, Shackelford said, "It was very disappointing. Houston was a team we should have beaten coming out of the dressing room. We played our worst game. Lew was the worst of all. The way he played, we could not win. Without him, we would have won. As it was, we only lost by two. I don't know why the coach didn't take him out. I'm not sure he wanted us to win that much. I don't mean he wanted us to lose. But when we did, it didn't seem such a terrible thing to him."

Wooden went to the basketball writers' luncheon the next week and said, "The loss can't hurt us, except maybe our pride. It was good for us, all our coaches, and, in the long run, good for college basketball. I had no valid aspirations of breaking USF's win streak, anyway." Later, he said, "I supposed I erred playing Alcindor the full forty minutes. I handled the situation rather poorly." By then he was being pressed by some who suspected his actions had been colored by a feeling his team would have a better chance at the championship if it was shaken up by a loss which would lift the pressure of the long winning streak. Dwight Chapin and Jeff Prugh, who covered the club for many years for the *Los Angeles Times,* say this flatly in their book *The Wizard of Westwood.*

Well, it is one way of rationalizing a loss in retrospect, but it is not realistic. Wooden may feel a loss here and there helps a team which seldom loses and needs to have its desire rekindled, and this feeling after a loss eases the pain of the loss, but for all of his speeches about winning not being everything, he always has done everything he could as coach to win, which he has proved by winning almost every game.

Shackelford, now colorman on the Lakers' broadcasting team, says, "There was no way that team could lose many games. If Alcindor had not had his physical problems that night we would not have lost any games. I think that was the greatest of my three teams at UCLA, the greatest team UCLA had, at least until the Walton teams. It is too bad it may not be so recognized because it lost one game.

"My sophomore season we did not lose any games, but we were young and inexperienced and I don't think our bench was all that good and we were unsure of ourselves in a couple of slowdowns we almost lost. But then we had our first ten players back plus Lynn and Lacey, who came back, and we had a year under our belt and we only had a couple of close games all year long and just breezed through the Holiday Classic at midseason and the NCAA championship tournament at season's end. By then we had lost Lacey, but we were still adequate in the corners, we had great guards and the greatest college player to that time in the center."

Lacey was a spectacular player. He was springy and quick and he had a marvelous shooting touch. He had been a high-school all-American nationally, but he returned to a team that had five other men who had been high-school all-Americans nationally. He thought he should have been a star, but all stars on this team were dimmed by the magnitude of Alcindor's star. He said openly he should score 30 points a game and resented it when he was told bluntly no one averaged 30 points a game on Wooden's teams at UCLA, and he was disappointed when he did not, but no one did, not even Alcindor. Lacey was satisfied that his team had won the title his sophomore season, but then he hurt his knee at the end of a disappointing junior season, and had to sit out a season, missing another title season, and when he returned his last season, he was unhappy at being placed at a high post to feed Alcindor instead of coming out of a corner to score from behind Alcindor's blocks. He said, "A lot of us were misused. I was."

He complained to black teammates who sympathized with him, forcing a bit of a black-white wedge which divided the team. When he was pulled out of and not put back into the Houston game, he called it "the last straw." He insisted he was itching to go back in and asked to go back in and was refused. Wooden said when he went to put him back in, he saw Edgar sitting with his head hung, dismal and disinterested, and decided against it. At game's end, a disappointed Lucius Allen went into the dressing room asking loudly, "Why didn't coach use Lacey?" In the bus, headed back to the hotel, he asked the question directly of Wooden, who took him aside and spoke to him privately. Wooden did not speak to Lacey, a brooder, who brooded privately.

"The Phantom," as he was called by his teammates, went off alone when the team returned to Los Angeles. He passed up practices, then quit the team, saying of Wooden, "I never enjoyed playing for that man." The talented youngster, who had been sought by the Boston Celtics, wound up with the old Los Angeles Stars of the American Basketball Association, lasted only one year, and went to work, wasted. It may have disappointed him, but the team went on winning without him.

There may have been players who were wasted by Wooden. There were. But there were not teams in his decade of domination that were wasted by Wooden. The team always came ahead of the player. The player was used in the ways that would most help the team. Some players have had their individual talents stifled when they were asked to make sacrifices to help the team and some were made unhappy by this, but they were all happy to be part of winning teams, and a great many of them were prepared properly for pro play and became professional stars. It depends on how you look at it, from the point of view of the team or that of the player.

That year UCLA had enough players to win with or without Lacey. They won their fifth straight Los Angeles Classic by 40, 41, and 32 points over Minnesota, St. Louis, and Wyoming at the Sports Arena. They won other games by margins of 31, 34, 34, 38, 41, 41, 41, 44, 48, and 51 points. The big rout was 114-63 over Notre Dame, but there were others that came close to that. They were extended only a few times.

In the opener at Purdue, Wooden's old school, a powerful team led by sharpshooting Rick Mount, battled the Bruins to a tie at 71-all with 10 seconds left and a mob of more than 14,000 fans going mad. But a short shot by Mount went in and came out, and Alcindor rebounded and passed to Shackelford, who passed to Bill Sweek, who shot with one second left and hit to win by two. After the Houston loss, the Bruins went to New York, Alcindor's old town, to show off in two games in Madison Square Garden, and after an easy win over Holy Cross, the Bruins were extended by Boston College.

It was easy after that. In the NCAA regionals at Albuquerque, New Mexico and Santa Clara were easily disposed of. In the tourney finals in the Los Angeles Sports Arena, the vengeful Bruins and Alcindor buried Houston and Hayes by 32 points, 101-69, forging a 44-point lead before easing off, then knocked down North Carolina by 23 points, 78-55, the largest margin ever recorded in an NCAA championship contest, to win their second straight title and the school's fourth in five years. With these four, Wooden surpassed Kentucky's Adolph Rupp as the coach who had won the most NCAA basketball championships. Wooden had been coaching at UCLA for 20 years. He overcame the difficulties that presented themselves during his Decade of Dynasty. And it was not all smooth sailing.

In May of 1967 Lucius Allen was arrested. His parked car was searched because it was without license plates, and marijuana and marijuana cigarettes were found inside. In June, a black woman judge ordered charges dropped because he had not been properly advised of his rights on his arrest. He was permitted to play in the season that was to come. However, in May of 1968, police stopped a speeding car containing five persons, including Allen and a coed who was to become his wife, and when the cops detected an aroma of marijuana, the occupants were charged with possession and arrested. He was fined $300 and placed on one-year's probation, but there was no problem of whether or not to permit him to play in the coming campaign because he already had dropped out of school because of scholastic failures. Later he was reunited with Alcindor on the Milwaukee Bucks, and in 1973 they were charged together with possession of marijuana in an incident that came to little.

Mike Warren had graduated and then Allen had gone, so Wooden was short of guards for the next season. He moved forwards Ken Heitz and Bill Sweek to guard, brought back a redshirt, Terry Schofield, and imported a junior college transfer, John Vallely. It was Vallely who wound up playing most of the time, with Heitz and Sweek alternating at the other spot. Vallely was good, but the others were ordinary. The Bruins were weak here. It didn't matter. After all, they still had Alcindor. And, with him, Shackelford, and two super sophomores, 6-8 Sidney Wicks out of junior college ranks and 6-6 Curtis Rowe from the freshman team, as well as Steve Patterson from the ranks of the redshirts. Wooden simply stockpiled talent collected by super-recruiter Norman, and when he lacked something, he simply picked it from junior college circles. Now Norman left, to become a stockbroker. Another of Wooden's former players, Denny Crum, became his right-hand man.

This team didn't quite steamroller foes as the past two had done, but they got past them without too much trouble. The Bruins won 45 consecutive contests in the conference, 41 in a row overall, and their first 62 played at Pauley when USC snapped all these streaks.

The night before, USC came close, behind Boyd's slowdown strategy at the Sports Arena. The Trojans tied the Bruins in regulation time and almost beat them in the first overtime when Steve Jennings scored on a lay-up to give them a 47–45 lead with only four seconds left. However, after a time-out, the ball was sent in, instead of to the defended Alcindor, to Shackelford, who had not hit a basket all night, and he hit a 25-footer that went through after the buzzer to force a second overtime, in which the Bruins pulled away to win 61–55.

Most assumed the Trojans had blown their only real opportunity, but they came right back the next night at Pauley with the same tactics that worked just as well, had the Bruins tied with one minute to play, and won 46–44 when Ernie Powell hit a 25-footer with seconds to go. Trojan supporters in their arch rival's home arena went wild and the USC players hugged one another in triumph and Boyd boasted of his first triumph over Wooden, "They're damned lucky we didn't beat them twice."

The Bruins sat sadly in their dressing room, but Wooden didn't seem too upset, pointing out his team already had clinched the conference crown and the berth in the NCAA tourney. Later, he reflected on the Trojans' bedlam of bragging and said, "When winning becomes that important, I'm getting out." Apparently he did not realize how frustrated his foes were, waiting to win over him. Some considered the comment hypocritical. This was the man who had made winning almost all-important at UCLA.

UCLA had the regionals at home and swept them easily. However, moving into Louisville for the finals, the Bruins were pressed by an underrated Duke team propelled by future pros Willie Wise and Willie McCarter. Drake used

UCLA's style. The Bulldogs were quick and aggressive and pressed the Bruins into many mistakes. However they did not shoot well enough to take advantage of their foes' errors, and in the end were shot down by Vallely's 29 points and Alcindor's 25. UCLA won by three, 85–82, leading by only one with seven seconds left before Shackelford was fouled and sank two free throws at the finish.

It was wild. Late in the game, Wooden signaled for Sweek as a sub, but when Sweek was slow moving, Wooden told him to forget it. Sweek snapped something at the coach and the coach snapped back and the two stood in front of the bench arguing publicly before Sweek sat down. As soon as the game was won and the team got back to the dressing room, Sweek rushed into the shower and Wooden rushed after him and stood at the entrance to the shower room, water spraying on him, shouting at Sweek, who shouted back. The team had almost blown a big one and tempers were short.

The team was tired and divided. Shackelford said, "We were so good we lost only two games in three years, it was easy for us, and we knew whatever problems we had we would win our third straight championship, but it was so easy it didn't seem to mean much and it had long since stopped being any fun. We'd had so many players with so many problems we'd long since stopped feeling love for each other as teammates, we weren't all that proud as a team. Maybe winning too much too easy is destructive. As our three seasons ran out, we just wanted to get it over with and be done with it."

They did that in the last game. Heitz hounded Mount, who missed 14 straight shots and went 18 straight minutes without a goal, and most of his 28 points came when the Bruins were beyond reach. The Bruins breezed in to beat Purdue by 20 points, 92–72, in the final to become the first team ever to win the NCAA crown three straight seasons. They were 29–1 for a second straight season, and with the 30–0 of their first season, Alcindor's Army finished at 88–2.

Wooden's Bruins had five championships in six years. Wooden seemed weary, worn by turmoil, pressure, and success. He sat tired, sucking on a cold drink, and said, well, they had proved they could win with a big man, but it was not as easy as some said it was, no man could win without super players, but some men might lose with them, and he was happy he had not and now he was happy to try it another way again.

4

The third of the four groups that put together UCLA's Decade of Dynasty was the one headed up by Sidney Wicks and Curtis Rowe. They were pals and problems as well as producers for coach Wooden. They almost took over the team. They wanted to win and then celebrate. During the second half of the preliminary freshman game, they'd show up in their latest fancy duds and strut the sidelines on their way to the dressing room as the band and fans whooped them along. After the victories, they partied and broke curfews. Wooden worked to keep them in line. He never kicked them out of line. They were sensitive to racial issues. They divided the team into black and white factions. Off court. But they pulled the team along behind them on court.

Wicks stood 6-8 and Rowe 6-6, and each weighed 220 pounds. Wicks was quicker. Both were tremendously strong. Both could shoot and rebound. They grew up in Los Angeles area high-school basketball opposing each other—Wicks at Hamilton High, Rowe at Fremont High. Rowe was City Player of the Year their senior seasons, breaking Edgar Lacey's league scoring record. As a freshman, he scored 51 points in a game to break Alcindor's frosh record of 48. As a sophomore he started ahead of Wicks. In fact, he went on to start in 90 straight games as his teams won three straight national titles. Lacking the grades to get into UCLA immediately, Wicks prepped one season at Santa Monica City College before joining Rowe as sophomores in Alcindor's Army. He was very displeased when Wooden used him sparingly that season. He knew he was the superior player. But he was not a team player. He was a soloist.

Steve Patterson moved up to play center between Wicks and Rowe. Wooden returned to the high post offense and placed him there. He didn't like having to feed them, but accepted it. He was as big as Sidney and Curtis and with them formed the most muscular front row UCLA has had. Henry Bibby moved up from the freshman ranks to team with Vallely at guard. Bibby had been brought from a tiny tobacco farm in North Carolina by Jay Carty in the only recruiting trip he made as a Bruin aide. Henry was the third black starter and even hungrier than the others. He had worked 12 hours a day on his family's poor place in the Deep South and practiced basketball at night by the light of a bulb hung on the barn. He had learned to shoot from the outside, shooting over his older and bigger brothers, one of whom, Jim, became a major-league pitcher.

Bibby was a sophomore, Vallely a senior, the rest juniors. It was another young team. It was thin on depth. More than any other team he had, Wooden went mainly with his first five. But the first five were tremendously talented. All five averaged in double figures. Wicks averaged 18 points a game, Vallely 16, Bibby 15, Rowe 15, and Patterson 12. They had balance, and between them averaged 78 of the team's 92 points per game. Wicks and Rowe averaged 10 rebounds a game, Patterson almost nine. When defenses sagged inside, Bibby sniped with fine .500 accuracy from outside. He never again shot as well as he did as a sophomore. Vallely was called "Money Man." He quarterbacked the club and came through in the clutch.

Wooden seemed relieved that Alcindor had graduated, as though now he could be credited with his coaching ability again. He admitted, "It was relief to begin coaching to win again, instead of playing not to lose." This 1969–70 team won 28 of 30 games, losing only two, though coming close to losing others. The next season it won 29 of 30, losing only one, though coming close to losing many others. It did not awe foes as Alcindor's Army had done, but still it scared them out of their games. Instead of blitzing them as the Hazzard and Goodrich teams had done, the Wicks and Rowe teams overpowered them. Alcindor's Army averaged 26 points more than its foes its first season and 24 points more for its three seasons. UCLA's first two champions outscored its foes by an average of 17 points a game, as did these next two. It was amazing how many close contests the 1969-70 Bruin team pulled out. This was true throughout the decade. If foes let the Bruins stay close, they would let the Bruins win in the end.

Oregon had a hot night in the twenty-second game of the season, did not let UCLA get close, and won going away by 13 points, 78-65. This was in Oregon, where the fans were ferocious. Many of the conference clubs have small gyms, where a visiting team may feel trapped. The noise is enormous and it can unnerve a visitor, who may feel he is about to be attacked. The game in Oregon ended UCLA's latest winning streak at 25 straight, 21 this season, and Wooden went to congratulate the winning coach, Steve Belko, before it ended because he knew there would be bedlam at the end.

While the winners were hollering happily, the Bruins sat silently in their dressing room. Wooden had been saying, "I'm very, very aggravated at my team." Now, he stood outside and said, "Subconsciously, a team that has won as many games as we have might get a little fatheaded. That's why I consider it almost a relief to lose. I could see it coming. Really, I expected it before this." His wife Nell stood by the bus, and when he got to her she told him, "They deserved to lose. They deserved it."

They lost again, too, and at Pauley, and to arch rival USC, the only team ever to beat them at Pauley. Bob Boyd was building a tremendous Trojan team. It had three players who would play pro—Paul Westphal, Ron Riley, and Mo Layton. The Trojans were a year away from reaching their peak, but they had almost beaten UCLA at the Sports Arena and they had beaten them at Pauley the year before and they were poised for an upset as they invaded Pauley to open the season-ending series in 1970.

Boyd did not feel he had to resort to the slowdown systems that had succeeded the season before. He ran his players with the Bruins. And when he switched from a zone defense to a man-for-man and his players played it with a passion, the Trojans roared from 12 points back in the last six minutes to tie it with less than three minutes left. Joe Mackey hit a jump shot to push SC on top with two minutes left. Wicks and Vallely missed clutch free throws, and Don Crenshaw hit one with 13 seconds left to give SC a three-point lead. Rowe hit from the field with three seconds left, but SC won by one, 87–86.

The Bruins had clinched the conference crown and the tournament berth, but as they drifted in despair into their dressing room, Wooden sat outside, visibly shaken, and he admitted, "I thought they might beat us over there at the Sports Arena in the last game, but I never really thought they'd beat us here again. If we now go over there and lose to them again, it may hurt our confidence a lot going into the tournament. Now I want this next ball game badly."

He got it. SC shot in front 10–2 and led by 10 after five minutes with nearly 15,000 fans, most of them SC students, roaring. An angry Wooden pulled Wicks out when Sidney did not go for a loose ball, accused him of not hustling, and told him he would not put him back in until he was told by Sidney he was ready to play. They argued in front of everyone. A few minutes later, Wicks went to Wooden and told him he was ready to play and Wooden put him back in and Wicks took the Trojans apart. The Bruins caught up around the ten-minute mark, led by 11 at 20 minutes and returned from intermission to put the Trojans away by 13, 91–78, with Wicks winding up with 31 points and 16 rebounds.

The regionals were set in Seattle. Jerry Tarkanian, who'd had an astonishing coaching record in junior college ranks, had moved up to senior college circles at Cal State at Long Beach, which had not had a top team before. He had built a contender, primarily from energetic recruiting of black players from poor areas from all over the country, with low grades and good ability, and he threw a good team, led by George Trapp, at the Bruins in the opener, but Bibby blew holes in his zone defense with deadly outside shooting and UCLA won easily by 23 points. Utah State stayed with UCLA for a while in the last round, but then the Bruins pulled away to win by 22.

The finals were played at the University of Maryland. The Bruins drew New Mexico State as its semifinal foe. New Mexico State had an outstanding team paced by future pros Sam Lacey and Jimmy Collins. But UCLA played maybe its most outstanding game of the season and, despite demon effort by Collins, clipped the Aggies easily, by 16, 93–77.

This put UCLA in the finals against Jacksonville, a small college club with a front line that averaged seven feet in height and had so surprised observers with its rise to the heights that some considered it a club which could beat the Bruins. Jacksonville in the semis had beaten a St. Bonaventure team which was without its star, ailing Bob Lanier. Jacksonville's star was its 7-2 center, Artis Gilmore, who has become a star pro, too, who was outstanding, who was considered by some as another Alcindor, and was also considered by some as a threat to a UCLA team without an Alcindor. But, Wicks, playing his greatest game, took him apart.

A Jacksonville banner put the school's sentiments simply: "Go To Hell, Bruins." Big Gilmore and his small sidekick Rex Morgan were nicknamed "Batman and Robin." So Sidney assayed the role of "Superman." Only he was awhile getting out of that damned telephone booth. Fronting Gilmore was a failure, and Jacksonville drove to a nine-point lead at 24–15 midway in the first half before a madhouse in Maryland, stunned and sensing an upset, the downfall of the king.

Wooden pulled Wicks behind Gilmore and had Patterson drop off his man to front the big man. Right away, Gilmore got the ball and went up to shoot. Wicks, six inches shorter, went up higher and banged the ball right back at the startled giant. It seemed to shake Artis terribly. Wicks blocked four more shots by Gilmore, who went 16 long minutes without a single basket. This took him well into the second half.

Vallely hit a basket to pull the Bruins within a point at 36–35 with two minutes to go in the first half, then hit Bibby with a pass for a basket to put them in front to stay, 37–36, then hit Patterson with a pass for a basket to increase the lead to 39–36, and it was 41–36 by the buzzer. And after intermission, the Bruins just kept pulling away, winning by 11, 80–69.

In the losers' subdued dressing room, coach Joe Williams accepted what had been inevitable. In a curious concession, he said simply, "It was a real honor and thrill for us to meet them in the championship game." Gilmore said, "They double-teamed me with two good men. Wicks is a fine player, but he couldn't do it alone. I didn't have room to breathe." With the winners, a realist, Wicks said, "I suppose we shook him up. He went bad awhile, long enough for us to win. But he's good. The Alcindor rule helped. He had to shoot, not stuff. I blocked some of his shots, discouraging him. I never could have stopped his stuffs, which might have discouraged me."

Despite Wicks's splendid show, Rowe said, "It was a team triumph." Both agreed they were especially pleased to have won without Lew. Wicks said, "Some said we couldn't do it without him." Rowe observed, "Look around this dressing room. The reporters are spread out among all five of us. If we'd had Lew, they'd all have been with the one." Wooden agreed that this made his school's fourth straight and sixth title triumph in seven seasons especially satisfying. "We won without a big man, although Sidney was ten feet tall tonight," he said.

He displayed a championship watch, awarded annually with the triumph. He smiled and said, "I gave my first five watches to my son, my son-in-law, and my three grandsons. I'm awfully glad to have one of my own now."

Some of the pleasure passed from it for him between seasons, however. At the Senior Basketball Banquet, attended by more than 800 persons at the swank Beverly Hilton Hotel, an affair which started out to be a victory party with everyone congratulating everyone else, substitute Bill Siebert stood up and stilled the celebration with a long speech in which he said that Wooden's concern for all his players as people was more fancy than fact, that he, the other coaches, and even the trainer gave preferential treatment to the starters and seldom spoke to the subs, and that when discipline was applied, such as after a wild water fight on a road trip, the reserves were reprimanded, not the regulars.

As he spoke, the listeners were at first surprised and shocked into silence. Then they began to shout at him to shut up and sit down. Even Siebert's father shouted this. Siebert's mother began to cry. It was a messy scene. When Siebert finally closed, saying the coaches lacked sensitivity, he was booed. Many went up to him, sputtering with rage. One threatened to punch him. Siebert went to Wooden, who said he was hurt, especially because his wife and family were hurt. Siebert said later, "A lot of people felt I had the right to speak, but thought it was the wrong time and the wrong place . . . but to me it was the only time and place."

The senior subs were beyond reach, but Wooden called underclassmen Terry Schofield, John Ecker, and Andy Hill into his office to talk over the problem with him and his assistants, Denny Crum and Gary Cunningham. They have since said these were extremely long and difficult sessions in which they all expressed some sympathy with Siebert's sentiments, were reprimanded and threatened with never getting to play. Later, they talked to returning regulars who sympathized with them, and who met with them once at Wicks's place and once at Sam Gilbert's home. Gilbert did not want them to act rashly. And they did not, though Patterson announced if any of the reserves were removed from the team, he would go with them.

When Wooden and J. D. Morgan heard about the meetings, they called a conference of all concerned, a sort of group therapy session, and everyone was heard. The players started to say then that they really didn't want to hurt the team, they just wanted to play for the team. Wooden said it was his job to play the players who could most help the team, and he was sorry if some didn't get to play much, and if anyone wanted to quit the team, he could without losing his scholarship. They said they did not. And Morgan said, well, fine, now we're agreed that the team comes first, let's all start to work together for the team.

Wooden later told this reporter, "It was just an unfortunate incident in which a young man who didn't get to play much complained publicly about it and sitrred up others who weren't getting to play. All coaches have to deal with this sometimes. We did not recruit the player, nor bring him in on scholarship, but we did give him a scholarship later, and we did not take it away from him, even when he embarrassed us as he did. I would not want a player who was not unhappy at not getting to play, but I do want players to recognize that every player on a team can't play all the time and some players are better than others."

This was a time in which youngsters and especially college students were becoming concerned about the way of the world around them and especially dissatisfied with war and when Wooden criticized their politics, they reacted, perhaps to prove their freedom, by drafting a letter directed to President Nixon, criticizing this country's activities in southeast Asia and the deadly firing on students at Kent State and asking withdrawal from Vietnam and Cambodia and a public investigation of the killings at Kent State.

It was signed by 13 players, including all the returnees and two who were departing, Siebert and Vallely, and sent to H. R. Haldeman, a UCLA graduate and one of the alumni who had helped raise funds to build Pauley Pavilion, a Presidential aide, and later a man involved in the Watergate scandal. Nothing came of it, except the comment from an unhappy coach that, "Players should not use their position as stars to try to influence the public politically."

Going into the new season, Wooden had four of his first five back. Vallely had to be replaced at guard. Hill, Schofield, Kenny Booker, Rick Betchley, and sophomore Tommy Curtis were available. Curtis was the most skilled of these, but was redshirted for the season. Two other splendid sophomores, Larry Farmer and Larry Hollyfield, moved up, but were not used much. Hollyfield was a flashy player, a sort of lesser Sidney Wicks, a soloist Wooden felt he had to discipline into becoming a team player. Schofield and Booker divided playing time at the one guard, opposite Bibby, and Wooden went with six men mainly. Four of them scored in double figures. Wicks averaged 21 points a game, Rowe 17, Patterson around 13, and Bibby around 12. Wicks averaged around 13 rebounds a game, Rowe and Patterson around 10 each. Bibby was the quarterback and outside shooter.

The team clubbed its first nine foes before getting into conference competition, all of them intersectional rivals, mediocre and none able to come closer than 12 points to the Bruins. Included among these were William and Mary and Pittsburgh, who were beaten as the Bruins won the Steel City Classic in Pittsburgh. As if to prove he did not observe what Siebert had called "a double standard," Wooden sat out Wicks and Rowe the first 10 minutes of an easy victory over Rice for having arrived to the dinner table late, and later Patterson was benched briefly because his sideburns were "too long." He briefly considered quitting the team. But these moments came and went, and the team continued to win.

After winning their first five games, surviving a slowdown at Stanford and finishing five points in front, the Bruins made their annual trip to the Midwest for two games. They took Loyola in Chicago Stadium by 25 points, then went on to Notre Dame and an annual nationally televised contest which brought a big buildup. Notre Dame had lost four of 12 starters, but the Irish had a superstar sharpshooter in Austin Carr, and campus pep rallies and pregame publicity stirred them up.

Carr was incredible and the Bruins could not contain him. He was averaging almost 38 points a game, and he scored more in this game. In desperation, Wooden called on Hollyfield to help out, but he could not handle Carr. It was the only time Hollyfield played extensively all season and it almost destroyed him. Carr scored 15 of his side's last 17 points in the last seven minutes to shut off a late UCLA surge and wound up with 46 as Notre Dame won by seven, 89–82. The crowd there went crazy, and Carr was carried off by his elated teammates, while the Bruins walked off with heads hung.

That UCLA team had won 14 in a row before this loss, which snapped another Bruin winning streak at 19. It was at this point the school began its record-breaking winning streak, but the Bruins could not know that then. They were shocked that one loss lost them the nation's number one ranking. Even more distressing, they were replaced at the top of the polls by their cross-town rivals at USC. It was an unusual situation when two teams in the same city rated one-two nationally in a college sport, but one which has been duplicated by the USC and UCLA football teams on occasion. USC was undefeated and rose to the top when UCLA was defeated. They would meet twice this season, which figured to settle not only the city title, but the conference championship, a berth in the NCAA tournament, and the national laurels.

Unlike most years, the meetings were scheduled far apart. The first came just after midseason, the second the last game of the season. The Bruins returned from Notre Dame to coast past Santa Barbara while building up for the big game against Southern Cal in the Sports Arena. The Trojans, despite their rise, remained overshadowed by UCLA and have had trouble getting students, much less the general public to go to their games, but they had no trouble getting a sellout house for this game.

Wooden had been nervous all week and critical of his players in practice, but he went into the dressing room before the game to tell them he thought they were the better team and if they played their game, the better team would win, which is about as much of a pep talk as he ever gave. UCLA led by nine in the first half, but the Trojans confused their foes by switching back and forth between man-to-man and zone defenses, caught up, led by one at intermission time, and went nine ahead with only a little more than nine minutes left in the second half. Had they continued, the complexion of this sport in the city and in the country might have altered right there and then. But they did not. They choked up and let it get away. They scored only one more point the rest of the way.

At a time-out Wooden told his team to stick to its style, that it had not been getting breaks which might begin now to even up, while Boyd, after deciding not to risk switching from a style of play which was succeeding to a slowdown which might have protected its lead, told his team to stick to its tactics. One cannot criticize the coach for this. It is sound strategy. It is the sort of strategy Wooden uses. But, Wooden's team, was, as usual, much more poised when it came to a crisis than was its foe, which, as usual, seemed unable to believe it could beat the Bruins.

SC began to miss and UCLA began to get the rebounds and Booker and Schofield started to steal balls and UCLA ran off 11 straight points before Dana Padgett of USC scored on a single free throw, to cut the lead the Bruins had taken to 61–60. Then the Bruins held the ball for more than two minutes to move the Trojans out of their zone defense, which it did, and when Wicks missed a shot, Layton did, too. Then Patterson came across court to block a shot by Westphall, Layton missed another, Rowe rebounded it, the Bruins returned to the stall, Bibby was fouled and made the free throw to make it 62–60. The Trojans brought the ball down court, but Bibby left his man to take a position in the path of Mackey, who ran into him for an offensive foul which returned the ball to the Bruins. Stalling at the finish, Wicks was fouled and hit two free throws to finish it off at 64–60, one of the most momentous victories in the decade of dynasty.

The Bruins had eight conference contests to go before the rematch, and they suffered a letdown after topping the Trojans. At Oregon, they trailed by four with four minutes to go, but as usual in a close contest the foe folded. The Bruins caught up and Bibby stole the ball and scored for a 69–68 triumph. The next night at Oregon State, the Bruins trailed by as many as 14 points in the first half and again trailed by four with four minutes to go, but caught up with half a minute to go and won, 67–65, with half a second to go when Freddie Boyd, the Beavers' good guard, dribbled the ball off his foot and out of bounds, and Wicks dribbled out the time and then hit a 20-foot jump shot.

Near season's end, the Bruins survived two more scares in the Northwest. At Washington State, they led by only two with only seven seconds to play when Schofield was fouled. The team's worst free-throw shooter, he was removed by Wooden, who said the player had suffered a severe leg injury, replaced by John Ecker, the team's best free-throw shooter, and Ecker hit two to sew it up, 57–53. The next night, at Washington, the Bruins blew a big lead at the end as their foes scored 10 straight points. In a time-out, a distressed Wooden said, "It's not your fault, but you've given in to a permissive society. You've lost the conference race and a chance at another national championship." He felt they'd gone soft and so lost and he couldn't stand it. But they were tougher than he thought. They had not lost anything. They hung right in there until finally Rowe twisted to pop in a jumper in the last half minute to win, 71–69.

Losing coach Tex Winter lamented that the Bruins were "lucky," which they were, but that was because their foes failed time and again in the clutch at the climax of close games. None of the Bruin teams during the Decade of Dynasty survived as many close calls as this one, but all of them had close calls and they won all but a few of them because they expected to win and their foes did not. They retained their poise while their foes collapsed. This club could easily have been blown right out of the conference race, but instead its foes collapsed.

In the last game USC still had a chance to catch them in the conference standings because it had not lost since its one loss to UCLA in the first game. The Trojans had their best team, they had beaten everyone else, and they had beaten the Bruins at the Bruins' home court, Pauley Pavilion, each of the last two seasons. But the Trojans were so tight they were behind by nine points before they scored a field goal, went another seven minutes without scoring even a point, fell behind by 21 points, and wound up losing by 11 points, 73–62, without ever having been in it.

The Trojans of Bob Boyd had twice beaten better Bruin teams when nothing was at stake, but its best team could not beat the Bruins even once when it was all on the line. USC finished with its best-ever record of 24–2, but was no better than second in the conference and had nowhere to go because it was another two years before the conference altered its rules so even if UCLA went to the NCAA tourney every year, the conference runner-up could at least go to the NIT in New York. And the Trojans were the first team to go, but by then it had just another good team.

In the regionals at Salt Lake City, the Bruins battered the host Brigham Young team in the first round, then survived another game it could have and probably should have lost against Jerry Tarkanian's team from Cal State at Long Beach. Thwarted in his efforts to schedule his next-door neighbors at USC and UCLA in an attempt to invade the big time, Tarkanian had his side sky high for this most important contest in their sports history.

Led by sophomore sensation Ed Ratleff and a host of talented recruits, who outhustled and outplayed UCLA from the opening tip-off, the 49ers almost put the Bruins away in the first half. Wooden was so distressed by his players' disappointing showing, he charged in the dressing room, "You're nothing but a bunch of all-American woman-chasers and hopheads." Stung, the Bruins returned to action in the second half angrily, but at first got nowhere. They still trailed by 11 with 14 minutes to play. And Wicks was on the bench in foul trouble. Bibby and Booker weren't hitting. Wooden went to subs and he had only an ordinary team on court. But Long Beach suddenly seemed to realize these were the Big, Bad Bruins it was beating and started to tense up, making mistake after mistake.

Bibby and Patterson scored nine straight points to close in. Long Beach pulled away again. Ratleff fouled out and the Bruins caught up. The score was tied when Tarkanian sent his side into a stall, playing for the last shot. They didn't get it. They waited out most of the last three minutes, but then, incredibly, Dwight Taylor, Ratleff's replacement, cut loose from a corner and missed and the Bruins got the ball back and Wicks was twice fouled in the fading seconds and hit the free throws for a 57–55 UCLA triumph.

Another miss that was momentous, another milestone made UCLA's somehow.

Almost right away Tarkanian and the Long Beach team started to say it would not blow the next shot at UCLA as soon as it got one, but to this writing it has gotten only one, and it blew that one, too, it had blown its best chance, and another strong, rising southern California club seemed to lose its momentum until it lost its coach, possibly as much to escape UCLA's shadow as for anything else.

In the Houston Astrodome, in the NCAA finals, UCLA stretched its shadow still further. There was no Elvin Hayes or Houston team to meet here now, which made it a neutral court, although almost all rooted against the Big, Bad Bruins.

Kansas wasn't competitive, and despite 24 turnovers, the Bruins coasted to a six-point triumph, 68–62. Crum wanted to make some adjustments early, but Wooden wanted to stand pat. Crum wanted Schofield in, Wooden didn't. They argued on the bench. Wooden won. After the last game, Crum was on his way to Louisville to become the coach there, and Cunningham had moved up to become the man most likely to replace Wooden when he retires, which most likely will be within a year or two.

In that last game, the Bruins faced Villanova, which had a jumping-jack superstar in Howard Porter and an accomplice in Hank Siemiontkowski, who had destroyed Jim McDaniels as Western Kentucky was outlasted in overtime in the other semi-final game. Villanova used a zone defense, which annoyed Wooden. After Patterson had one of those halves players have sometimes, scoring 20 points to pace UCLA to a 12-point lead at intermission, Wooden sent his side into a stall, an unusual switch which frustrated the fans, who cursed the champs. It interrupted UCLA's tempo, too, and Villanova closed in at the finish. Ahead by 12 with 15 minutes to play, the Bruins saw their lead drop to three, 63–60, with almost two minutes left.

Almost desperate in their deliberate game now, the noise of the fans in that madhouse washing over them, the Bruins killed off 40 seconds before Bibby was fouled. He made the free throw to make the score, 64–60. Villanova got its shots. Tom Inglesby missed. Porter missed. Wicks rebounded and threw down court to Patterson. Somehow, Porter got there to block Patterson's shot, but was called for goal tending, a crucial call that killed the Wildcats. It made the score 66–60 with 38 seconds remaining. It was 25 wasted seconds before Siemiontowski could sneak in for a lay-up to cut the count to 66–62.

The Bruins held the ball. Bibby dribbled it. When Siemiontowski fouled him, the lead was safe. Wooden shook a fist in a small gesture of triumph. Three seconds remained and Wicks walked over to the bench and stuck out his hand to Wooden. Startled, the coach put out his hand and they shook hands. Then they smiled at each other, sharing their secret. Opposite personalities from opposite poles of the earth, they somehow had made it through together to the ultimate triumphs. At the buzzer, UCLA was cheered, but the Bruins showed no celebration. They shook hands, but hardly altered expressions. They were cool, as though they could not have cared less. They cared, but they were cool.

Outside the dressing room, Wooden was buttoning his brown suit coat as he said, "The slowdown is permissible under the rules. You never have to shoot, and I used a deliberate style of offense to force them out of their zone defense. I didn't feel we would lose at any time," smiled the self-satisfied Wooden. He felt he had proved a point. It is a pet project of his to get college basketball to adopt a 30-second clock similar to the ABA's 30-second clock or the NBA's 24-second clock in which each side has only that long to shoot on each play. At this time, a pointed smile on his face, he said, "Maybe now the rules committee will think a little more about putting in a 30-second clock." Apparently it didn't think much more about it. It didn't put one in. It may have felt it would favor UCLA, which now had won five straight titles and seven in eight years.

Porter was later revealed to have signed a pro contract before the finals, causing Villanova to forfeit its record in the finals, but that didn't matter, either, for UCLA already had topped a Villanova team with Porter, who had been good, but not good enough. Now UCLA was about to lose its entire and fine front line of Wicks, Rowe, and Patterson, who had won 57 of 60 games the last two seasons, but that didn't matter, either, because it had another Alcindor, another one-man front line moving up, Bill Walton, who had finished a fabulous freshman season, who Wooden and the Bruins had been waiting for all year, while almost as a matter of fact finishing off another championship season. He had distracted them, but not to the point Alcindor had distracted another team, which wasted its year. Now the Bruins had 15 victories in a row banked, and with Walton, many felt Wooden would at last surpass the USF record of 60 straight and perhaps go on to 105 in a row, and to 10 national titles.

5

Elkhart officials announced that South Bend Central's basketball coach, Johnny Wooden, would speak at the winter sports banquet, although they had hoped to line up some prominent college coach.

Elkhart, Ind., newspaper,
February, 1946

John Wooden has carried the clipping of the above around with him many years. He feels it helps him to be humble in the spotlight of success. He carries many clips around with him to inspire him. He carries with him a crinkled piece of paper on which his father, Joshua Wooden, composed his creed: "Be true to yourself, make each day a masterpiece, help others, drink deeply from good books, make friendship a fine art and build a shelter againt a rainy day."

The walls of his office are covered with messages of merit and photos of men who inspired him. Prominent is his "Pyramid of Success," with which he seeks to inspire the young men who play for him and other men, and many copies of which he distributes annually. It consists of a series of squares in which he has composed his creed under such headings as Industriousness, Friendship, Loyalty, Cooperation, Enthusiasm, Self-Control and so forth. The squares are stacked as blocks narrowing to the top. Framing them to form a sort of pyramid are angled lines on which are inscribed the words Ambition, Sincerity, Adaptability, Honesty, Resourcefulness, Reliability, Fight, Faith, and Patience.

Wooden reads and writes poetry at home. He has said among his favorite works are Shakespeare's *Hamlet,* Gray's "Elegy," Milton's "On His Blindness," and Bryant's "Thanatopsis." A sample of his own poetry follows:

> Remember this your lifetime through,
> Tomorrow there will be more to do,
> And failure waits for all who stay. . . .
> With some success made yesterday. . . .

He also reads the Bible daily. He is a deacon of his First Christian Church in Santa Monica. He is a religious and a moral man. He does not drink hard liquor, nor smoke, nor does he curse, which is enough to make many hate him, nor does he accept happily these things in others. His verbal outbursts consist of such as "Goodness gracious," or "Goodness sakes alive."

He strives to protect his players from falling victim to such bad habits and is distressed by modern manners and morals. He does not like long hair, sloppy dress, and the disordered life favored by young people today, but he has had to accept some of this to survive. Free sex does not fit his framework. One reason he gives for barring reporters from his dressing rooms is he does not like the thought of outsiders seeing his players naked.

He insists he is as much a teacher as a coach and as concerned with his players' studies as their play. He tells them college is a place to learn, and he encourages them toward graduation. Some, pointing at pro ball, couldn't care less. Some call him, "Saint John." Although there is little evidence that he does not for the most part practice what he preaches, some see him as too good to be true. At least two players on his last team call him, in their own words, "a hypocrite." Players on each of his teams have called him this. But as time passes and they are apart from him awhile and review him in retrospect and at a distance, most see him as someone who helped them, and their respect for him seems to grow.

Although his wife, Nell, insists he has not changed in 40 years, success inevitably has altered him. He is more sure of himself and his methods than he was 10 or 20 years ago and he has a sort of haughtiness about him, although he would not like this in himself. After he philosophizes on some subject, he will say, "Of course, this is only the way I see it. Someone else may see it differently." He tries not to say immodest things, although some come out immodestly. He is not too tolerant of those who disagree with him and looks unkindly on what he considers to be impertinent questions. He does not like his attitudes or tactics to be questioned, and he draws back from such questions and smiles thinly at them as though only fools would ask them.

You suspect he would if he could cane you or court-martial you, and a rival coach comments, "Beneath his kind exterior he is a killer. If you do wrong as he sees it, he would see the wrath of the gods descend on you in claps of thunder and flashes of fire." Another said, "Beneath his skin he is a shark, who denies it but would do anything to win, including, if necessary, sneaking up behind you and snapping off a leg."

Of course he wants to win, which is what distresses so many, but this is not inconsistent with his creed. He believes in making the most of yourself, in doing the best you can at whatever you do. He once told this writer, "Basketball is something I do best. A long time ago I found my niche in teaching and coaching. I know sports is a toy part of the world, but through sports I have reached a great many young men and perhaps influenced some for good. I believe sports to be mostly good—an entertainment for escape from the pressures of our world, a physical and emotional outlet for players and fans, alike, a challenging competition which can develop those who are in it in many ways.

"I am as concerned with setting my players out on the right roads in life as I am in winning with them. Not all agree with me or listen to me, but I continue to try to reach as many as I can with what I believe in, which is all any teacher can do. I do try to win with them—but by preaching self-sacrifice, unselfishness, and team play. If I did not try to make them the best players they can be, I would be remiss in my profession. I want them to win what they can win throughout their lives. But I do not teach them to cheat or deceive the other man. If beaten, I want them to be gracious losers.

"I have been as happy with teams that did not win much as with those which won everything. I have been prouder of lesser players who reached their potential than of superstars who did not. I have been disappointed by some young men, but not disillusioned. I do not demand gratitude, so I cannot expect it. When it comes, it is coveted, but I do not do as I do because I wish to be admired, nor do I teach as I do because I expect to be thanked. I do as I do and teach as I do because of my beliefs."

He was 62 years old when he entered 1973. His brown hair was turning gray, but cropped close to his skull. As a popular young player in Indiana years ago, he helped popularize the crew cut. His skin is seamed from the years, but he does not seem old. He has thin, hawklike features, narrow lips, a narrow nose, narrow eyes. He wears glasses with thin metal rims. His blue eyes are warm or cold, depending on and giving away his feelings. He speaks softly, but with a sort of Biblical pretension, as do some teachers. He seems more a teacher than anything else. Or a minister. Lew Alcindor's mother said he seemed more a minister than a coach. He dresses well, but conservatively. His shoes always are polished. One would not expect to find a fleck of food on his lips or a stain on his shirt.

Kareem Abdul-Jabbar, who played for Wooden as Lew Alcindor, has likened him to the little old man in the horse and buggy in the Pepperidge Farm ads. Told this, Wooden smiled and said, "I suppose that is not far from the truth. I am old-fashioned and from the farmland. I was brought up by poor but proud people, who were religious and moral, and I remain true to my upbringing. I hardly feel everything old-fashioned is finished and everything new and modern is proper. I am an old-fashioned man in a modern society. I believe in old-fashioned virtues and believe they apply today. I have gone out in the world to make the most of myself, but I still try to live the sort of life that was lived in that tiny part of the world, the small communities in which I was reared."

John Wooden was born near Indiana University, but starred at Purdue and later coached his most momentous triumph at Notre Dame. But it is high-school basketball that is king here. John Wooden went to Martinsville High School. Martinsville had a population of 5200 at the time. The high school played in a gym that seated 5520. It was filled for every game. They came from the surrounding countryside to root for the home team. They still do in many gyms which seat more than the population of their town.

Every school in the state starts again at season's end in the state tournament. When a small-town team reaches the semi-state or the finals, all of the town may turn out, with a neighboring town protecting the deserted town. The state tournament started in 1911, and John Wooden led Martinsville to the finals in 1926, 1927, and 1928, and he won in 1927, and he lost in 1926 and 1928.

John Robert Wooden was born on October 14, 1910, in Hall, Indiana. His father, Joshua Hugh Wooden, was a tenant farmer. A few years later, the family moved a few miles to Monrovia, where the father worked a small farm and was also a rural mail carrier.

Everyone in the family worked in the fields and barns, picking potatoes and tomatoes, feeding and milking the cows and other livestock. Mom canned fruit and smoked meat. When their work was done, the boys could play. Dad hung a tomato basket at one end of the hayloft. Mom stitched up old rags into her hose to make a basketball. Later, Dad hung up an iron ring and bought the boys a real basketball. John remembers his father as a strict, but gentle man who read from the Bible daily, would not tolerate profanity, and imposed on his sons a rigid code of behavior. Like so many who become straight and strict, John was a bit wild as a boy and received whippings which helped reform him.

When John was 14, his family moved to Martinsville. His dad had made bad investments and lost his farm. John Wooden met Nellie Riley in this town. She played trumpet in the school band. The Rileys and Curtises were back-fence neighbors. Glenn Curtis was a famous coach in Indiana who coached at Martinsville High at the time. He did not want his players to date during the season. Johnny had to sneak around to visit Nellie without neighbor coach Curtis noticing in season. They went to band concerts and dances and hayrides and played tennis.

John feels each of his coaches gave him something special. His first coach was his grade-school coach, Earl Warriner, who also was his principal. Warriner once disciplined him by making him sit out a game their team lost, then put his arm around him and said the team would have won with him, but it was far more important if he learned a lesson than any victory would have been. John learned. He says, "He motivated me. He made me want to be the best student and the best player I could be." At the time, Wooden preferred playing baseball to basketball. He was a slick shortstop, who later had a pro offer. But he hurt his arm, couldn't hit well enough to play another position, and decided to stick to basketball. His high-school coach, Curtis, was a brilliant tactician and strict fundamentalist, but he also was a tough man who rubbed Wooden the wrong way. Curtis had used John's brother, Maurice, who was called "Cat," as his sixth man. Cat thought and John thought he should have been a starter. John arrived on the team with resentment for the coach. Reprimanded after fighting a teammate, John quit the team. But Curtis talked him into coming back, and from this John says he learned to be tolerant of players with whom he has disagreements.

John was short at 5-10, but muscular at 180 pounds, and strong and aggressive, and he was to become known as "The Indiana Rubber Man," because while you could knock him down, he always bounced back up. He could handle the ball and dribble it and shoot it and he was smart and tough and he became a regular as a sophomore and went on to win all-state all-star honors all three years he played varsity ball. He is remembered as one of the greatest players ever to play in Indiana. He sparked his team to the state finals three straight seasons. Only two other teams ever have reached the finals three straight seasons.

This was a different, early era of basketball from that he has come to coach. Teams did not run much. They dribbled and passed carefully to set up shots. Almost all shots were taken two-handed, set shots, from the outside or one-handed, lay ups, inside. The ball was returned to midcourt for a center jump after every basket. Play was rough and scores were low. There were few big men playing.

One early big man was 6-7 Stretch Murphy, who later played at Purdue with Wooden. In the 1926 state final he led Marion past Martinsville, 30–23. Wooden went scoreless. Wooden's 10 points were tops in the 1927 final as Martinsville nosed out Muncie, 26–23. He scored five as Martinsville lost to Muncie, 13–12, in 1928. Wooden never has forgotten this defeat:

In the last minute, his team led, 12–11, and had the choice of taking the ball out of bounds or shooting a free throw. Captain Wooden wanted to take it out to keep it, but coach Curtis chose the shot. Wooden shot and missed. The Muncie center, Charles Secrist, took his own center jump and heaved the ball underhanded from far outside and it went high in the air and came down right through the basket as Butler Fieldhouse exploded in a frenzy. There was still time for Wooden to pass to a teammate for a shot at the other end, but it spun around and out while a player who might have tipped it in to win was jumping for joy, thinking it was in. Ever since then, Wooden has told his players to assume every shot will miss and to get in position accordingly. This is a man who always learned as he went along.

Throughout high school, Wooden worked. He graduated with honors. He was recruited by the top college clubs in Indiana at the time and picked Purdue because it was the most powerful team in the Big Ten at the time and was led by a coach, Ward "Piggy" Lambert, who was known to coach the running game Wooden wanted to play.

He got no scholarship and had only a few dollars and a handful of clothes packed in an old suitcase. He had been promised only jobs waiting tables and washing dishes at a fraternity house and taping ankles in the athletic department. He also mimeographed and supervised the sale of programs at games. And sold snacks walking the aisles of special football trains going back and forth between big games out of town. He made the sandwiches himself. He was ingenious. Discovering that those on the dean's list got free tuition, he studied hard to earn this each semester.

Somehow, he also made all-American in basketball all three seasons he played varsity ball at Purdue and was selected this country's College Player of the Year his last year. He also played freshman football at Purdue, but hurt a knee, which finished his football, to go with the hurt arm, which finished his baseball. He was always getting hurt in basketball, too, but he played hurt. His team won the league title his last two seasons, but there was no national tournament to enter at the time. Wooden says he learned the free-lance, hard-running, fast-breaking offensive game from Lambert. Wooden says he learned the value of being better-conditioned than the other guys. He says he learned to stick to his system, no matter what.

Graduating in 1932, Wooden was awarded the Big Ten

Medal as the outstanding scholar-athlete in the conference. Later, he was named to the College Basketball
Hall of Fame as a player, and still later as a coach, the only
one ever selected from both categories.

He had been appointed to West Point, where he would
have been eligible for further college-level play, and was
tempted, but turned it down when his schooldays
sweetheart, Nell, said she could wait no longer. To raise
money for marriage, he went to Chicago to play three
games for George Halas' basketball Bears for $100 a game.
Here, he met Frank Kautsky and agreed to play for the
grocers' Indianapolis Kautsky Athletic Club for $50 a game
whenever he could. However, he turned down a $5000-a-
year offer to barnstorm regularly with the Original Celtics
of New York, whose roster included Joe Lapchick and Nat
Holman, two future coaching immortals. He also turned
down an offer of a fellowship to teach English at Purdue.

He had decided he wanted to coach, and he accepted an
offer of $1800 a year to coach basketball, baseball, and
track at Dayton High School in Kentucky. On the side he
was asked to be athletic director, supervisor of the physical
education program, and an English teacher. They also
wanted him to coach football, but he drew the line there.

He went to draw his savings from his bank only to find
the bank had gone bust. He married Nell, anyway, on
reluctantly borrowed money, that August of 1932, in Indianapolis, took her to the Bamboo Inn downtown for
dinner, took her to the Circle Theater to hear the Mills
Brothers sing, and then the next day took her home to
Martinsville and took off for a week to help out at a
basketball clinic for $25. Some say Nell has regarded him
cynically ever since. She is not afraid to say she can do
very well without his poetry and his fancy philosophy.
Clearly, Saint John's wife can be irreverent. But she has
been his constant companion throughout life, a sympathetic sidekick, and he was thoughtful enough to pick
her up on his way to Dayton.

Here, in 1933, John Wooden commenced his coaching career. He has told this reporter, "I had studied my coaches and learned something from each of them, but at first I had to learn to coach for myself. The system you use, the way you adapt it to the players you have, the way you deal with your young men are developed as you go along. You learn a lot in your first years of doing something. In fact, I believe I have learned something every year since I started. I was not born a coach. I had to become one."

From the first, he stressed conditioning, fundamentals, and a running game. He did not have talented basketball players at Dayton. He won six games and lost eleven with them his first season there. It was the only losing season he has had in coaching.

After two seasons he returned to South Bend, Indiana, where he coached Central High nine seasons and won 197 games and lost 28, giving him an 11-year high-school-coaching record of 218 victories and 42 defeats. He won no state tournament.

After the Japanese attacked Pearl Harbor on December 7, 1941, Wooden, a patriot, in his early thirties, enlisted in the Navy, became an officer, and was discharged in December, 1945.

He returned to South Bend, but he did not want to stay. His house had been lost. Purchased only three years earlier for $6000, it had been leased out to someone who had failed to meet the mortgage payments. Wooden felt he was not welcome back at Central, which now had another coach. He wanted to move up to college coaching, anyway. He had received several offers from high schools and colleges and accepted one from Indiana State University, a teachers' college, in Terre Haute. If the school was not nationally known, a sort of big-time, small-time basketball was played and still is at such schools, some of which, such as Evansville, Butler, and Ball State, produce pro players, turn out strong teams, upset name schools, and have seasons in which they reach the fringe of fame.

Wooden coached two seasons at Indiana State. His record was 18–7 his first season and 29–7 his second, 47–14 for both. His first team was invited to the NAIA tourney in Kansas City, but Wooden declined because one of his players, a black reserve, was barred. His second team went to the tourney when the player was permitted to play, but lost in the finals to a Louisville team led by future pro Jack Coleman. Other future pros in action were Mel Hutchins of Brigham Young and Vern Mikkelson of Hamline. Wooden's record with what he had at Indiana State was well regarded. His all-star performances as a player were well remembered. He was a prominent personality at that time in the Midwest and was sought by big-time basketball schools.

Minnesota wanted him and he wanted Minnesota. But UCLA also extended him an offer. Bob Kelley, who had broadcast basketball and football in Indiana, had moved on to broadcast Rams games in Los Angeles, and he had recommended him to UCLA athletic director Wilbur Johns, who had been having little luck coaching basketball and wanted to turn that over to someone else. Johns researched Wooden, reacted favorably, and asked him to take over. Wooden preferred Minnesota, but he did not want to keep, as athletic director Frank McCormick of Minnesota wanted him to keep as his assistant, the man he was succeeding as head coach, Dave McMillan. Wooden told McCormick he would take the job if he could have his own assistant. He set a day as his deadline and asked McCormick to call him by 6 P.M. with the decision. He asked Johns to call him by 7 P.M. for a decision. McCormick did not call at 6. When Johns called at 7, Wooden accepted the post at UCLA. When McCormick called at 8, telling him he could have his own assistant, Wooden told him it was too late. A snowstorm had prevented McCormick from getting through earlier. This was fate, Wooden sighs. Once he had made a commitment, he would stick by it. He was sorry about it, however.

So he left his beloved Midwest and moved to sunny southern California, where the life-style was so different. He was 37 years of age and had won 265 games and lost 56 in 13 years of coaching basketball at the high-school and small-college level. He was not then the coach he is now. Winning came harder. He had not won so much and was more impatient with losing. His teams had never won a tournament, which had turned him tense. Despite preaching purity, he smoked nervously for many years until the cancer scare caused him to quit.

At South Bend Central he had a fistfight with the Mishawpaka coach after a game. At Indiana State he had to be restrained from attacking the officials after a game. In his early years at UCLA, his sharp tongue regularly raked officials and foes. At Berkeley in one game he accused a Cal player of being a crybaby, and the youngster yelled at him, calling him, "a goddam son of a bitch."

His first 15 years at UCLA were filled with disappointments. He was successful short of the ultimate successes. He lost the conference race nine times, he lost every game that counted in the national tournament all but one time, and he failed to win the title that time, too. It was many years before he became comfortable in southern California. He had many mediocre "home courts," improper practice facilities, and there was little enthusiasm for his sport in the Far West. He did not like the life-style. He longed to return to his beloved Midwest, where the living was easy, the basketball was beloved, too, and the facilites were fine.

Today he is making $25,000 a year, according to public listings, but his income, with television shows and other side moneys, amounts to around $100,000. He had been offered more, but does not need more. However, in his early years at UCLA, he was making $6000 a year and was hungry for more. After his second year at UCLA, his alma mater, Purdue, offered him $15,000 or so a year for five years, a free insurance policy, a free car every year, a home on campus, membership in the local country club, and so forth to return as coach. He accepted on condition he could be excused from the final year of his three-year contract at UCLA. But Johns and Bill Ackerman, an official at UCLA, refused and offered to increase his salary for his last year. Wooden refused, but agreed reluctantly that he would abide by his contract.

They kept promising him what had been promised him from the first—a new basketball building—but never produced until he bought it, himself, with his super teams. Purdue came after him again another year. Other schools—Indiana, Michigan, Notre Dame, and many others—considered him or came after him other years. He was offered more money, better facilities, more recruited talent, better support, a life-style more in keeping with his own. And he was tempted many times. But he couldn't bring himself to leave. He was not a man for much moving around. After a time, his roots had taken in California. He had come with a young son and a young daughter, and they had sprung roots and were happy. They were growing up, and he didn't want to upset them with a move to a part of the country they hardly remembered. So he stayed, and still attacked, seeking success, never growing complacent, never settling into a groove as most others would have.

He was 53 years old and had been coaching successfully for 28 years before he attained the ultimate success in his profession. Since then, he has had more successes than any of his rivals. His record for the last decade of 285 victories and 15 defeats is unrivaled in the annals of college coaching in basketball. His record of 613 victories and 154 defeats for 27 years is by far the best of any veteran college coach in the country. His record of 813 victories and 196 defeats for 38 seasons of coaching over 40 years is simply astonishing. He has won eight of every 10 games he has coached.

In the last 10 years he has won 19 out of every 20. Since then he has been sought by the pros as well as the collegians. Twice the Los Angeles Lakers temped him with tremendous offers, but both times he refused them. And he has refused others. They suggest he should try to prove himself as a pro coach, at the ultimate level, and he just laughs at them.

"Coaching is coaching, on any level," he pointed out to this writer. "The challenge is comparable. If you start out approximately even with your competition, the achievement of reaching the top is the same on any level. The real difference is in the state of development of your players. I am a teacher, and pros do not require much teaching, nor is there much time for it during the pro season. The players are more fixed in their philosophies and life-styles. Most are married and have children and basketball is a job to them and they are in it for the money. I am not motivated by money.

"I like to play a personal role in the development of young men. Accordingly, I rather wish I had not left high-school teaching and coaching. If I had it to do over again, I would have remained on that level. Because there you truly were working with boys at the most formative stage. I would rate that rather higher than making national champions and gaining fame with less impressionable young men at the next level, in college. But whatever else I do, I will continue to preach old-fashioned virtues to young men who may not be totally receptive to them, but who may be marked for the good by them."

He is 63 now, a legend in his own time, loved by some, hated by a few, respected by almost all. His wife says, "Those who hate him, envy him and are afraid of him." He is getting older. He has a bad back. And a heart problem. But his eyes are clear and his hands steady. He seems to some a warm man, but he can be as cold as a chip of ice. He seems to some soft, but he is as hard as a piece of steel. Sparks glint from the corners of those eyes and his hands flex into fists. Cross him and he can cut you to pieces with his cunning and sarcasm and success.

He has been inspired and he is inspiring. He takes comfort in his poetry and philosophies and feels strengthened by living the good life by the golden rule, but he gives little comfort to his enemies; he beats them, he beats them fairly, he beats them at their own game, he beats them too much, he beats them so much he frustrates them and steals their sleep from them, and he makes it worse for them by saying winning doesn't mean that much to him, which maybe makes it easier for him to win. He says he wouldn't mind losing more than he does, but he is not going to lose more on purpose, he is not going to give them games, they are going to have to take them, they are going to have to beat him themselves.

They claim they could beat him if they had his players. They said just as he could not beat a San Francisco team with a Bill Russell, so, too, they cannot beat a UCLA team with a Lew Alcindor or a Bill Walton. They say he had only one player good enough to play pro before his Decade of Dynasty, Willie Naulls, and a dozen since—Hazzard, Goodrich, Erickson, Shackelford, Lacey, Alcindor, Allen, Patterson, Vallely, Bibby, Rowe, and Wicks—as well as others who will—Wilkes, Farmer, Nater, Curtis, Lee—and Walton. They say you can take all the goodness and good coaching and trade it all for a Walton and you will win.

6

William Theodore Walton III was born on the fifth of November, 1952, in the San Diego suburb of La Mesa, California. Growing up, he and his brother, Bruce, a year older, loved all sports and played one game or another almost every day in the warm, sunshiny climate enjoyed the year round in this beautiful Pacific Coast beach area.

Bill grew tall and thin, though he did not become a giant until his height accelerated in his teens. Bruce wasn't quite as tall, but was built thicker. Bruce preferred football, Bill basketball, but both played both, often on the same teams.

Bill recalls, "I played basketball every day, well, almost every day, from the time I was seven or eight. It wasn't a conscious effort. I just did it. It was a lot of fun for me just to go out in the backyard and shoot baskets, even by myself."

While he was a student at Blessed Sacrament Elementary School, from the fourth through the eighth grades, Bill played various sports under the coaching of Frank Graziano, a fireman who volunteered his services to the school kids. Graziano taught Walton the fundamentals of basketball. He played him at center defensively, but at guard offensively, because Bill was his best ballhandler.

He has said, "Bill always was ahead of others his age, even before he was bigger than them"

Bill has said, "I always enjoyed playing against bigger, older kids because it was more challenging. I sometimes played in four or five leagues at a time the year around."

He played end in football, but just before he entered high school, Graziano talked Bill into dropping the sport because he was so frail he might get hurt, which might hurt his basketball chances, and because basketball was his best bet.

Bruce went on with both football and basketball in high school, but by the time he got to college he gave up basketball.

They went to Helix High School, where the basketball coach was Gordon Nash. The injury to Bill's knee, and the operation to repair it, came in his freshman year. With exercise, he recovered, but slowly, and he stayed on the junior varsity team most of his sophomore year. Nash brought him up to the varsity late in the season, but used him in only six games. "He was a pretty good rebounder even then, but he was inexperienced," Nash recalls.

Bill was only 6-1 then, but between his sophomore and junior years, he shot up six inches to 6-7. He weighed only 180 pounds. He was skinny and had little endurance and could not play complete games. Nash recalls, "He would simply get too tired to go on. When that happened, he'd tell me, and I'd take him out."

Because of his frail looks, foes would shove Bill around some. When that happened, however, brother Bruce, two inches shorter, but 100 pounds heavier, would play policeman for him. He says, "When they would begin to rough up Bill, I would look at coach and he would give me a nod, and I would get to work." Mother Gloria says, "When the referee wasn't looking, Bruce would give the player an elbow and let him know that the skinny guy was his brother." Brother Bruce smiles and says, "After that, they wouldn't rough up Bill anymore."

However, Bill rapidly began to reach the point when he could take care of himself. For a fellow his height, he had quickness and agility. He could get the ball up and into the basket when he got it inside, and he had a soft shooting touch from outside. Although his knees began to bother him from his accelerated growth as his tendonitis developed, he could block shots and rebound missed shots and he concentrated on making the fast outlet pass to his teammates, who were fast breaking down court.

He was the key man on a team which won 29 of 31 games and won the California Interscholastic Federation district tourney title.

He was not fully developed yet and was not locally acclaimed as a coming star. He missed the first five games of the season with an ankle injury, but played the rest. He played in both defeats, the last one 58–52 to Monte Vista early in January. After that Helix High won its last 16 straight. Walton averaged only 17 points a game and scored only 13 in the title game, an 87–82 triumph over Madison of San Diego, so there was no reason for anyone to go overboard on him, but after the club climaxed its long streak with the championship, the big young center began to attract attention.

Between his junior and senior years, when his brother had graduated and had accepted a scholarship to play football at UCLA, Bill added another three inches to reach 6-10 and another 15 pounds to reach 195 and he became an even better and more durable player, although the tendonitis troubled him. He has said, "I was getting older and smarter. I put on pounds and I learned not to waste so much energy on the floor.

Nicknamed "Mount Helix," he was a sensation. He averaged 29 points and 24 rebounds a game, yet played unselfishly and led Helix High to an undefeated 33–0 season, which brought its winning streak to 49 in a row, and another CIF title, over Chula Vista, 70–56. Walton dominated the championship game with 31 points and 31 rebounds, and now he was acclaimed as a budding superstar almost everywhere.

By then, almost every major college in the country was courting him. He was not only a big and a brilliant and unselfish basketball player, he was white, he came from a good background, he had been in no trouble, and he was an excellent student, who was to graduate twenty-ninth academically in his senior class of 575. Coach Nash commented, "Bill is an excellent student, and not necessarily because he is a super brain, but more because he's a super achiever. I've known him to spend all weekend on an English paper he wanted to get an A on. And he got those A's. . . . And he used the same dedication to make the most of the great gifts he had as a player. He was a fine boy from a fine family."

Bill's father, William Theodore Walton, Jr., known as Ted, was a district chief of the San Diego Department of Public Welfare. He headed up a crew of 200, which dealt with 15,000 welfare cases annually. All of which may have stirred in his son sentiments for the underprivileged in our society. Bill's mother, Gloria, was a librarian, which may have stirred in her son a certain bookishness. Bill has said, "We were not rich, but we never wanted for anything. However, we had feelings for those who had less than us. We had discussions about the good things and the bad things in our world. We all had our say. We were not ever stifled."

Bill, his older brother, his younger sister and brother, and his parents lived in a sprawling white house on a hillside. Within, Mom always seemed to be cooking—heaps of hot dogs and hamburgers for lunch, steaks and roasts for dinner—in a desperate attempt to satisfy the large appetites of her large family. Bill has said, "There is no doubt in my mind that Glo's cooking is the reason I grew to be 6-11." His reference to his mother as "Glo" reveals the informality within the family. It is a warm family, which likes to do things together.

Sometimes the after-dinner period was passed with music. The parents loved music and saw to it that their children had music lessons. At the family gatherings, Pop played piano, Bill baritone horn, Bruce trombone, Andy sax, and sister Cathy drums, flute, or tuba, while Mom played audience or sang with the rest of them. The shyest of them, Bill was at home at home, taking part with his family in family things. Even now that he has grown apart from them, a maturing young man who often prefers solitude and wants to go his own way, he still feels close to them. He spends a fair amount of time with his sister, for example.

Bill now is somewhere around 6-11 and 230 pounds. Bruce played football at UCLA at 6-5 and a slimmed-down 250 pounds. He was an outstanding offensive tackle who won some all-American mention, was drafted by the pros, and was prepared to play for pay in 1973. At 16, Andy was a 6-5 forward at Helix High who hoped to follow in the footsteps of brother Bill. Even sister Cathy, 5-11, played girls' basketball at Berkeley, where she was a student at the University of California.

The father is 6-4 and the mother 5-10. Father Ted has said, "I never tried to steer my kids into sports. I encouraged them to play, but only as a broadening experience to complement their music. So wouldn't you know that they all give up music and wound up in sports?"

Nevertheless, he and his wife are their most enthusiastic fans and regularly travel wherever necessary to see their sons in action and root almost hysterically for them. They are expressive people, who jump up and down, shout, cheer, clap. Their expressions reveal their worry when Bill is bothered by his bad knees.

Bill told us, "They are great people who have encouraged us to do whatever we wanted to do and be whatever we wanted to be. They wanted us to go to college. While we were not poor, they could not have afforded to send all of us if it had not been for the athletic scholarships Bruce and I could get."

Tom McMillen of Pennsylvania was the most hotly pursued high-school basketball prospect in 1970, but Bill, who became the better of the two by far, was sought by more than 100 universitites, too. They stopped counting at

100. He was 17 and unsure of himself, but he had his own strong feelings. He disliked those who made too much of him and mistrusted those who offered too much. He did not wish to go to a sports factory. Nor a place where he would attract too much attention. He already was resistant to too much personal publicity and was giving few interviews.

An instant celebrity, he once took a girl friend to a concert and was distressed to see it reported the next day in a San Francisco newspaper. He expected attentions paid him by the San Diego press, but not a city as far removed as San Francisco. He complained to his coach, "I can't do anything without reading about it in the paper." At Walton's request, Nash helped protect him from the press. And Walton relied on Nash and on his parents to help him handle all the attention he received from recruiters, while reserving the right to a final decision for himself.

Walton has said, "If people wanted to see me, the coach asked me. It was clear between the two of us that if I said yes, I'd speak to them, and if I said no, I wouldn't, and it was entirely up to me." When recruiters reached La Mesa and offered to take Bill and his family out to dinner, they were refused. A friend says of Bill's father, "Ted has a lot of character. He didn't want to feel obligated in any way."

As had been the case when brother Bruce was being recruited for football, a favored few were invited to dinner at the Walton's home, where they could make their pitch between courses. Notre Dame's Johnny Dee, San Diego State's Dick Davis, USC's Bob Boyd, and UCLA's John Wooden were among those who broke bread with the Waltons. Wooden says this is as far as he's gone personally to recruit a player. He ate roast beef and impressed the Waltons with his manners and low-key soft sell, as well as with his reputation and record.

Bill has said he narrowed his choice to six schools—the University of California, UC Santa Barbara, USC, San Diego State, and Duke as well as UCLA. He says the fact that his brother Bruce already was at UCLA played no part in his decision to go there. In fact, he says it almost swayed him away.

He says, "I suppose the school asked him to and at first Bruce tried to talk me into joining him at UCLA, but then he seemed to see he was a negative factor and the real decision had to be mine. I had lived with him all my life and gone to the same classes and been on the same teams and I didn't know if I wanted to anymore. I care for my brother and I never want to grow too far apart from him, but we are different people, we have entirely different personalities and interests, and maybe there comes a time when you just don't want to be with your brother all the time. There is a certain stage in your life when you need a change. I did decide to go to the same school, but we do not room together, we do not see a lot of each other, and we go our own ways."

He might, instead, have gone to UC Berkeley, where his sister was headed, and he has admitted to us he rather regretted he didn't, but might yet if he goes on to graduate school. Presumably he dropped Duke from his list because it was too far away. He may have dropped Santa Barbara, where protesting students rioted regularly a few years ago, and San Diego because these schools did not play big-time basketball. He says he selected UCLA because of its combination of scholastics and athletics. He insists its history of championships and domination of college basketball were not decisive factors, but it was the championship team which dominated its sport which needed him least which got him instead of schools which wanted him more and might have ended the Bruin dynasty with him.

Walton complains of comparisons made between him and his predecessor, Alcindor/Jabbar, but he knew when he went to UCLA he inevitably would have been termed a new Lew, a white Alcindor. When Walton made his decision, Wooden was delighted. He knew now he would stay at the top awhile yet. He commented, "He is as good a prospect at this stage of development as anyone I have ever seen." Sighed San Diego State's Davis, denied the super-prospect, "He is the best high-school player I've ever seen." Maryland could have McMillen, UCLA had Walton.

First, he was selected to an AAU All-Star team which was to tour Europe. It was a rare honor for a recent high-school graduate, but older players from college or service ranks were used ahead of him, he did not play much, and he did not enjoy the experience much. The high point came when he was assigned to play for a mediocre foe in Czechoslovakia to even things out some. He did such a good job against his own teammates, the Czech fans stood and cheered him at game's end. In Italy and Yugoslavia and other countries, he was appalled by the poverty of much of the people. A young man with feelings for his fellowman, he already was as much interested in the politics of his world as in its sports.

As a freshman at UCLA he led a tremendous team, which included also Keith Wilkes, Greg Lee, Tommy Curtis, Vince Carson, and Gary Franklin, which walloped 20 straight foes. Walton averaged 18 points and 16 rebounds a game, while backing up and setting up his teammates. Wilkes averaged 20 points and 12 rebounds a game. Lee averaged 18 points, Curtis 16, and Franklin 16.

Gary Cunningham was the freshman coach who brought along his balanced bunch in the Wooden system. It was his last season as freshman coach before moving up to become Wooden's number one aide. It also was the last season for freshmen basketball teams, since freshmen were declared eligible for varsity play by the following season, and those who could not make the varsity began to be grouped with some sophomores on junior varsities, currently coached at UCLA by Frank Arnold, who doubles as varsity assistant.

Walton would have made the varsity and would have been a starter and a star right out of high school unless Wooden had chosen to hold him back a season when he didn't need him. Of course he didn't know that then. And with him, Wooden would not have lost even the one game he lost, at Notre Dame. There is no way Notre Dame, even with awesome Austin Carr on a tear, could have topped Rowe, Wicks, and company with Walton. So, UCLA had one less unbeaten season. How bad do you have to beat your foes, anyway?

While waiting for Walton and accomplices, the UCLA varsity was winning by 30 and 31 and 34 and 35 points and once by 46 points and by an average of 15 points. Meanwhile, Walton and his teammates were waiting to move up while walloping San Diego by 50 points and Santa Barbara by 60 and such as Antelope Valley and Chaffey by 72 and 77, averaging 34 more than its foes. "It was no fun," admitted Walton. "There was no challenge and no goal to go for. We were too good for the teams we played. We couldn't wait to move up to the varsity where winning would mean something, where we could go for the national championship as a goal, where we would play better teams."

It didn't matter. The first Walton Gang riddled foes by 47 and 50 and 56 and 61 and 64 points, and by a national varsity record 30 points a game over 30 games, and it won every one.

7

"The Big Man" was what his teammates called Bill Walton. Keith Wilkes was "Silky," as in "smooth as . . ." Larry Farmer was "Bullwinkle" because some said he looked like a cartoon moose. Some simply called him "Moose." Henry Bibby was "Charlie" because that was his real first name. Some called him "South," because he came from North Carolina. Greg Lee was "Greg" because no one had thought up a good nickname. Tommy Curtis was "T.C." Backup center Swen Nater was "Nate the Great," because he acted as if he was.

They were a compatible crew, "The Walton Gang," Bill Walton's first UCLA varsity team and his first championship team. He said of the too-cool, sadly divided UCLA team led by Sidney Wicks and Curtis Rowe, "I wouldn't have been happy if I'd had to play with that team, but I'm happy with this team; with these guys it's great fun." They were young, Bibby was the only returning regular from the previous team. Everything was fresh to them. And fun for them.

Athletic Director, J. D. Morgan said, "Bill Walton may be a very private person away from the team, but he is very much a part of the team, compatible and fun-loving. He is very spirited, and his spirit is very contagious and infects the other players." Coach Wooden commented, "This is the most coachable team I've ever had."

Walton said, "I wish we could be called the UCLA team instead of The Walton Gang. The team doesn't feel it's my team. This is *our* team. Everybody does something for the team. Everybody realizes that everybody on the team is valuable to us. We'd really be in trouble without anybody that we now have. It really hurts me to look at the guys and know that no matter how much I want it to be the UCLA team, it will be The Walton Gang. You can't change that.

"With the exception of myself and Henry, it's so hard for the rest of the guys to be in the role they are. As great as they are, they don't get the recognition. These guys have sacrificed so much, but they don't complain publicly. We talk about it a lot because we are a close team.

"Take a guy like Greg. Greg and Tommy Curtis, both high-school all-Americans, Greg averaging 29 points and Tommy 32 in their senior years. The most shots Greg has taken in a game this year is eight. It's really hard for Greg to take only eight shots because he's been *the man* for so long, he's been *the man* all his life in basketball, and now he's put in a situation where he doesn't take all the shots, but it hasn't affected his personality or his game or the way he is. A lot of guys have made this sacrifice. I just think our guys deserve a heck of a lot of credit for making this team what it is."

The starters were Walton at center, flanked by forwards Farmer and Wilkes, with Bibby and Lee in the backcourt. Nater was the backup center, Larry Hollyfield the extra forward and Tommy Curtis the extra guard and sixth man. Wooden felt Lee worked with Walton better, passed better and complemented the outside-shooting Bibby better than did Curtis, who shot better from outside than Lee and was superior coming off the bench to give a lift to a team which might have gone flat. Hollyfield was flashier than Farmer, but far less steady. Nater could have been one of the country's better scoring centers, but he did not defend well and could not compare to Walton.

Unlike Alcindor, Walton was played primarily in a high post and used defensively more than offensively. The other players played off him. He was to roam the pivot area, blocking shots and rebounding missed shots, passing off to trigger fast breaks, following his fellows down court while serving as safety man in case of interceptions, then moved into offensive position as much to rebound missed shots as to shoot. He shot less than outside-shooter Bibby.

Wooden went with these eight men. Sophomores Vince Carson and Gary Franklin and seniors Andy Hill and John Chapman seldom played. Bibby was the only senior of the first eight. Farmer, Hollyfield, and Nater were juniors, the rest sophomores. Farmer, Hollyfield, and Nater had two seasons to play, the rest three. And there was a splendid freshman bunch, including Peter Trgovich, Dave Meyers, and Andre McCarter, recruited and ready to move up in another year. If UCLA had frightened foes in the past, the future was terrifying for them.

Except for the 6-11 Walton and Nater, it was not a tall team. Wilkes was 6-6, Farmer and Hollyfield 6-5, Lee 6-4, Bibby 6-1, and Curtis 5-11. Walton averaged 21 points a game, Wilkes 13, Farmer 10, Bibby 15, Lee 8, Hollyfield, Nater, and Curtis 17 among them. The team averaged 94 points a game, its foes 64, a startling spread of 30 points a game, best in NCAA history.

The spread fell off only two points a game against the best teams in the tournament, for it was a record 32 points a game through the regular season. The Bruins played their first nine games at home in Pauley Pavilion and 17 of its 26 regular-season games there. They had to play half their conference schedule of 14 games on the road, otherwise they played only three of 12 rivals on the road.

Going in with 15 straight victories left over from his last team, Wooden sourly asserted, "We are a very young and inexperienced team. There certainly shouldn't be any pressure on us to win. But you writers will put pressure on us. You'll pick us to win everything again. I really can't understand it. Everybody knows USC will have better material. Only a lame brain would pick us for national honors with a completely new team." Lame-brained or not, the press picked UCLA to win it all nationally, and they were right and Wooden was wrong.

The Citadel, from Charleston, South Carolina, came in first for the season opener and was sent home defaced, 105–49. The next night, Iowa of the Big Ten was beaten 110–81. Next, Iowa State, stopped 110–81. They play basketball on the side in the Southwest Conference. Texas A&M arrived and was trounced 117–53. Notre Dame was savaged, 114–56, TCU came in to be beaten 119–81, then Texas, trod on, 115–65. Against Texas, Walton totaled 24 rebounds. The Big Ten tried again with Ohio State, but it wasn't close, 79–53. Walton took big Luke Witte apart. The last two completed another holiday Bruin Classic conquest for the Bruins.

Early in January, the conference campaign commenced, requiring the Bruins to hit the road. Headed for Oregon, they flew first class, as they usually do when the flights are more than an hour or two. They kidded the stewardesses who served them, but they were reserved and behaved. From Portland, however, they had to take a tedious two-hour ride by chartered bus south through the Willamette Valley to Corvallis, where they would meet Oregon State. Acid rock screamed from a portable tape player, but most players slept. As the bus pulled into Corvallis on an overcast, cool afternoon, Wooden, who had been seated near the front with wife Nell, rose and spoke to them:

"This is our first road trip. I hope you will act as gentlemanly as you always do in your homes. You're always to be on your special best behavior with those you come in contact. And I want to impress upon you to keep your rooms neat. This is directed at two of you—and you know who you are—who had to be called back to your rooms about this last year." He sat down. He said, "One rule we insist upon while we're on the road is that the players, if they're going shopping or for a walk, go in pairs, especially if we're in a big city, such as Chicago or New York. We believe in the buddy system for personal safety."

The players practiced for an hour in the Oregon State field house, then went to their motel to rest. Whenever possible they put up at a first-class hotel, plush rooms, two to a room. "If you're the best, you deserve the best," one player shrugged. At 10:30 game-day morning, they had breakfast together, then started to wait out the time. At 3:30 they had their pregame meal together, strolled through downtown, then lay restlessly to nap awhile. Finally, it was time to go to Gill Coliseum. The players were quiet during the bus ride to the arena. As it arrived, Henry Bibby from the back yelled, "Hey, whattaya say? Hey, whattaya say we play some ball tonight?" His teammates agreed it was a good idea.

They got off and went into their dressing room and got out of their fancy civvies and into their blue and gold uniforms and out onto the court, where 10,500 hostile fans booed them. But they played some ball and, after being extended awhile, beat the Beavers, 78–72. It was the closest any team would come to them all the regular season. More at home on the road after that, more relaxed, they moved on to Eugene, where Oregon was routed, 93–68. And then they went home.

In Pauley, UCLA shredded northern California foes Stanford, 118–79, and California, 82–43. Walton flipped in 15 fielders against Stanford. Then came the final four non-conference goes. Santa Clara came in and was crushed, 92–57. Opposing center Mike Stewart was so frustrated he threw the ball into the upper stands at one point. Denver arrived and was sent back, 108–61. The Bruins left on their annual visit to the Midwest. In old Chicago Stadium, Loyola was walloped, 92–64. On to Notre Dame, where a roaring crowd and an Irish slowdown fell far short, 57–32. These weekend games wrapped up January. The Bruins headed home for February.

Senior Henry Bibby had come a long way from the farm and the Deep South where as a black boy he cultivated tobacco, convinced 'he would not have much as a man. "With Walton, this team can win many more ways than the last teams. Wicks and Rowe were powerful players, but they weren't big men the way a Wilt or an Alcindor is and Walton is, and the big man is the most important man, especially when it also has players who are better than people realize. Wilkes is super-smooth. And we have a lot like him, right back on the bench.

"I have a job to do, I do it. I'm the field general. I quarterback the club. I handle the ball and pass it and shoot when we need shooting from the outside. I'm good at what I do. I know I'm appreciated by the players and the coaches. I don't need a lot of glory. I don't think many of us do. It's all right if most of it goes to The Big Man. He deserves it. But he doesn't ask for it. He's a super guy. He's unselfish on and off the court. He's my man."

Walton sighs and says, "I knew our team would be harmonious this year. I knew there wouldn't be any problems from the guys from our freshman team last year. I knew them really well. The only problem that could arise, I thought, was Henry. He'd be the top man, the returning senior, and he could just as easily have played the role of Mr. Cool, or Mr. Above Everything, but he didn't, and it's so great for us that he's playing the way he is and being the kind of person he is. That's one of the reasons for our team's success, because Henry is one of the team. Everybody looks up to him and respects him, but he's also one of the guys.

"As a team, we're playing both ends of the court. I think its wrong when they say I'm primarily a defensive player. I've been a defensive and offensive player all my life until I came here. We're playing a high-post offense and the high post just ruins centers offensively. It's a terrible offense for a good center, because a guy does nothing but set picks and rebounds. But it's our offense, so I play defense and pass off for the fast break and don't initiate many shots. I think I'm equally as proficient at offense as at defense, but the offense we've been using has minimized my offense.

"I make it a point of knowing where all the guys are all the time, so when I get the ball, even with my back to everyone, I know Henry is over here and Keith is close by and Farmer is within at least 10 feet of me. I know where everybody is all the time, so when we get the ball, I don't have to look all around for somebody. Coach doesn't want me to have the ball going down. If I did it, he wouldn't get upset or anything, but I know there are better guys on the break than I am. My job is to get the ball for them, not bring it up court or come down the sidelines and take the jump shot off the fast break.

"My knees *are* bothering me, yes. I have to take care of them. I have to heat them before games and ice them after games. I have to pass up some practices, which I feel bad about because I don't like getting special favors and I don't like it looking like that but I guess it has to be done. My knees hurt a lot sometimes, but we're winning, so that makes the pain bearable. I have to bear it. These are good guys on this team and I'm with them all the way. Some of our games are too easy. But I don't think they'll all be easy. The other teams can't expect us to lose to them or let up on them. We have to be free to play as well as we can, no matter the score. If they want us to lose, they have to beat us. We're not going to just let them do it to us, they have to do it themselves. If they can."

Returning to conference competition at home, the Bruins routed USC, 81–56, which was supposed to have superior material. Then they whipped Washington State, 89–58. Washington came in with its star center, Steve Hawes, supposedly the best center north of Walton, saying he was not afraid of Walton, he was sure he could do a job on him and he was sure Washington could do a job on UCLA and could beat the Bruins. His first three shots were blocked by Bill and Hawes seemed to shrink. He scored only one basket in nine attempts the entire contest. Walton scored 11 in 16 tries. He even threw in twisting jumpers over Hawes's outstretched reach and he took him apart inside. He outrebounded him 24 to nine, which matched what was to be Walton's season high in rebounds.

In the *Los Angeles Times,* Jeff Prugh wrote, "Walton outclassed Hawes so badly that the officials should have stopped the contest and ruled it a technical knockout." Washington coach Marv Harshman said, "I've never seen Hawes dominated by anybody that much. I don't know if Walton's better than Alcindor, but he sure plays with more enthusiasm and he covers more area out there. Now I kinda wish Alcindor was back. Walton does even more. He utterly destroyed us. There's not much you can do against him, except grap him whenever he gets the ball, but then, of course, you lose a lotta people that way. We lost Hawes that way, with half the second half still to go and that was the last straw." UCLA outscored the Huskies in the second half, 63–38, and in the game, 109–70.

Wooden said, "Well, Lewis was an overwhelming player, but so is Bill. It's hard to imagine anyone playing a better game than Bill did. He was just tremendous." Later, the coach added, "Bill is certainly deserving of all the credit he's received. His abilities enable us to bring out the best in the other players, but its's still a team effort. Certainly Walton is the difference between us being good and great. He is a remarkable young man.

"He is going to get better, too. He's so young he still tends to get down on himself when things don't go just the way he thinks they should. He has to have the experience to learn to shrug off things that don't seem to go quite right. Sometimes this team seems to show more emotion than reason. Again, that's because we're basically young. But this is a fine group of young men. They seem to accept my beliefs better than some of our teams in the past. Not that I had any real troubles before, but I think our team this year may reflect a desire of young people to want direction and leadership. At least that's the way it seems right now. We're all having fun."

Wooden insisted his club should not be conceded any championships. He sort of smiled and said, "You have to accept being ranked number one because that's the way it is in the newspapers, but I can't honestly say that I really believe it. We have to be truly pressed by someone before we can be measured. If we are pressed badly and come back to win, then you can talk about greatness."

UCLA was ranked number one because it has been ranked number one the better part of nine years now and usually has finished number one and everyone accepted it that this one would finish number one, too. When it beat old rival USC, UCLA stretched its undefeated streak to 17–0 this season and 32 straight over two seasons. In mid-February, the Bruins took care of Washington and Washington State, home and away. Washington State fell, 89–58, and Washington, 109–70, at Pauley, then in the Pacific Northwest the following weekend, Washington went down 100–83, and State, 85–55.

Already trimmed in the Northwest, Oregon and Oregon State were trimmed at Pauley on consecutive nights by the almost identical scores of 92–70 and 91–72. UCLA was coasting. In the first contest, Walton let loose with what were to be his season highs of 15 field goals and 37 points.

The first weekend in March, the Bruins have to play their annual pair in Northern California. Wooden says he used to require his players to be in by midnight after games, but, devilishly, he says if they win over California tonight, clinching the conference crown, it may be even later. They win easily, 85–71, clinching the conference crown. And some stay out quite late, indeed.

Midday the next day they bus to Rickey's Hyatt House in Palo Alto to rest before the game with Stanford that night. That night, Stanford stays with them until it leads, 5–3. Then UCLA scores 11 straight points and it is all over. UCLA wins, 102–73.

The regular season ended with USC visiting UCLA at

Pauley. UCLA won, 79–66, but not without trouble. It was a rough, physical game, during which Ron Riley's elbow struck Bill Walton in the mouth and Walton got all upset, especially when no foul was called.

Later he complained, "That was the cheapest shot I've ever seen. I was elbowed and it jarred a tooth loose. I was elbowed five or six other times. It's supposed to be a basketball game, not a wrestling match."

Riley said, "It was accidental. I wasn't trying to hit him. If he feels that's what I did, that's just his tough luck."

Wooden angrily commented, "I suppose that was a 'phantom punch.' He should have been kicked out of the place."

Several USC players called Walton "a crybaby."

Walton said, "They can call me whatever they want. If I have a complaint, I'm going to complain. I can't stifle my emotions."

8

The pros were pursuing him now. His college class still was two years from graduation, but the courts had ruled that no longer mattered, in the Spencer Haywood case. If a pro team wished to sign a player and he wished to sign with them, he was free to do so. He could not be deprived of the right to earn a living on some saintly pretense he had to finish college. The pros used the devices of declaring collegians who wished to join their ranks "hardship cases." Walton's family were comfortable, middle-class people. He could not claim financial hardship. But with bad knees that might cave in at any time, he could claim physical hardship. He could say he had to cash in while still able. Dallas of the American Basketball Association drafted him and offered to let him cash in on a $1,000,000 long-term contract.

Even before the NCAA championship tournament began in 1972, Walton said he was going to refuse the professional offer. Many did not believe he would. Many who would not earn nearly a million dollars in a lifetime of hard work did not believe he should. But Walton had his principles and he felt he should stick to them and he would. "I'm not interested in money," he said. To prove it, he pulled out his wallet and pulled from it a single dolllar bill, which he said was all the money he had at the moment. "I don't care about comfort or possessions," he said.

He said, "I'm not ready to play pro yet. I'm not nearly the player I hope to be. I'll get heavier. I'll get bigger and better. My knees may get better. It is hard for me to play 30 games a season now. How can I expect to play 80 to 100 games? I find it hard to play back-to-back games now; how can I expect to play four or five nights in a row the way they do in pro? If I play pro, I want to give the people who pay me their money's worth. But I don't need a whole lot of money.

"As a pro I'll be even more in the spotlight than I am now," he sighed sadly. "I'll have those guys coming at me for 10 or 20 interviews a night. Who needs it? Or wants it? Besides, I don't want to play with a lot of 40-year-old guys. I want to play with the guys I'm playing with now. Young guys. Guys who feel about things the way I do. They're a great bunch of guys. I'd never be able to forgive myself if I deserted them."

"The NCAA Tournament?" asked Loyola's coach George Ireland. "You mean the UCLA Invitational." He wasn't in it, but he knew what it was.

In 1972, it opened for UCLA with regionals in Provo, Utah. UCLA had to open Thursday night against Weber State, then if Cal State Long Beach got by USF, it would be the long-awaited Bruin-49er rematch on Saturday afternoon.

"My players are not looking past Weber State to Long Beach," John Wooden insisted. "They respect Weber State. They know enough not to take them too lightly. They know any team which gets this far can be tough. I expect a tough game."

Weber was a soft touch. Before the sellout crowd had settled into the 23,000 seats in the mammoth Marriott Activities Center, home of host Brigham Young University, the Bruins scored the first seven points. They shot off to a 12–1 lead before Weber hit its first field goal with more than six minutes gone.

Weber State tutor Gene Visscher put all his players on Walton. Which stopped Walton. But left all the other

Bruins free. Walton hit only one basket, but Lee hit three and Curtis hit three and Wilkes hit four and Farmer hit seven and Bibby hit seven and, with the game won, Wooden brought in the reserves and Franklin hit a couple and Hollyfield a couple and Hill three and Nater five, and it was easy.

Later, Visscher said if he had it to do all over again, he'd do it the same way. Why not? They'd only lost, 90–58.

Wooden was dissatisfied. "We were miserable. We weren't sharp at all. If they hadn't given us the shortest open shots we've gotten all year, we might not have won. Subconsciously," he sighed, "I doubt we had much respect for Weber State. I suppose we were looking forward to Long Beach."

Long Beach, having beaten USF, was waiting. For a year, since bowling a big lead and choking in the clutch when it had the Bruins reeling in the last regional, Long Beach had been waiting, its fans preparing banners to demean the Bruins, its players saying the Bruins were mortal, just another team, a team they should have beaten and now would beat. Star Ed Ratleff vowed, "We're gonna take it to 'em. They're gonna know they've had a game." Coach Jerry Tarkanian said, "It's a game. We've got a good team and can win any game. They have a good team, too. Their record shows that. But they can be beaten."

Long Beach was good, but not good enough, not nearly good enough, and they played as though, down deep, they knew it all along. They had been good enough to get back into the regional finals, to get another shot at the big team they knew would be there, too, but their talk was just talk; they played rough, with a sort of desperation, as if they knew they were not good enough. They had stirred up UCLA enough to inspire the Bruins to put out their best, and that was more than enough.

It started when the UCLA band decided to rehearse at three in the morning in their hotel, the same hotel that housed the Long Beach team. As if that wasn't enough, they decided they needed another practice period at nine. By then, the 49ers were roused from the sleep they had sought through the long, noisy night. Irritable and wearily edgy, Tarkanian first took his team out to the parking lot to run through plays, then to the arena early and was insulted by slanderous signs raised high by Bruin supporters. "I just wish we had more time to prepare," he said warily. Wooden said, "We're ready."

The game started and the players started to rough each other up, cursing one another, too. Walton and Nate Stephens went at each other. Lee and Chuck Terry went at it. Farmer and Ed Ratleff went at each other. Even little Bibby and big Nate Stephens went at it. Bibby was knocked down several times. He kept getting up. From 6-6, Farmer and Bibby spurted to put their foes away early. The 49ers draped themselves all over Walton, but Farmer hit inside and Bibby from outside. Bibby hit three in a row from what appeared to be just outside the stadium and it was 17–7 and it wasn't a contest after that.

Wooden worried awhile yet, but during one time-out when Wooden was talking fast, Walton put a hand on the coach's arm and said, "Hey, hey, easy, easy." Then as the coach turned in astonishment, Walton turned to his teammates and said, "Get it to me over their heads. I've got it beat." And he did, starting to score when he wanted to do so.

Under pressure from Farmer, Ratleff missed seven of eight shots the first half. By then it was 34–23. Under pressure from Lee, Terry hit only two baskets the entire game. Under pressure from Wilkes, Gray hit only two baskets the entire game. Under pressure from Walton, Stephens hit only one basket the entire game. The Bruins steadily pulled away in the second half.

During the second half, Walton pulled up in pain, clutching his ribs and calling time. He said he was elbowed. When Walton was taken from the game with more than 10 minutes to play and his side safely ahead, 51–38, Wooden met with Long Beach assistant coach Dwight Jones in front of the scorers' bench and told him it was disgraceful and unethical the way his players were roughing up the UCLA players. Then Wooden went to one of the officials and complained that the 49ers were committing intentional fouls, especially the way they had been elbowing Walton flagrantly. He was asked to sit down, and told it would be watched.

There was not much left to watch. At the buzzer, the 49ers had the fewest points they had scored in a game all season and had lost, 73–57. Despite the wide margin, the Bruins seemed relieved, betraying the emotion they had felt going into this game against their next-door neighbor who had embarrassed them the year before and talked big about the rematch ever since.

As they stood courtside awaiting regional trophy presentations, the Bruins slapped hands, embraced, and laughed happily. They threw cups of water at one another. Wooden pretended not to notice. He stood smiling, with his arms crossed across his chest, waiting for the winner's rewards. When water splashed on trainer Ducky Drake, he growled, "Cut it out." But the Bruins pretended not to notice him. Tommy Curtis grinned, "Oooohhhh, it's so good."

Walton had hit seven of 10 shots and scored 19 points, but he was one who did not seem excited. In fact, he seemed unhappy. And, later, as he left the dressing room, he, as usual, said he did not want to discuss it, but he confided to one that he felt he had been slugged by Nate Stephens and roughed up by other 49ers and he was fed up with it.

Bibby, who had scored 23 points, took the same tack, observing, "Every year we play Long Beach we get slugged." Lee displayed a fat lip and observed, "I didn't give it to myself, it was given to me." Wooden commented, "There wasn't much basketball being played out there. What there was, we played it. Any time this team expects a tough game, it plays a good game. It rises to the occasion.

In the 49er dressing room, Gray said, "Walton is a crybaby. And that little squirt, Bibby, was mouthing off all day. I couldn't do anything because he's small and I'm big and I'm supposed to be a bad guy. If I'd done anything, I'd have gotten run out of the country to Cuba."

Ratleff sat silently a long while with his head down. Then he looked up and said, "The officials protect UCLA. They were fouling us a lot and we didn't get the calls. They get away with so much because every time you touch them it's a foul." Tarkanian said, "Ratleff is black and blue. His arms are sore. He's sorer than he's ever been after a game. And he says he's never been knocked down so many times."

Ratleff said, "I really thought we had a better shot at them this year than last year. Bibby hadn't been hitting that well last year. But he hit today against us. And they have Walton now and he makes a difference. With him they take a close game and make it not close." Terry said, "You've got to change your game when you face a Walton. You can't use what works for you against anyone else. You know you want to win a game like this so much. You look forward all year to playing in it. And then you play it and suddenly it's all over and your whole year is lost."

Tarkanian said, "We went in hoping to take away the middle from them. But some passes got through to Walton. He's so good. And Bibby beat us from outside. We knew if Bibby was hitting we were in trouble. Well, with Walton in there we were in trouble anyway. We were beaten by a better team. They're a great team."

Some of his players squirmed at such talk. They were disappointed, depressed, looking around for something to cling to. Soon they were talking about next year again. Most of them would be back. "We'll beat them next year," Ratleff promised, almost aimlessly, as if he did not believe it himself, gathering his guts.

Meanwhile, UCLA was on its way to the finals this year back home in Los Angeles, at the Sports Arena. Who was there to trouble them? Louisville, coached by the Bruins' old assistant coach, Denny Crum? North Carolina, with big Bob McAdoo to challenge Walton? Florida State's towering upstarts?

"I'm the coach of this team and don't tell me how to coach my team." Wooden to assistant Denny Crum during the 1971 NCAA finals when Crum persisted on a point Wooden wanted to banish his assistant to the end of the bench, but Bibby, the captain, calmed the coaches.

Now it was the 1972 NCAA finals and Crum had moved on to become head coach at Louisville and he had won 24 of 27 games there and now he confronted his old boss at UCLA, who had won 28 straight, in the second game of the first round. It was pupil versus teacher, which added spice to the contest, though few felt it would be a real contest.

Still, the Sports Arena was sold out months in advance, mostly to UCLA supporters, and it was, for the finals, their home court again now, not USC's, this circular, baby-blue building, seldom filled since Jack Kent Cooke built his Fabulous Forum in the suburbs to house his professional basketball and hockey teams five years before, but still almost like new, sparkling amidst the old, black ghetto which surrounded it.

On a warm spring evening, 15,189 fans flowed into the arena, turned up high, and they began to make a lot of noise. There were quiet people there, NCAA officials, coaches conventioning, observing with scholarly intensity, but the noisy ones dominated—the cheerleaders screaming in their sexy costumes, the bands blasting, the fans yelling.

After Florida State upset North Carolina, the team rated second best in the nation, UCLA, in its blue and white uniforms, and Louisville, in its cardinal red and white, came out, and the noise threatened to carry the roof off. The television cameras were blinking their red eyes, carrying the contest coast to coast. Broadcasters were breathlessly speaking into their mikes. The typewriters were click-clacking.

Before the game began, Wooden said, "We are pleased to play a team led by one of our own, proud that Dennis Crum has taken his team this far, and we expect a difficult game." And the 34-year-old Crum said, "I know them. I know what to expect from them." And he smiled and said, "I don't think Mr. Wooden will give me anything."

As the UCLA and Louisville players stood together in the corridor while waiting to be called on court, Walton was so cool he was kidding Crum. "Where's all that money you promised to pay me under the table last season?" he asked the coach, who was startled into a little laughter. They went out to a thunderous roar and Walton stood near midcourt, smiling, part of the time appearing to be paying no attention to the warm-ups, his mind maybe elsewhere. He kept time to the music with snapping fingers.

From the opening tip, Louisville went to UCLA. Crum's Cardinals swarmed all over the Bruins, surprising them some, using an energetic man-to-man defense, which made them make mistakes, and appeared ready to rough up Walton as much as necessary to slow him down. After seven minutes they were within 12–10 of the Bruins and the anti-Bruin fans were roaring.

At one point, Walton exchanged comments with Mike Lawhon and was punched by him. Bibby barged in, blocking Lawhon down. Another time, Walton, fouled by Lawhon, yelped at him. Lawhon shouted, "You big crybaby. What a candy you are." Walton fumed at the free-throw line. "These two are for you," he growled at Lawhon, then sank two. "And I'll see you after the game," he challenged, but he did not do that later.

Walton went to work. Doubling on him, Al Vilcheck and Ron Thomas could not contain him. Lawhon just volunteered his services, sometimes tripling on the big man to no effect. Walton whirled for hook shots and forced his way inside for follow shots and his foes began to collect a lot of fouls trying to keep up with him. In three minutes, Walton scored his team's next eight points and UCLA went ahead, 20–14.

Louisville refused to crack. Paced by a super player, slick little guard Jim Price, the Cardinals hung on. Bibby was not hitting and was benched for three personal fouls midway in the first half. Walton turned an ankle and had to call time, limping away in that agonized way of his, before returning nimbly and seemingly none the worse for wear. But the Bruins kept building a lead, little by little. Despite 14 turnovers in the first half, the Bruins went to intermission ahead by 11 at 57–46.

At the start of the second half, the Bruins scored the first six points. But a goal-tending call on Walton's block of a shot that seemed a foot short of the basket gave Louisville a lift, and the Cards came back a bit and drew within seven points.

Then Thomas drove under Walton on a shot attempt and the big man fell flat on the floor and lay as though dead, or at least dying, and another time-out had to be called as the Bruin supporters held their breath. But Bill was helped up and he used those remarkable recuperative powers of his and returned to action, sinking a free throw, then frustrating his foes again, complaining on almost every call, but playing splendidly between complaints.

Farmer got five straight points and suddenly UCLA led by 13 after five minutes. Louisville fought back to within eight, but then Vilcheck fouled out with 12 minutes left. Then Thomas fouled out. And UCLA started to pull away again, leading by 12, then 15, then 19. Wilkes and Larry Carter took swings at each other, but Louisville's fight was fading. Only the jumpers popped in by Price kept the Cardinals from total collapse.

As so often, a foe stays close and stays close and stays within striking distance, and then, suddenly, it is no longer close, the foe is finished and it is all óver and UCLA has a lock on it. Wooden cleared his bench and the Bruins coasted home, 96–77, and their fans stood and cheered them and Wooden went to Crum and accepted congratulations from him.

UCLA had shot 57 percent, Louisville only 40 percent, more than making up for the Bruins' 21 turnovers. Walton had hit 11 of 13 from the field, 11 of 12 from the free-throw line and scored 33 points to go with 21 rebounds and six blocked shots. His foes, Vilcheck and Thomas, had been destroyed, left with five field goals and four rebounds between them.

Only Price with 30 points and flawless floor play had performed as though there was no pressure playing at the top. For UCLA, Farmer had 15 points, Wilkes 12, Lee 10, six others 26 among them. Bibby had only a single field goal before fouling out. It wasn't his night, but with 10 men scoring, the Bruins had managed without him.

In the Louisville dressing room, an angry Vilcheck snapped, "We need neutral officials. Walton and UCLA got all the calls. He's a great player, but he cries more than any player I've seen. For being as good as he is, I don't know why he cries constantly like he does."

A depressed Price, soaked with sweat, looked up from his seat by his cubicle, and said, "We lost and I'll make no excuses. UCLA played better and it won, so it is the better team." Asked if he was satisfied with the way his team played, Price smiled and said, "Man, we lost and I'm never satisfied when we lose. If we played the Lakers and lost by one, I wouldn't be satisfied."

Crum stood solemnly outside the players' portion, his face pale, and he said, "I think this is the best UCLA team I've seen. We did our best to win, but it wasn't enough to win. I think Florida State has a chance to win, but, no, I don't think they will win."

Wooden sat in his sector, sipping an orange drink, and he said, "I thought we played well. We won, didn't we? I thought Louisville played a fine game. I expect Florida State will play a fine game. I haven't thought much about Florida State yet. Now I have to start thinking about them, don't I? Well, I suspect I'll use Walton in near the basket against them," he said. And smiled that smile of his.

Minnesota had upset mighty Marquette in the regionals, but Florida State had upset Minnesota and Adolph Rupp's last Kentucky team to reach Los Angeles and the NCAA finals and now it had built a 13-point half-time lead and a 23-point second half lead and then held on to knock North Carolina and McAdoo from the race by four, 79–75. And now it had to face UCLA in the final.

Florida State, hungry from three years on NCAA probation, paying for recruiting violations, had rounded up a bunch of brilliant black players, flamboyant with Afro hairdos. Coached by Hugh Durham, the Seminoles had two 6-10 giants, Reggie Royals and Larry McCray, and two 5-7 flashes, Greg Samuel and Otto Perry, to go with 6-4 Ron King, 6-4 Ron Harris, and 6-6 Rollie Garrett. They had won 27 of 32 games and insisted they could win one more. Cocky little Petty, their spokesman, said, "No one knew us before. Now they know. We can play with anyone. They have the greatest coach in the world in Wooden and the greatest player in the world with Walton, but we just might upset them."

Florida State was upset mentally first. Bill Wall, coach of mighty MacMurry College of Illinois, president of the National Association of Basketball Coaches, spoke at a press conference, saying, "I resent the fact Florida State is here, and a lot of other coaches do, too. Our coaches are amazed, disgusted, and disillusioned at this. Their coach was caught with his fingers in the till not once, but twice."

A commotion was stirred up. Florida State officials were stung by the criticism. University president Stanley Marshall called a press conference to say, "Wall's remarks were inaccurate, totally untrue, and damaging to us. We are considering legal action."

Coach Durham said, "Wall doesn't know what he's talking about. He doesn't know the facts, but I will not get down to his level to answer them. We've paid the price. We accepted punishment. We didn't debate it in the press or in public. Now we just want to play."

At Friday's practice, Wooden, who did not want his coming triumph tainted, offered his regret to his opposing coach: "I'm sorry about this. I want you to know we don't feel the same way," he said. Durham said, "Thank you. I'm happy about that." His outspoken player Perry said, "It won't affect us in any way. That's off the court. Our job is on the court. We got a job to do."

They worked at it. But Walton seemed to upset his rival center, McCray, by standing around in blue jeans and button-down shirt watching him work out. It was a lay-up drill and Larry blew six straight, his head turning over his shoulder to see if Walton still was there. Walton waved with a lifted fist. McCray waved a fist back and smiled, but he stopped shooting until Walton left.

At nine Saturday morning, a few hours before the game, Durham brought his team back to the Sports Arena for an additional shooting practice. They were alone with the ghosts in the empty place, shooting at shadows. UCLA did not work out. To accommodate national television, it was an afternoon game and Wooden did not want to weary his Bruins. But Durham was ready to try anything.

Some 15,063 fans moved out of the warm sunshine outside into the arena. UCLA had more supporters than any of the four teams, of course, but it seemed the other fans were all for Florida State, sympathetic to the Seminoles, wanting them to upset the big team, wanting any team to end the dynasty.

Warming up, the Bruins were relaxed. The bands blared away and Walton stood near midcourt moving up and down on his toes and snapping his fingers in time to the music. He seemed almost ready to burst into song or dance. Curtis ran around slapping his teammates on their rear ends. They smiled and seemed loose. Meanwhile, Florida State was all business, eyes burning darkly.

Florida State missed its first two shots, but then hit seven straight to take a 21–14 lead, with the fans standing and screaming in surprise. Seven points was the most the Bruins had trailed in any game all season. Big Reggie Royals was dropping off Wilkes to help big McCray on Walton, and the game was nine minutes old before Walton banged in his first basket.

But this freed Wilkes, who started to shoot and hit. At 18, Wilkes was a wonder under pressure and wound up with 23 points. Bibby began to cut loose from the corners and he hit, too. He wound up with 18. Tommy Curtis came in, cool in the clutch, to take charge. He hit a 12-footer to put the Bruins ahead to stay, 27–25. By then, McCray was sitting down, saddled with three fouls.

Curtis was from Tallahassee, home of Florida State. He had played on the playgrounds with some of the school's players and had been recruited eagerly by the school, before leaving town for Los Angeles. He seemed especially inspired in this situation, playing in the title tilt against his hometown school and boyhood buddies. He hit four baskets and assisted on six others in a brief brilliant stretch.

Wilkes hit 13 points in the first half, Bibby, 16. Walton started to take charge, rebounding, passing off and scoring. He hit hooks, follows, and short shots from those high lob passes. By half time, the Bruins were ahead, 50–39, and seemed safe. The crowd's early hysteria had faded and everyone was accepting the inevitable.

Throughout the first half, Walton had appeared to be angry at the rough treatment dealt him by the Seminoles' giants. He complained a lot to the officials. After he was fouled, he complained to his foes. In the second half, he started to fight back. His side led by 13 points, 67–54, when he picked up his fourth foul with between 11 and 12 minutes left. Within one of fouling out, he had to be benched.

In the next six minutes, McCray murdered reserve center Swen Nater, and King, who wound up high man in the game with 27 points, began to connect from the corners. The Seminoles outplayed and outscored the Bruins and began to slash away at their lead and the fans who wanted the upset had their hopes revived and began to holler for Florida State again and all was bedlam in the building.

Walton was rushed back into action and the Bruins hung on, but for the first time this young team seemed shaken and uneasy. Three times the Seminoles cut their deficit to seven points, fell back to nine, then went to seven again, the last time with four minutes left. Suddenly they seemed to realize they had the Bruins reeling on the ropes, and, as it had been for so many teams before them, they began to tense up. Wooden sent in Lee and orders to stall.

Bibby missed a jumper, but Royals lost the ball to Wilkes. The Bruins ran out a minute before shooting. On an inbounds play, the Seminoles threw the ball away. Again the Bruins ran out a minute before being forced into a jump ball at midcourt. Wilkes took the tip. The Bruins ran down the clock some more before the Seminoles got the ball back. Then McCray was called for traveling.

McCray was saddled with four fouls. Royals was fouled out. Florida State forced another jump ball at midcourt, but Lee controlled it. He got it to Walton who got it to Wilkes who streaked in to score uncontested to sew it up. Ron Harris scored, then scored again, and Florida State was within five, but it was too late, time ran out and UCLA had won by the fewest points by which it had won all year, 81–76, and its fans cheered them, while other fans sat down in disappointment.

It was all over again and UCLA had won again, the first title for this young team, but the sixth straight and eighth in nine seasons for its school's teams. This team had completed a perfect 30–0 campaign and stretched the school's winning streak to 45, now within reach of USF's enduring record of 60 straight. Only in 1956 and 1957 when USF and North Carolina did it in consecutive years had any other schools produced undefeated national champions, and this was the third UCLA team to do it.

Bibby said this team was better than the Wicks and Rowe teams he had played on the previous two seasons, "because they never went undefeated and this team did." Wooden would only say, "It is one of my best teams." But most felt if it was not then, it soon would be his best.

It seemed curiously dissatisfied with its triumph, title or no title. As the players were held on court for the awards ceremonies, they lolled on the bench almost indifferently. After a brief burst of hand-slapping enthusiasm at the finish, there had been no sign of a real celebration. Walton, who had scored 24 points and collected 20 rebounds and had held McCray to three baskets and six rebounds, was announced as the tournament's Most Valuable Player, and he was cheered as he walked up to take his trophy, all loose and shrugging, unexcited.

In the losers' locker room, coach Durham seemed drawn and disappointed. He said, "I thought we had a chance. We played well while we had our starters in the game, but we kept having to take them out with fouls and then we lost a big man. It's hard to keep a game going against UCLA. They take the ball inside to Walton and you pick up fouls trying to contain him. We came close, but he put it away."

McCray said, "I'm really 6-11 and he's supposed to be 6-11, but he's taller than that, he's taller than me." Royals stared sullenly at the floor and said, "If we played again against them, we'd beat them."

The Bruins weren't worried about that. Walton worked his way into the Bruin quarters through a crowd of fans and writers, asking, peevishly, "Whose dressing room is this, anyway?"

Inside, by NCAA edict, covering the championship contest, it was open to reporters for the first time all season. Asked how tall he was, Walton snapped, "I'm 6-11, just like it says in the programs. It isn't how tall you are, anyway, it's how tall you play. How can you tell how tall I am? You've got a bad angle. You're looking up at me."

They clustered around him, looking up at him, who towered over them. The sweat streamed down his pale skin, which was discolored with a welt on one arm. His reddish hair was mussed. He seemed weary. He said, "I'm really embarrassed. I can't believe how bad I played. I'd have to say it was one of my worst games. We should have beat these guys with ease. I guess I should be happy that we won, but in all honesty I'm not. Of course, I'm glad for the team we won, but in all honesty I'm really upset with myself the way I played."

The only really happy player in the locker room seemed to be Curtis, who had cut down one net, and now showed off his championship ring and smilingly suggested, "It will be something to show the people back in Tallahassee." Bibby, who had put down the other net, shrugged and said, "We didn't play well, but we won. We never think about losing. I was never worried. We were behind early but we've been behind before and we caught up early. We were far ahead at the finish and I never thought they could catch us. We won easily enough." It was his third straight title. He said, "It gets to be old after a while."

Wooden said, "I understand why Walton and some others aren't satisfied. Bill, for example, sets high standards for himself and is displeased when he doesn't reach them. But I don't think we played as poorly as the players do. Very few championship games I've seen or been in have been exceptionally well played. There's too much emotion and too much at stake for that. I was especially pleased when we fell behind but didn't lose our poise and showed patience. I was not so pleased when we got cautious and started to stand around near the finish, which is why I went to a slower game, to protect our advantage. I'm satisfied.

No, this isn't my most satisfying championship. The first one stays that."

Walton was asked how his team remained so invincible. He looked to Lee and said, "You're the man with the words; you tell them."

Lee looked at the reporters and then he said, "We're integrated."

When Walton was called to a press conference, he went, but reluctantly. When NCAA publicist Jerry Miles put a microphone up to his face, Walton asked, "Can't you put that down?" When reporters complained they could not hear, Walton snapped, "I can hear myself. My voice is bouncing off the wall back there. There's seats open up front. If you can't hear, come up here."

Then he said, "We didn't dominate the game like I knew we could. Florida State has an excellent team, but we just didn't play that well. We like to win convincingly, so the other team can have no complaints. We don't like to back in. I'm not elated by it at all. I'm very upset. I feel like we lost. I don't even feel like we won."

He spoke sarcastically, in mumbles, and then stormed off, saying, "I've answered enough questions." When more questions were asked as he went, he snapped, "No comment . . . no comment." When fans pushed forward for autographs, he ignored them. When a lady took his picture, he said something to the effect she wasn't supposed to do that. And he went on his way, getting away as fast as his long legs would take him.

Bill Walton taking charge of "his gang." (UCLA)

Upper left: John Wooden at 38 shakes hands with Wilbur Johns, his predecessor as coach and his athletic director at UCLA as he takes over the Bruin basketball team in 1949. *Upper right:* Walt Hazzard, senior star of UCLA's 30–0 team in 1963–64 season, dribbles by Jeff Mullins, Duke star, in NCAA title finals at Kansas City. *Lower left:* Kenny Washington, sixth-man supersub and surprise star of 1964 and 1965 championship finals, flies through the air while teammates Gail Goodrich (25) and Jack Hirsch watch. (UCLA)

The second Bruin title team: *Upper left:* Gail Goodrich lays one in from behind the basket against archrival USC. *Upper right:* Keith Erickson comes down with a rebound against Michigan in NCAA championship final in Portland, Oregon. *Lower right:* Hazzard calls for ball while Goodrich drives in during final. Michigan star Cazzie Russell (33) is in center. (UCLA)

UCLA's Pauley Pavilion, inside and out,
opened in the fall of 1965. (UCLA)

Pauley Pavilion did not open with a champion. The 1965–66 UCLA basketball team, led by Edgar Lacey, left, and Mike Lynn, here in action against Illinois, was the only one in a 10-year period which did not win the Conference crown, make the NCAA tournament, and win the title. But Lew Alcindor was a freshman that year, and the Bruins soon bounced back with more national crowns, giving the cheerleaders something to shout about. (UCLA)

Alcindor takes down rebounds. In 1967 NCAA title victory, he outleaps Dayton's Don May (21), an all-American. *Lower right:* Brilliant Bruin guard Mike Warren moves in to go up for a shot in championship contest, played at Louisville, Kentucky. (UCLA)

The great Elvin Hayes of Houston goes high to shoot over reach of Lew Alcindor, his vision impaired by an eye injury, in stunning midseason upset of UCLA early in 1968 in awesome Astrodome before record college crowd of 52,693 fans. Mike Warren is 44, Mike Lynn 35. (UCLA)

After blasting Houston in rema
in NCAA tourney semifinals at I
Angeles Sports Arena, the Bru
ripped North Carolina for crown
1968. *Upper left:* Mike Warren
bounds one home. *Upper right:*
cindor hooks another in. *Belo*
Bouncy Lucius Allen bounces hig
than the ball. (UCLA)

Third straight college crown for "Alcindor's Army" and fifth in six years came in 1969. *Upper left:* Star guard John Vallely shoots over reach of Drake player in three-point semi-final triumph at Louisville *Upper right:* Lynn Shackelford prepares to pass against defense of Purdue star Herm Gilliam. *Lower left:* Ken Heitz blocks shot of Purdue's supershooter Rick Mount. *Lower right:* Alcindor rides high to hook one in. Purdue had third star in Billy Keller, but fell by 20. (UCLA)

With Alcindor graduated and gone on to become Kareem Abdul-Jabbar, pro star, the Sidney Wicks-Curtis Rowe group took over to win two more titles in a row. *Upper left:* Curtis Rowe retrieves a rebound from New Mexico State star Sam Lacey. *Upper right:* John Vallely dribbles away from all-American Jimmy Collins in NCAA 1970 tourney semifinal at College Park, Maryland. (UCLA) *Below:* Shooting over Sidney Wicks, Austin Carr of Notre Dame knocks UCLA down, ending their winning streak in midseason, 1970–71. (Photo by Jim Hunt, courtesy Notre Dame)

pper right: In 1970 final against
cksonville at Maryland's Cole
eldhouse, little Henry Bibby goes
gh to get off a shot between two
ants—the great Artis Gilmore (53)
d Bob Burrows. *Lower left:* In
71 final against Villanova at
ouston's Astrodome, Steve Patter-
n leaps to lay one in despite bump
hefty Hank Siemiontowski, while
llanova's standout Howard Porter
) and UCLA's Terry Schofield (43)
atch. *Below right:* Wicks blasts past
rter. (UCLA)

Enter The Bill Walton Gang to stretch UCLA's domination still further with an unbeaten season in 1971–72. *Upper left:* Big Bill Walton outleaps teammate Jon Chapman to clamp on a rebound against Iowa at Pauley Pavilion. *Upper right:* Overhead shot shows Walton's rebounding style against Notre Dame. *Lower left:* The big guy grabs another against Louisville in NCAA tourney semifinal at L.A.'s Sports Arena. *Lower right:* UCLA coach Wooden accepts congratulations from first-year Louisville coach Denny Crum, formerly Wooden's assistant with the Bruins. (UCLA)

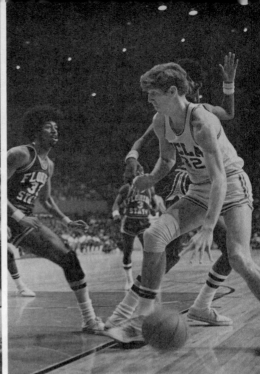

The 1972 title contest in the NCAA championship tournament at L.A.'s Sports Arena and the first crown for The Walton Gang. *Upper left:* Walton goes high to block shot attempt by 6-11 Larry McCray while Keith Wilkes (52) watches. *Upper right:* Big Bill dribbles against 6-10 Reggie Royals and little Ron King. *Lower right:* Wilkes stretches to pull in rebound on fingertips from waiting King. (Upper right photo from UCLA. Others from James Roark, *Los Angeles Herald-Examiner.*)

UCLA's eighth NCAA basketball title in nine years won, Larry Farmer (54) lays one on Henry Bibby (45). Keith Wilkes and Vince Carson are in center. Carson looks as if he feels he did not have a major part of it. He did not. *Upper right:* Walton whispers condolences to losers' Reggie Royals, whose expression indicates he could have lived without them. Bill is smiling, but later complained his club let foe come close. *Below left:* Wooden gets game ball and captain Bibby championship plaque from NCAA official. (Right photo by James Roark, *Los Angeles Herald-Examiner.* Others by UCLA.)

After the basketball season ended, during the long, hot summer, in May, 1972, Bill Walton joined others in barricading Administration Building on UCLA campus during antiwar demonstration. (James Roark, *Los Angeles Herald-Examiner*)

John Wooden moves out to lead the applause as his UCLA star Bill Walton, sore knees bandaged, leaves late in another triumph. (James Roark, *Los Angeles Herald-Examiner*)

9

He slouches some as though to hide from his height and he shies from interviews as though this will turn off spotlights and when he speaks to an outsider he stammers some as though reluctant to give much of himself away, but it is impossible for Bill Walton to slip unseen through the shadows. He is almost seven feet tall, he swiftly has become the center of attention on the most successful sports team in the nation, and his Huckleberry Finn face has been displayed on television, on magazine covers, and in newspapers for all to know in this sports-mad city and this sports-mad country.

There are celebrities who feel scorched by the spotlight, frozen by their fans, insulted by invasions of their privacy, and he is one. He is only 19 years of age and he has been shoved suddenly into that spotlight and he is not used to it and he does not like it and he does not think he ever will like it or get used to it. He could turn if off by turning from the sport which has made him famous almost overnight, but that would be a denial of his natural size and ability, though he admits he sometimes is tempted to do it.

He says, "I enjoy basketball. I enjoy playing the game. I enjoy going for goals, so I enjoy playing for the championship. But I do not like all the publicity, and the pressure put on us, and the big crowds. I might enjoy playing pickup games in a gym with no one watching just as much. I want to win every game we play, but I don't want to have to win. I don't even want to think about long winning streaks and breaking records. I like to think we could lose without it being the end of the world. I'm just starting in sports and already I'm being called a superstar and I don't think it's right. I'm nowhere near the player I can become. I don't like people telling me how great I am. Or reading that stuff. It's a team game and I like to think of myself as a team player. I think it matters more how the team does than how I do. Whatever I do, I get help. I give help to the other players and I get it from them. They're as important to the team as I am. I wish everyone would just treat us as a team and not single me out individually."

He sighs and says, "Basketball is not always fun. The publicity and the pressure spoil it for me. No one enjoys a game as a game, not the coaches, not the players, not the fans, and not the press. All that matters is whether you win or lose, and I don't feel that way. It matters more to me how I play, how we play, then whether we win or lose. Maybe it's easy for me to say because we win, but I don't like playing not to lose.

"I don't enjoy being everyone's target. Everyone thinks because I'm so big and supposed to be a superstar and on a team that wins that it's all right for me to be roughed up. Well, I don't. I'm emotional and when I'm wronged I complain. And when I complain I'm called a crybaby. I don't feel I'm a crybaby. I'm determined to try to control my emotions. I'm learning I have to expect abuse. I'm beginning to understand my position. So, if I can, I'll let them do their thing and I'll do my thing. But if that's the way the game has to be played, it's not going to be much fun for me. Just because I'm big, it's not easy for me, you know. You have to work your butt off out there. My bad knees bother me. I have to spend a lot of time taking care of them, and they still hurt like hell a lot of the time. There were times I felt like quitting this past season. Who needs the pain? But the team needed me. When the time comes I'm not needed, when it's just me that matters, I may not want to play anymore. My idea of living is just to enjoy life. Life is too short to feel any other way.

He insists he was not tempted by offers of $200,000 a year to play pro ball. He says, "That's a lot of money, I know. But money doesn't mean a lot to me. I'd like to have a lot of money. What matters is what I'd have to give up to get it. Money can't buy happiness. I know a lot of people with a lot of money who aren't happy. And I want to be happy. I just don't know yet what will make me happy. I'll probably play pro ball because that's the best basketball and basketball is maybe the thing I do best, but I'm not sure it will make me happy. I'll be exposed to even more publicity and pressure. I'll be hounded for interviews. I'll be out in the open and I might have to change my life-style. I'd be traveling all the time. And I'm not sure my knees would hold up over the longer, harder schedule. I wish sometimes I'd been blessed in something besides basketball, something I could pursue off by myself without all the attention."

It was pointed out to him that offers to him were especially high because of bidding between rival, warring pro basketball leagues, and if the leagues merged, as they might at any time, the offers might at any time decline drastically. He said, "I'm not worried about that. I'll take my chances. I'm not going to be pressured into jumping, into leaving my friends and teammates prematurely. The money just doesn't matter that much. If I'm a better player two years from now, and I sure should be, I should be worth even more. And I don't know now if I'll want to go into pro basketball then. I want to do more with my life than just win a few games. I'd like to make more of a contribution to mankind. If I graduated today, I'd be tempted to go to law school tomorrow. I like to do things for people they can't do for themselves. There are a lot of needy people in this world. I like the thought of opening up a law office and offering a free service to needy people. I think the laws in this country screw poor people, minorities, and the needy. I like the idea of serving people instead of just serving myself by playing ball for money."

He said, "I don't need luxury or a lot of possessions. Material things don't mean much to me. I don't need fancy clothes or a fancy car or a big house. I don't even need a house. I could live in a camper. That way I could live out in the open away from most people." It was pointed out to him that if he did not want to spend his money on himself, he could spend it on others, that he was being offered a lot of money and a lot of things could be done for a lot of people with a lot of money. This seemed to make him uncomfortable. He said, "Maybe, but I'm not sure you can buy happiness for people. Anyway, if I took the pro dough, a lot of my friends would consider it a cop-out. I don't worry about what people think of me, but I've made it clear money doesn't mean much to me, and I wouldn't want anyone to think I made the move to make money."

He stood there in the campus sunshine, a curiously solitary figure, strangely imprisoned by his image. We walked from the athletic department at UCLA to the parking lot, where my car was parked. Heads turned to stare at him as he passed, but he pretended not to notice. He had just completed his first championship season as the Bruins big basketball star and he was not at ease with it.

He said, "I guess I'll have to go on with the game if I'm to make the most of myself and I suppose I'll have to get used to the attention and I'll have to find a way of dealing with it without wrecking my way of life, but I don't know if it will work out. I don't worry about it. I just take life as it comes. I live a day at a time. I've already forgotten about yesterday. And I don't care about tomorrow. Like they say, it may never come.

"People think I'm all caught up in basketball, but it's just something I do. I don't do it for fame. Or for the fans. I do it for myself. I don't want to do it all the time. I don't want to talk about it all the time. There are other things I want to talk about, other things I want to think about, feelings I want to express, but I don't want to use my position in sports to push off my feelings on people. In today's society, athletes are made out to be much more important than they should be.

"I don't think being an athlete has determined my personality. I'm other things, too. I don't know who I am or where I'm at yet. I'm only 19. I'm just trying to get myself together. I'm not sure my head is screwed on straight yet. I don't know why people want to talk to me, to interview me. I don't know enough about basketball or anything else yet. Who cares what I think or what I say?"

He shook his head, wistful with wonder. He said, "I know if I go with basketball, I'll have to give up something of myself. But, jeez, I won't have to give up everything, will I?" he asked, and it was almost a plea.

We drove through the tree-lined streets out of the campus and down Wilshire Boulevard to a fancy restaurant frequented by some of the UCLA athletic crowd. Entering, he was noticed. He pretended not to notice. Waiters asked for his autograph. Other diners asked for his autograph. Even the owner came over and asked him for an autographed picture.

We remembered an incident described by another writer. A pretty girl came up to him and looked up at him, up, up, up.

"Boy, you must be a basketball player, huh?" she asked.

He smiled nervously, head hung, feet shuffling. "Yeah," he replied, almost inaudible.

"You play professionally?"

"No," he said.

"Oh, just messing around?"

"Yeah," he said.

Some see him only as a very tall person. He has heard all the jokes: "How's the weather up there?" . . . "Do you have to duck for airplanes?" . . . "I could use you to replace some light bulbs for me." He has heard them all and he no longer

finds them funny and does not laugh at them. He says he
has been poked at with umbrellas as if to see if he is real.
Often? "Once is enough," he says.

He says, "I'm used to being tall. I accept it and all that
goes with it. If I was shorter, I wouldn't be noticed so much,
but I wish I was taller because it would help me to be a
better basketball player and that's something I'm doing
now so I'd like to do it better. I'd like to be able to do a lot
of things better. I'd like to be smarter. I'd like a lot of
things. I guess I'm a perfectionist in those things that
interest me. In other things, I couldn't care less."

However, he closes his eyes then and leans back, hiding
his thoughts, and betrays himself by asking, "If I was this
tall and not a basketball player, would I be considered a
freak?"

Around us, others whisper about him, call the attention
of their women to him. He ignores it until they come up to
him to speak to him or ask for his autograph. He is basically
shy, distressed by such distractions, and he replies in
mumbles and rushes his signatures in scribbles. Alone
again, he says, "I stay away from places where I'll be
hassled, but I go where I want to go because you can't let
other people run your life. I just don't pay any attention to
the fuss made over me by strangers. These people don't
mean anything to me. They're nothing in my life. They
don't mean me any harm, so I do what I have to do with
them, but I don't get involved with them. When they come
up to me and speak to me and ask for autographs, I smile
and I say 'hi' and maybe I answer a question and I sign. I
sign only because it's easier than not signing and maybe
having some sort of scene over it. I'm not even aware of
what they say to me or what I say back to them because it's
all on the surface and it doesn't sink in and I don't think
about it. As far as I'm concerned, it all has no meaning. I
shut them out and give them only a little corner of me.
Even while I'm dealing with them, my mind is on other

things. My mind is always working. I operate in everyone else's world, but I live in my own world."

He was silent a moment, then he said, "Autographs are the most meaningless things I can imagine. What do people want with them? What do they do with them? Getting mine, do they think they have a little piece of me?" he asked. He is an intelligent, sensitive person. Asked a question, he thinks awhile before answering. He wants to sort it all out in his mind and get it straight so he can say it the way he sees it. Asked about not giving many interviews, he said, "I don't give many because I don't want to parcel out pieces of myself. I don't think I'm all that important and I don't think my opinions are all that important. I don't want to be made into some sort of cardboard cutout and I don't want them to be disappointed when they find out I'm something other than they want me to be. Some people have the idea that a UCLA athlete has to be an all-American boy. But what is an all-American boy? Someone who wears his hair cut short, who helps little old ladies across the street and spends most of his time studying to get ahead? Someone who thinks it's the most important thing in the world to win games or the most noble thing on earth to give your life for your country?"

He shut his eyes against the thought of it and hunched forward a little, his reddish hair falling over his freckled face. The waitress, came to ask him if he wanted soup or salad with his meal, and he said he wanted both and not one of those small cups of soup, either but a big bowl. As the food came, he shoveled it in. As he finished something, he asked for something else. He eats four or five major meals a day and snacks in between.

He said, "Sometimes when I'm with my girl, we don't say much. She's quiet, like I am. I like that. It's nice to be with someone sometimes without speaking. You know what I mean? To be content without conversation. Sometimes you want to talk, sometimes you don't. It's great when you can feel comfortable enough with someone that you can be content just to be together and you don't have to speak, you don't have to entertain them or prove a point or make something of yourself. I hate people who put on a false front."

I told him a story about jazzmen Miles Davis and Gil Evans. One day Gil called Miles to say he'd be in Chicago the next day. Miles said come early and come over. Gil did. Miles let him in. Some records were spinning out music. Gil took a drink, sat down near Miles, and listened with him. A couple of hours passed without a word, just the two of them listening together to music they loved. Finally, Gil got up and said he had to go. Miles said, OK, it was good being with you. Gil agreed it had been a ball. They shook hands and Gil left. They had not exchanged a dozen words but they'd had a happy visit. Bill Walton smiled and said, "Yeh, man, that's what I mean. That's cool. That's the way it should be."

He spoke of his life at UCLA. He lived in Dykstra Hall his freshman year, but moved into a small apartment in a converted frat house his sophomore year. It is a small apartment with a large bed, a lot of books and records, but no telephones. He lives alone. He goes around in jeans and T-shirts and an old car, avoiding the main roads and the bright lights. He has a few close friends and a steady girl friend, but he would not name them.

He said, "I lived in a dormitory my freshman year and I hated it. I liked a lot of the guys, but I simply didn't want to see the same people every day of my life. And I don't need a whole lot of people. Now I live alone. And I really enjoy living alone. I live simply. Living alone, I can live any way I want to live. I can do what I want to when I want to. I can go for weeks without seeing anyone if I want to. If I want to see someone, I can go to see them."

"What if someone wants to see you?" he was asked.

"They can come to see me," he said.

"What if you don't want to see them?"

"They know which ones are welcome. I don't advertise. I don't give out my address a lot. The people I know know how I feel about them."

"They can't call you because you don't have a phone."

He said, "I don't need a telephone ringing all the time. People become prisoners of the telephone.

"For one thing, I don't need all the calls from the pros. I put out the word they can speak to Sam Gilbert if they want to speak to me. He takes care of my business. There is none. He gives the word to them: Don't raise the offer. It won't matter. I'm not ready. I'll let them know if the time comes I'm ready.

"If you have a phone, people call up asking you to go somewhere or do something. It's like living in a dorm. I don't want to have to make excuses if I don't want to do something. If I feel like doing something with someone I can go to a pay phone and call them up."

"What if they don't have a phone?" he was asked.

He laughed. "Forget it, I guess," he said.

What does he do in his room? He said, "I study. Not a whole lot. I'm majoring in history, but not because it will lead to anything, only because I like it. I'm interested in finding out about other parts of the world and how they live. I take other courses. A lot of my teammates are black. I'm interested in their origins, their backgrounds. I can't be black, but I can find out as much as I can about what it is to be black.

"I study to learn, not to get good grades. I couldn't care less about grades. I don't care about graduation. The diploma means nothing to me. It's just a piece of paper. If I've learned something, fine. If not, I've blown a helluva opportunity.

"I read a lot. I listen to a lot of music. I go to movies. I don't want to single out any book or record or picture I liked because some people will say, 'Hey, if Bill Walton liked it, it must be good,' which, of course, is crap. I go out. I won't be hassled into being a hermit. I pick my spots. I stay away from most public places. I go to parties, but I don't like big, formal parties. My brother Bruce says he likes parties with 25 screaming guys and 25 screaming girls. Well, that's one way we're different. I prefer parties with just a few people. I'm happy sitting around rapping with a few people.

"I don't have many friends. I have a few real good friends. Not too many. I have a few friends because I won't force myself on anyone and won't let anyone force himself on me. Friends are important to me, so I'm selective about them. I don't want a friend if it's not someone I would do anything for, who would do anything for me. I feel I can sense sincerity in people. I think most people are insincere. I'm suspicious of strangers because I sense they see me only as some sort of sports superstar and aren't interested in me as a person. Most are obsessed with me being Bill Walton, basketball superstar. Writers are, of course. They paint a one-dimensional picture of me.

"I like people who let me be myself. I guess most of my friends are my teammates because they're going through some of what I'm going through and they just want to be themselves, too, and I can relax with them. But I have other friends, too. I have different friends for different things I do. I like to do some things with some people who like to do the same things, other people I like to do other things with. I date. I have a girl, but I'm a long way from marriage. I don't go overboard. I go my own way. Beyond the basketball court, even coach Wooden doesn't know where I go. That's my business."

In a *Boys' Life* article, Tom McMillen said he sets himself a strict schedule daily, hour by hour, so he could cram the most into his time. Bill Walton, cut from a different cloth, shudders at the thought. He says, "Aside from commitments I have in season and with some classes, I don't even want to plan what I'll do an hour from now or two hours from now or tonight or tomorrow. If tomorrow comes, I'll let it take care of itself. I want to live now, not in the future. I don't know what I'll do with most of my life. I'm not even sure I'll stay in college. I'm not sure you have to go to college to have a good life. I don't buy that stuff about studying hard and getting good grades and getting a good job and working hard to get ahead all your life. I don't believe in the old concept of a nine-to-five job. I don't want to be stuck with a suit and tie. The Protestant ethic doesn't mean much to me. If I find that's the way to go for me to be happy, that's the way I'll go. If not, I'll look for some other way to go."

As we left, a fellow who passed us coming in nudged his girl and said, "That's Bill Walton, the best basketball player in the country." She said, "Ohhhh, he's so tall." Walton winced perceptibly. He was treated with extreme courtesy. The owner and waiters bowed his way away. Outside he blinked into the sunshine. Asked, he admitted such special consideration annoyed him. He confessed he feels the eyes on him and hears the whispers. "I hear the whispers as I walk around," he said. "People avoid my eyes, but I sense when I'm being watched. It bothers me, but I have to learn to live with that, too. What the hell is it I do that's so wonderful? Put a round ball in a round basket? How can you measure that against contributions others make to mankind? On the world scale, basketball doesn't mean much."

He folded himself into the car and we drove through Westwood toward campus. He said, "People make too much of sports and athletes. It's all out of proportion to its place in the overall scheme of things. After graduation when I took that AAU tour through Europe, I saw people starving in the streets. Then I came to UCLA and I saw people waiting hours just to get into Pauley Pavilion. When they're inside, they go stark, raving mad. I laugh at them. I can't believe them. What are we doing that's so important? Why should we have to have such huge arenas?

Why shouldn't they take the money it took to build the Pavilion and the Forum and all the big sports arenas and use it to feed hungry people?

"When basketball season is over, I've had it. That's why I go to the mountains or someplace like that where I can be alone, away from the insanity, where I can maybe think things out and reach for reality. I like football, but I seldom go to a game. I seldom go to baseball games. I'm not a fan, really. Sports are fine, but why do they have to be blown all out of proportion?"

I parked on a tree-shaded side street just off campus, near where many of the players lived. He'd said he had a class to make. Now he said he'd skip it. I offered to excuse him, saying I'd taken up a lot of his time. But, he said he had time to spare and would like to go on talking. For some reason, this time he felt like talking.

"I don't like being with older people," Bill Walton said. "They've given up. They say you can't change things. Maybe you can't, but you can try. All our leaders are old. They're trying to hang on to their positions. They want the status quo. They don't want to change things. They don't even want to look into things. They don't want to be blamed for wrongdoing. But as far as I can see, they're corrupt. Power has corrupted them. They think they can do anything they want to people. I have no patience with the politicians who run our country today because they are ruining it. So many people get screwed by our political system. So much crap is fed us. A lot of lies. A lot of covering up. Do what you want to do, then lie about it and cover it up. You have to be able to see through things. But they don't give us much to say in the selection of candidates. Or much choice in candidates. They keep giving us the same old faces. One candidate is as bad as another. Am I supposed to trust Nixon now? McGovern talks some of our ideals. But I doubt he'd live up to them. Anyway, there is no way he will win.

"You can't be President until you're 35. No man should

be allowed to be President after he's 35. The job needs a young man. The young haven't been disappointed or corrupted. Being young is the greatest gift you can have. The young are the only hope of the world. My generation has made mistakes, but at least we're trying to make things better. When we see wrongs, we want to right them. We don't have much power, so we have to make our feelings felt any way we can. We hold rallies. We demonstrate. We protest. We speak out. At least we try to make people think about things instead of just accepting them the way they are.

"One of the biggest problems is racism. People can't accept the fact that some people are black, some yellow, some red, some white. They can't see past their skin. They think color makes people different. Backgrounds make people different, not color. If you're raised in a rich suburb you're going to look at life different than if you're raised in a poor ghetto. Opportunity makes people different. If you know you have no chance to get ahead the right way, you'll take what you can the wrong way. But it isn't color that makes people different. Under our skin, we're the same. The whites have gotten it into their heads that because they're white, they're right. Well, they're wrong. You have to look at each person as an individual.

"I don't blame the blacks for hating the whites. The blacks have gotten a raw deal for a long time. A lot of my teammates are black and I really admire the way they've risen above their raw deal. They're my friends and I feel for them. I know I've gotten twice as much as I deserve because I'm white. I'm ashamed of the way whites have denied rights to blacks and I don't want to hear about how things are better than they used to be because they're not how they should be.

"When people say things are getting good for the blacks, they stop working to make them the way they should be. One hundred years after the Civil War the blacks are still trying to get where they should be. I wouldn't blame the blacks for any steps they took, violent or nonviolent. I can't blame them for hating whites." He turned intensely and said, "If a black man gunned me down right now, I'd figure it was all right because of what whites have done to blacks."

It was a startling thing to say. He was silent awhile. Then he said, "I wouldn't blame the blacks if they took up arms and went into outright revolt. I don't like violence, but violence scares people, and sometimes you have to scare people into doing right, into acting. If revolution comes, I'm ready. The history of this country is it took violent revolution to get our freedom, but people tend to forget that. They hold George Washington to be a hero, but he was a revolutionary soldier. They put down Jerry Rubin because he is a revolutionary and so considered a radical, but he should be just as big a hero today. People dislike it because the young people are stirring things up, but things have to be stirred up."

Walton is one of our immature revolutionaries. Their ideals are high, their tactics often low. He said, "I think sometimes I'd like to be a farmer. I'd like to be alone with the earth and live off what I could grow with my own hands. There'd be no one to tell me what to do or what kind of person I should be. I think that bugs me more than anything.

"This is one of the differences between coach Wooden and myself. He is not of my generation. I can't expect him to see things as I see them. He sees things from another point in time. He tries to bridge the gap. He will listen to your side of things. He is a very logical man, and, when we have been able to show him the right of something logically, he has been prepared to go along with it. But he has a different set of standards than his players do. His morality is different from that of young people today. We live a freer life. We believe if you want to do something, you should do it. He is concerned with convention. For instance, I wish he didn't insist on short hair. Maybe it's a little thing but it touches on our freedom to do our thing. He's one of the older people who believe the length of your hair and whether or not you wear a coat and tie matters. He's concerned with how we look. I couldn't care less. I'm concerned with what's inside.

"He thinks it's a great thing, those television commercials athletes do condemning the use of drugs. I don't believe athletes or anyone else should go on television to tell people what to do. I don't use drugs, but if someone else wants to, that's his business and I'm not going to tell him how to live his life. Everyone should be able to do his own thing and not worry about what others think about it. They're trying to restrict us too much. They shouldn't have so many rules and laws for us."

"What about murder?"

He shrugged. "If you really think it's right, commit murder," he said. "Personally, I don't recommend it. I hate killing. Taking someone's life is obviously the ultimate taking away of their rights. But I don't want to be the one to judge what's right for someone else. We let many murderers go free because we decide they acted in self-defense or something; they were justified. We draw lines. The lines are not always clear. I don't want to be one to draw lines."

He was silent a few seconds. Then he said, "When we make war, we commit murders. It's legalized murder. Many innocent people are inevitably killed. And who knows who's guilty, anyway? If you refuse to fight, you're breaking the law. I'm against the draft. I won't be drafted because of my height, but I sympathize with those who are drafted. They're told to go and kill. They're asked to risk their lives for no real reason. And they had no say in it. We didn't vote to have war. Congress didn't even vote to have war. Our Presidents put us in war and have kept us there. I sympathize with those who went to Canada, who fled rather than fight. If I *was* drafted, I'd go somewhere else, too, to Sweden or anywhere. I wouldn't want to go into the Army to kill and I wouldn't want to go to jail, which is like going to the Army except there's less chance you'll get killed.

"Why do we have to have wars? Why do people have to kill one another? Can anyone answer that? I hate it when people say you should be proud to die for your country. What does death prove? Wouldn't it be better to live for your country? Why can't we live and let live? Why can't we cherish life instead of worshiping death? What do wars prove, anyway? Is war justified to force our system on another country? Who says our system is the best? It isn't working very well right now. I don't know a better one, necessarily, but I still wouldn't want to force it on someone else who didn't want it. I'd sure like to make it better.

"Heck, I even get annoyed when players fight on a basketball court. I don't know why players can't just play the game. Is it so important to win? Why do we have to win all the time? Why does this country have to win all the time? Why is it so important to be the biggest and the best? Why are we so hung up on it in this country? What does it matter which country is the strongest? We're not animals. We're human beings. We're supposed to have some sense. We're supposed to use reason. Let's be friends. Let's live together in peace. Let's not live everyone else's lives for them. We could end this war so easily and we don't do it. What does it matter how we look? Why not just end it? Why not start living better todays instead of worrying about building better tomorrows?

"I think the most important thing in life is to live and enjoy life. Have fun. Enjoy what you're doing while you're doing it. Help one another. Be yourself. If you can be honest with yourself, that's all that matters. Let's get to the point where we can be honest with one another. Let's be able to trust one another. I think the black race is the greatest race on earth because they're so together. They really believe they're all brothers and sisters. No matter what a black man has done, his family always will welcome him back and try to help him. A black man can go anywhere and be welcomed by other blacks. None of this is true of whites. We're suspicious of one another, much less of other people. We judge each other as well as everyone else. We divide ourselves up by classes. We don't feel a kinship for one another."

He sighed. He said, "One of the the things which has disturbed me at UCLA is there is no togetherness among the students. The school is in a wealthy area and most of the students come from well-to-do homes. They are not hungry and they do not feel for the hunger of others. Many go to their fancy homes at day's end. They don't really live together. They're not typical of young people today. I think sometimes I should have gone to Berkeley. The students are much more together there. They're aware of the wrongs in our world and they act to try to correct them. A university is supposed to be a place for young people, and I think it's right young people should have a say in how things are run, as they do there.

"I grew up comfortable. I never was hungry. But I do feel for others. I do want to help others. I want to see the end of wars. I want to see people set free, their individual rights restored. There are some people on this campus who agree and are ready to act. Well, I intend to act with them. I think I have been more guilty of not acting than of acting more up to now. I don't care how it looks. I'm warned it will reflect badly on me as a basketball superstar. I'm warned Mr. Wooden will be unhappy. But I have to live my own life and do what I think is right. I'm not on a crusade. I don't think the world will change. But I have to live with myself and I do think I have to try to change things I think are wrong."

Along the way, I had pointed out to him that he was saying some strong things and he was asked if he really wanted to permit them to be published. He said, "Why not? I said what I believe. Why should I care if it comes out?"

He stretched in the sunshine, shrugged, smiled, and went on his way with a little wave, the tall, loose redhead trotting around a corner.

At the time, few knew of his political commitments. Soon, everyone did, as he in May of 1972 participated in antiwar demonstrations staged primarily by UCLA students on and off campus. He took part in a sit-down on much-traveled Wilshire Boulevard and in the barricading of a main building on campus with demands that the university be shut down. He exchanged harsh words with a school official. He stood out, of course, and was one of those arrested. As he was taken away, he yelled, "The whole world is watching."

He was charged with unlawful assembly, disturbing the peace, rioting, and failure to disperse when ordered by police. His brother Bruce bailed him out with money obtained from Sam Gilbert. Eventually, Walton went to court and got off with a $50 fine and 12 months on probation. UCLA also placed him on probation.

Wooden said, simply, "It was a most unfortunate incident." Privately, other school and sports officials spoke more strongly about it to him. Typically, Sam Yorty, then L.A.'s mayor, called him "a communist dupe." But Walton expected this. What seemed to bother him was that so few of his teammates and fellow students supported his stand. He was put down by most, who mocked him and seemed to suspect his sincerity. Reportedly, some of his teammates even suggested he be dropped from the team. He was not, of course. He was too good a player and there was never any chance of that. And Bill saw that, too, and in a way seemed disturbed even by this. Clearly, he grew somewhat disillusioned.

He also was criticized for refusing to play on this country's Olympic team in Munich. When the U.S. basketball team lost for the first time, the controversial championship contest won by, of all countries, Russia, Bill's critics intensified their attack on him.

By then, he had made his move to get away from it all. He went backpacking with his sister in California's Sierra Mountains and the Canadian Rockies. Then he hitchhiked across Canada from Vancouver to Montreal. A couple of times he sent home for money, but mostly he managed. He was gone most of the summer. When he came back, it was almost time to start back to school.

On his return, he tried not talking about the controversies of his life, but he gave into temptation a couple of times. He said, "I've been taught all my life to be peaceful and to respect my fellowman. So when I see my government annihilate a whole country, I just have to do something about it. . . . Fascism was taking over. We had to stop it. We had to do something to raise the consciousness of the people around us. . . . I'd really rather not talk about it. I feel a certain way about it, but it might not come out right."

He insisted he had not boycotted the Olympics in any protest against his country's policies, but simply decided not to play. He said, "I respect the investment UCLA has made in me. I have knee problems and considered the risk of playing more games after the season too great. Also, by the time basketball season ends I've had enough of it for a while and want to do other things for a while, which I did. We had good players over there. I can't agree we'd have won with me. Anyway, is it so terrible we didn't win for once?"

However, later, in the spring of 1973, when the Russian team came to this country for a series of games with a U.S. All-Star team, Bill agreed to play in some games. And he did play in the opener in the Los Angeles Sports Arena and did dominate the Russians while he played, but he wrenched his knee severely during the game, left the game, and did not play any more games. The rough Russians proved their Olympic triumph was not purely a fluke, extending the Americans throughout the series, although losing finally to them.

Much as Walton resents comparisons with his predecessor at UCLA, Alcindor/Jabbar, the similarities between them are striking. When boycotts of the Olympics were urged on political grounds, these were two of the few who chose not to participate—Alcindor in 1968 and Walton in 1972. Both have been politically passionate and therefore generally unpopular when they have spoken out at times against discrimination and war and the waste of money spent to fight people instead of poverty, though Walton has acted more, at least publicly. Neither ever would speak much to anyone, requesting they be protected from the press and the public, refusing most interviews and requests for autographs. In recent years, they have been the only two to go this far. Each feels accountable only to himself. Each is a uniquely private person.

And, of course, each is a towering center, so especially skilled as to be set apart from all but a few, unselfish team players, who, no matter what, always were welcomed back to the leadership of the UCLA teams they took to national titles.

10

The players have been outstanding, but they come and go. The team turns over completely once every three or four years. The one constant during the Decade of Dynasty at UCLA has been the head coach, John Wooden. One wonders what is his system of success, why it works so awesomely well, and why was it that it suddenly and almost without fail started to work? There appears to be no single answer, but a number of answers, though some more important than others. Those who are in a position to judge such things give some of the same answers and some that are differen from those others give. Wooden, himself, has his own answers, but all do not agree with him, and with vanities and being so close to the situation, he may not necessarily see the overall view as well as others.

It has to start with talent. Other coaches could have won with an Alcindor or with a Walton, especially when they have been surrounded by outstanding players. Wooden has had so many outstanding players that some of them seldom got to play and got lost. Some were red-shirted, sitting out a season or two so they could play a later season when they were needed. He has had many more outstanding players than any other coach in the country. He has far more playing pro ball and far more starring in pro ball than any other coach has produced.

From the time of his first two championship teams, more talented players have wanted to play for Wooden than for anyone else, and recruiting the ones he wanted has not been a problem. But those first two teams did not have the greatest gifts, the most natural talents, and it was winning with them that helped him with those which followed.

Wooden always has been strong on conditioning and on fundamentals. Still, he has been willing to permit his players to gamble. Since the base is sound they do not make many fundamental mistakes and can afford the mistakes that come from applying pressure to the opposition. Wooden is a great believer in applying pressure to his foes. He applies it with a controlled fast break on offense and a zone press on defense. He switched from a hard-running fast break to a controlled break, experimented with a man-to-man press and went to a zone press on defense at the time he began to win titles.

Some of his assistants, especially Jerry Norman, were partly responsible for these shifts in tactics. Wooden was willing to listen to his aides, but it was he who decided to put the tactics into play, and he polished them. Some give his assistants more credit than they deserve. Wooden was generally regarded as a better offensive coach than a defensive coach, but when he started to stress defense, he started to win titles, and now he is known as equally good coaching defense and offense.

With his shift in tactics, he started to pick the players who suited his system best. He took the best players he could get, but he also took lesser players who had the specific skills he sought. He was willing always to fit his system to his talent. An Alcindor required adjustments in tactics, so Wooden went that way. An Alcindor was worth it. Walton is more flexible and less adjustments in Wooden's basic system were necessary to suit him, but Wooden made those he felt he should make.

Now, his system is no secret, nor are any of his tactics. They are out there for all to see. But Wooden teaches his tactics well. He organizes his practices better and conducts practice with greater intensity than almost any other coach. He believes that you play the way you practice.

Some say he is a better teacher than a coach, that he conducts practices better than he runs games, but this is nonsense because if he made mistakes in games, if he was slow to make adjustments, he would lose games, and he doesn't lose any more games than he does practices.

He insists on team play and even the most selfish of soloists he has had have been in time bent his way. Of course all coaches want conditioned clubs of players who play unselfishly for the team, but not all can get their players to bend to their wishes. It is nothing another coach can copy; it is a chemistry a John Wooden has and a few others have had which compels others to listen to them and accept their wishes.

He scouts his foes less than other coaches. He tells his players to play their game and they will win and they accept this. He doesn't worry about his foes, they worry about him. They say they are not, but they are afraid of him and his teams. His players play with confidence, the confidence that comes from his teams almost always having won, and their foes play scared, feeling the fear that comes from almost always having lost to his teams. It affects them, twisting their games tight. Only super-players among the foes rise above it. They swear they do not, but players on other teams expect to lose to UCLA now. Come the clutch, Wooden's players stay cool, keep their poise, keep doing what almost always has worked for them in the past, and it works again because their foes feel the enormity of what is happening, a possible upset of the champs, and they are awed by it, and it makes them nervous and they get tense and they choke up and suddenly the upset has gotten away from them and they are only another loser. Foes give away a lot of games to UCLA. So success has bred more success.

It could come apart on him at any time. Wooden knows this. He protects it with a passion. He is calculating. He says what will help him. He says it is no use to play slow-down against his teams, and so many do not try, although it is this tactic that has threatened his teams more than any other. He says ball-control offenses and zone defenses are not truly in the spirit of his sport and should be legislated against, but when he needs these tactics, he uses them. He is above it all. He has, we suppose, earned the right. He is, after all, at the top.

He is tough and he is no fool. He says he doesn't have to win all the time, but he does everything he can to win all the time. Why not? That's what he's there for. He doesn't get his teams up for the harder games, because he doesn't want to seem to take the easier games for granted. He holds his players on an even emotional level. He tells them any game can be hard for them if they give in to taking it easy. And it is part of his incomparable chemistry that he gets his players to accept this, and they seldom suffer the severe letdowns that lead to the upsets others suffer. And if they do let down a little, they are good enough to get by.

He will not let it come apart on him. He is tough, but he knows when to go easy. He prefers a certain type of straight, dedicated person to play for him, but he has had problem players who felt there were other things in life besides books and basketball, and he has somehow managed to keep them on the team without their destroying it. And this is the toughest sort of thing for any coach to handle, and it goes against the grain of a moral man. He has had homesick kids and wild kids and cutups and women-chasers and even boozers and drug addicts and thieves on his teams, and he has lost a few of them, and maybe saved a few, and somehow kept most of them in the game, and they helped him win, although he says he is more interested in helping them survive.

He survives. He survives bad guys such as have destroyed many good coaches and good teams all by themselves. He survives crises. He keeps secrets. He holds silences. He protects his players. If one wants privacy, they all get it. He will not expose them to any elements that might upset them. He holds it all together. If he had to change in the way he treated his players, in the paths he had to take that he had found led to the top, he changed. He made himself over and his teams and his style and attained such success that by now it almost sustains itself.

He has had help, of course. J. D. Morgan became athletic director in 1963, and in Morgan's first year, Wooden won his first national title. There has been talk of disagreements and jealousies between them. Wooden says, "We do not agree on everything. But we are able to reach agreements. We are able to work together. I am not jealous of his position. There are coaches who double as athletic director, but it is difficult. Athletic directors at major universities such as ours which participate in more sports than most colleges by far have their work cut out for them. J.D. is a worker and he has relieved me of many responsibilities which might distract me from the thing I have wanted to do most—teach and coach my young men."

Morgan was born in Newcastle, Oklahoma, on March 3, 1919. He was a four-sport athlete in football, basketball, baseball, and tennis at Cordell High in Oklahoma. A back injury limited him to tennis at UCLA, but he was a four-year letterman, number one player and captain in the net sport. He graduated from UCLA's School of Business Administration in 1941. During World War II, he commanded a Navy torpedo boat. After the war he returned to UCLA and has moved up through the positions of accountant, associate business manager, and now athletic director. He coached tennis 16 seasons before retiring from it in 1966. He coached eight NCAA singles champions, including Arthur Ashe and Charles Pasarell, and seven team champions.

As athletic director, he has presided over enormous improvements in UCLA's physical plant and record of success. Married to the former Cynthia Gray Crane, they have a son, Kevin, 19, and a daughter, Pamela, 12. His wife is active in university affairs. His life is devoted to his university and its athletics. He is a boss. He runs the show.

He is a brilliant man. He also is a hard, proud man. He denies it, but he has a large ego. Sometimes he seems haughty. He tends to talk down to people. He has a domineering manner. He is sure of himself, and secure in his success. But he is the sort of man you would want running your business. And in his hands, sports has become a successful and profitable business at UCLA.

He denies it, but he is accused of wanting the spotlight and envying Wooden's place in it. He says, "It simply isn't true. As athletic director I am a power behind the scenes, but it is my job to wield power properly and stay behind the scenes. I could not have coached our basketball team as successfully as John has done, nor could anyone else. He is not the sort of man to seek publicity, but he has earned all the attention he receives. I surround him with a smooth-running organization so he can operate efficiently. I give him what help he needs. I relieve him of details so he can be free to do the job he does so well. We discuss schedules, recruiting, trips, and so forth. We do not always agree. Sometimes he gives in to me, sometimes I give in to him. But we do not have arguments as such and never has there been left the slightest bad feelings from any disagreements."

Wooden has hired his assistants with care. Usually these have come from his former players. His assistant when the Decade of Dynasty began was Jerry Norman, who played for John in the early 1950s, became UCLA freshman coach in 1957 and assistant varsity coach in 1959. He recruited many of the players who carried the Bruins to their first championships and suggested some of the shifts in style and strategy which Wooden put into practice, though they did argue at times. Norman left in 1968 to begin as a stockbroker. Denny Crum, who played for Wooden in the late 1950s, then coached in junior college ranks, replaced Norman as Wooden's right-hand man and chief recruiter, argued tactics with him, and left to become head coach at

Louisville in the fall of 1971 after an especially angry argument in the tournament that spring.

Gary Cunningham played for Wooden in the early 1960s, returned to UCLA in 1965 to become freshman coach, and replaced Crum as varsity assistant in 1971, with Frank Arnold taking over as coach of the freshman team, which, when freshmen became eligible for the varsity in 1972, became the junior varsity team. Cunningham says, "An assistant coach is just that. It is his job to assist the head coach, not try to take over. When and if we are head coaches, we can run the show our way. Until then, we run it the head coach's way. This is easy since Wooden's way is obviously the best way. Who can match his record? Oh, there may be some things I or anyone else would do differently, but we don't while we are here only to help him. We played for him and coached under him and we know what he wants us to do to help him.

"We see things, we develop theories, we make suggestions. Some of us have put these more forcefully than others. I've probably argued with him less than some of my predecessors. Maybe I agree with him more. In any event, John is not afraid of arguments. He wants his assistants to have imagination and make suggestions. And he listens. He probably is less in a rut than any coach in the country his age with his experience. He always is innovating. He changes and makes changes. He's dynamic. He hires assistants to help him and he lets them help.

"I know they say I will succeed him, but I don't say that. I don't know it. No one does. You can't count on such things. He may coach for years to come, anyway. If you were in charge, you'd want him to coach forever, with his record. Meanwhile, whatever my future, I learn every day I coach under him. This is the best assistant's job in the country. It is by far better than being head coach at most schools. I want to be head coach someday or somewhere. When the time comes, I will be prepared."

Wooden says, "The biggest change in my treatment of players over the years is that I have come to see that saving troubled players is the single most important thing I can do for them. It is easy to say we simply should dismiss a young man involved in wrongdoing or some problem. It would save me being accused of keeping someone simply to help my team. But these players seldom help your team. Some outstanding ones do, perhaps, but, more likely they contribute to disharmony. It is more trouble to keep them and work with them. But that is one reason we are here. Not to impose our view of life on them, but to help them find their own way. We do not reach them all, but we can try."

Lucius Allen's life at UCLA was marred by marijuana raps, Mike Lynn's with a credit-card theft. If you coach hundreds of players over the years, some of them will cause a coach trouble, on and off the court. Others resent it when they are not played as much as they feel they should be. Edgar Lacey hurt his team and his personal career when he quit in midseason one season. "I did not give up on him, he gave up on himself," Wooden says. Bill Siebert shook up the Establishment by blasting the coach's supposed lack of consideration for the team's lesser lights at the annual basketball banquet. There has been no banquet since. But when the youngster wanted a teaching and coaching position in Australia, Wooden recommended him for it and helped him get it. Siebert says now, "I am grateful to Wooden. He is not perfect. But I have had second thoughts about the speech. And if I had it to do over again, I would not attack so bitterly."

One of his early players, Eddie Sheldrake, says when his wife was critically ill, the Woodens not only raised money for them, got them their doctor, but even helped out at their home. Others report similar incidents. Wooden shrugs and says, "You become attached to players, as if they were your sons. Some disappoint you, but they remain your sons, and you hold your feelings in and do what you can for them."

Wooden says, "I sometimes am troubled that the price of success may be too high. Not for myself, but for my players. It is very difficult for them to see things in perspective. It is hard for them to keep their lives in balance. Their lives may not always be filled with success as they have been here. Accordingly, I always have stressed that my players work toward graduation and if at all possible graduate because I know those who say they will come back to finish up later seldom do and because I know athletes at many universities do not graduate. Nine out of 10 of my players have graduated. This is an unusual record.

"Frankly, I do not feel it is difficult for a person to achieve success in both athletics and studies at the same time. I know sports takes time, but it is a matter of budgeting your time and disciplining yourself. Most of my players achieve higher grades in season than out because they are better disciplined in season than out. Many who play here are potential pros. But this is misleading. Most will not play pro. Even if they do, they will play only a limited time, almost certainly less than 10 years. Unlike other professions, players can pursue sports only a limited part of their lives. Few will coach. Most will live most of their lives away from their sport. Some will have made a great deal of money, but must know how to put this to use. Many will come out with little. They must have something to fall back on. Thus, I must make them feel their studies are more important to them than their basketball. If they have not prepared themselves for alternate ways of life, their time in school has been wasted.

"I am a basketball coach, but I also am a teacher of young men. The nature of sports is that the coach comes closer to his players than do most of their teachers. Sometimes closer than their parents. They will not let me come as close as I would like, but I still come closer to my young men than will most adults in their lives. I must use this opportunity to try to reach them. I feel I have reached many, and I am as proud of this or perhaps prouder than of any achievements in coaching."

Walt Hazzard, now Mahdi Abdul-Rahman, says, "He reached me. He may have had more influence on me than any man in my life." He sends Wooden telegrams of good wishes before and after every season and tournament without fail, and often telephones him, too. He was a problem for Wooden, but Wooden worked with him and reached him.

His players sometimes are elusive. He is the saint, after all, not they. They are human, young, subject to temptation, prone to pleasure. They have had at times parties that surpassed the stories that were told about them. One time, four girls were found in rooms with four players. Well, that was only one per player. And aren't girls and guys supposed to get together? Is a player supposed to see a cheerleader as a doll, unreal? Famous, is he supposed to slug the girl that dares approach him on campus or outside the dressing room? A fellow has to relax. Bill Walton's beer busts already are legend. All things considered, Wooden's teams have been straighter than most. Imperfect, but more perfect than most. He has seen to that.

Lynn Shackelford says, "John was always willing to meet you halfway. Some have felt he doesn't care, but I think he does, he just can't always get through to show it. However, some of his message does make it. You know he's right and you respect him and it tends to make you do right more than you ordinarily would. If he disapproves of something, he tries to hold it in."

He has not always held his feelings in. But he has lost his temper less by far than most, and if he has not forgotten, he has forgiven many their "sins" as he saw them and always was willing to go on helping them. Some resented the lectures. But some were helped by them. Gail Goodrich grins and says, "At least I found out where the library was." Jerry Norman was dropped from the team for using profanity at practice and being insubordinate, but he was not only taken back, but became Wooden's aide later.

Wooden says, "I was hot-tempered myself as a lad, strong-willed, sometimes insubordinate, not always respectful of my coaches. I was kicked off teams myself. But coaches took me back and taught me a lesson which I have applied myself in my coaching. The worst thing a person can do with children is fail to correct them at the right time, which is when they do wrong. But they do not always see right and wrong as you do, and you must accept this and be patient with them and tolerant of the trouble they cause you and continue to work with them as best you can."

Hazzard and Wicks resented having their soloist styles stifled, were benched awhile, and had to fit themselves at least partly into the coach's system before he relented. However, he did relent and no one who saw them play for him can say they played just the way he wanted them to play. Hazzard says, "You don't come off the playgrounds and adjust at once to team play. I was never selfish, but I could do flashy things and liked to do them. Wooden would chew me out in front of the entire team. He didn't do that with many players, but he knew it made me mad and he knew I played better mad. He's a master psychologist who treated each player different according to his personality. Once I saw that there was no point making a pass a player couldn't catch, I toned it down. Wooden's way worked. I was still free to do a lot of things. He didn't tie me up in knots. He made me use better what I had to use." Wicks shrugs and says, "You did it his way or you didn't do it. Most of the time. You got a feeling for what you could get away with."

Gail Goodrich resented having Hazzard handle the ball. He had been spoiled and resented the shadows. But he played his part and helped Hazzard, and, when Walter left, Gail got his shot at the spotlight and made the most of it. Gail says, "Wooden takes a selfish player and makes him play unselfishly. This is his greatest gift, the ability to get team play out of individuals. Most coaches want it. Not all. Some stress the play of their stars. But Wooden believes his way is best and he has the knack of getting you to believe it. Of course it's easier now that he has this history of success behind him and is getting better players. But he is the one man most responsible for his teams' success, no question about that.

"I had some disagreements with him. In my sophomore year he played me a lot at forward when I knew my future was at guard. But he made me see you have to make sacrifices personally to help the team. And it made me a better all-around player, too. He didn't favor me over Walter. Heck, he would leap all over Walter. But Walter was more experienced and a better ballhandler and he made me see my job was to do what I could do to help him. I was a shooter and he let me shoot. And when Walter left, I was ready for responsibility. He prepared you properly for every game. He gave you confidence in your game. That the dynasty has gone on as far as it has is just astonishing, but I could see the groundwork being laid when I played.

"You must remember, I'm 30 now and I look at life differently than when I was 20. He gets kids when they are 18, 19, 20, and they are cocky and want to have fun and resent discipline. Sooner or later he gets everyone who plays for him to respect him. I really respect him. He's a great man. His life-style is different from that of young people today, but he's reasonable about differences and is able to bridge the gap. He not only cares about you as a player, but as a person. He does what he can to set you straight. You may not agree with him, but he's really right most of the time, you know. He taught me to budget my time and discipline myself to study and try to learn. I was hung up on basketball, not books. Without him, I'd have gotten very little out of college. And the basketball was beautiful. It was fun, sure. But we didn't have any dynasty to sustain. And we were winning. Let any team lose some games and the sport stops being so much fun."

Wooden says, "You just don't reach every player. All Keith Erickson wanted to do was have fun. And I never could convince him there was more to life than that. All I could do was get him to stay in school as long as he could play basketball. When it ended, his college ended. But he did become a good basketball player and does have a fine pro career now. He wasn't a good player when we took him, you know. He was a good athlete, but not a good basketball player. No one else wanted him. His junior college coach didn't go overboard in recommending him. But we thought he had the tools to make a good player and he did become one."

Erickson says, "I had potential, but he did make me a player. We were good players and he made us into a great team. He can coach great players, but he is at his best turning mediocre material into something special. Most coaches get too much credit. I've been around awhile now and I know. I've seen a lot of bad ones. A few good ones. John is one of the very few great ones. He belongs with the legends, like Lombardi. Hey, you don't always love your teammates. Today I play happily with Goodrich. Back then, I didn't like him. He was a spoiled kid. All he wanted to do was shoot. When Wooden got his game with ours, it was a wonder.

"He's the kind of man you come to believe in, the kind of man you'd like to be. I see that now. I didn't then. All I wanted to be was a beach bum then. He tried to reach me. He insisted education came ahead of sports. He said hitting the books was more important than basketball. I thought it was less important than anything. He wanted very much for me to graduate. I'm sorry I didn't, for his sake. The only thing I graduated from was the beach. But that's something, anyway. Without his help, I might still be in the surf."

Some do put him down. Jack Hirsch, the free soul who has had his ups and downs since departing the campus, says, "He comes across as a little too Puritan. Sometimes I pick up the papers and say to my wife, 'Oh, no, they're making him out to be a god.' Really, he's just a human being with faults like the rest of us. College basketball is big business. A man does the best job he can to keep his job. They say Wooden doesn't relate to his players? He relates to the players who win for him. Hell, it's hard for him to put anything ahead of winning. That's his job, isn't it?"

Eddie Sheldrake says, "I think in the early years he really enjoyed coaching and in looking at what his players did and became after they got out of school. Now I think he just wants to win. And get the season over with."

Although Curtis Rowe has said, "He sees only the player, not his color," Wooden has had some troubles relating to blacks, as have all coaches since blacks began to take great pride in themselves. They demand rights they deserve, but are super-sensitive to the color of their skin, sometimes blame prejudice on their own failures, and do a lot of muscle-flexing. Mike Warren has said, "The coaching staff was seriously interested only in us playing, studying, and keeping out of trouble. . . . Wooden didn't understand us. We are, of course, different. I was dating a white girl and he got terribly upset at this." Fred Slaughter has said, "He comes from a white background. He relates to blacks as well as his background lets him. That's better than most. He may not understand the black man, but he has never been deliberatly prejudiced and I think he learned a lot during Alcindor's time here."

Alcindor told Wooden, "You can't understand us completely because you're white." Wooden said, "I can try, can't I?" Alcindor said, "Yes, but it won't work because you're not black." Willie Naulls says, "He is the greatest coach. He does what he gets paid to do—he produces winning teams. But I don't think he does much to make the college experience more beneficial to his players. . . . He gives you his slogans, but not so much himself." Naulls was one of many UCLA players who threatened to quit, but did not. When Sidney Wicks wanted to quit, Naulls talked him out of it. "In the long run, it's wiser to stay," Naulls has said. "If you want to play pro, this is the place to prepare."

Naulls, a black man, today is rich from investments in shopping centers and such, mainly in Watts and such depressed centers. He has offices in Beverly Hills, but he does much in the ghettos and for the people there. He has no official status at UCLA or with the Lakers or any others, but he always is in the locker rooms and with the players, especially black players, and he is enormously influential. When Wicks wanted to quit, Naulls took him to Sam Gilbert. Gilbert negotiated Alcindor's pro contract and is taking care of Bill Walton's business. Gilbert, a white man, also has no official status at UCLA, but he also is enormously influential with the players, black even more than white, and seems to be encouraged by school officials to remain involved because he is not as restricted as they are.

Gilbert has made a million dollars in contracting, He has fancy houses, one in the Lake Arrowhead mountains, and Bruins always are welcome and many hide out there. He is in his sixties, married, has three children, and seems to regard the Bruin basketballers as part of his family. He sits near the bench at home games and makes many trips, rooting hard for his players. He wears a feathered fedora which he calls his "rooting cap" and which makes him immediately recognizable. He calls himself a "fat little matzo ball." But he is a shrewd man who counsels players and negotiates for them without taking anything from them.

Bill Walton said, "Sam Gilbert doesn't try to tell you what to do. If you ask it, he will advise you. I don't want a boss, not Sam Gilbert and not John Wooden. If they tried to run my life, I would put them out of my life. But if Sam wants to help me and if I want him to help me, that's fine. And if Wooden wants to give me advice, that's all right too, as long as it's understood I don't have to take it. I understand that he is the boss on the court. But he understands that I am my own boss off the court.

"It impresses me that we are able to talk despite the differences in our ages. We disagree on many things. He doesn't agree that his and your generation has screwed up the world. He doesn't like me to say 'screwed up.' His morality is different than that of young people today. But he does coach you as a human being and he does try to help your total life. He is more important to his teams than I am or Lew Alcindor was. We come and we go, but he is the one who stays and wins. He is a fine man and a super coach."

Alcindor adds,"His ability to coach is incomparable. He gets more out of you than anyone else. He can help anyone. He is the greatest. And he is a good man. And it is a good experience to be around that man awhile. But he is not always influential. He is a narrow man, set in his ways. He says he changes, but he does not change much. He has a set, narrow set of values and he wants to impose them on everyone. If you do not do as he thinks you should do, he is disappointed in you and dissatisfied with you, and he takes it out on you."

Wooden does impose some startling restrictions on his players. He insists on cleanliness in their rooms on the road and their dressing rooms. "I don't want to invade the players' privacy," he says, "so I seldom go into their rooms, but sometimes I do and they don't know when I'm coming. I like to make spot checks on lockers to see that they are not getting slovenly. Wherever we are, we will leave our dressing room every bit as neat as when we came in. There will be no gum wrappers on the floor. No tape scattered around. No orange peels. All will be placed in a container. And I don't expect our manager to be the pickup man. Our players understand this. I help. If I start picking up things, the players soon join in. We'll have equipment managers around the country tell us no one leaves the dressing room like we do. Well, I think that's part of better basketball. Now I'd have a hard time proving that, but I think it is.

"The waitress at a hotel will say ours was the best-behaved group of athletes she's had. Our players compliment her on the way she served them and she can hardly believe it. I was disturbed once when a hotel manager complained about the way some of our players left their rooms. Since then, I have stressed that they treat these rooms as if they were their own, in their own homes and not to expect any more of the cleaning lady than they would of their own mothers.

"It is important to be tidy. If you are sloppy off the court, you will play sloppy on the court. That is why I prefer short hair. I want my players to have a neat, uniform appearance. I always wanted them to wear coats and ties on the road. But I am not as strict about these things as I used to be. I am not as happy with the appearance of my players, but I have to accept a certain amount of their doing what they want to do. I used to kick a player off my team for smoking or drinking. Now I only ask that I not know about it."

He sighs and says, "I preach homely virtues. Perhaps it is out of fashion, but as Lewis Alcindor suggested, I am an old-fashioned man. I believe many who felt me too tough a coach are referring to the past. I always felt an apt description of me would be as a stern father. This still is true, though I have changed over the years. The times have changed and one must change with the times. I am more permissive than I once was, but so is society in general. As I have grown older, I may have mellowed, I have become more tolerant. I still have rules. I still believe in old-fashioned virtue. But then I was brought up that way and we cannot alter what we believe in. Nor would I wish to, because I believe sincerely in virtue. Players may resent my speaking of this, but, if I keep speaking, perhaps some of it will sink in.

"Young men are not as coachable today. There's a rebellion against supervision of almost any sort. To accept discipline for many young men now is almost a badge of dishonor. It hurts their pride to accept discipline, even though deep down they know any group activity must be disciplined or it will turn into chaos. You have to go along with them in many respects. If a certain type of style is desired by black players, for example, the players must be permitted to express their individual personalities. The Good Lord in His infinite wisdom chose to make each of us different and we must accept these differences. However if I feel some extreme would present a poor image of our school, our team, and myself, I will rule against it. Judgment is used. It is my judgment.

"A coach should not be a dictator, but a team cannot be a democracy. A coach rules with the advice of his players. I listen to their opinions, then make a final judgment. If a player disagrees with me over something, I welcome him speaking out. In place. By this I mean I will not permit being challenged in practice, for example. Practices are planned carefully and time budgeted carefully. To have practice disrupted by individual argument or group discussion would be to cheat the team. However, after practice, the player may speak his mind. And I will listen with understanding.

"I truly do try to be understanding and I have been changed by my players. I always referred to my players as 'my boys.' I considered it a term of endearment. I cannot do that anymore because players resent it. At first, blacks resented it because it had been used in a depreciating way by whites. Now, whites resent it because they wish to be considered men. They are not all men, in my opinion, but if they wish this form of respect from me, they are entitled to it. They are my young men now. I was very much struck by something Wilt Chamberlain said when someone wondered how a new coach would handle him. Wilt said, animals were handled, not men. This changed my way of thinking. Now I try to work with my young men. I do not handle them."

He sat in his office, the walls covered with inspirational slogans and pictures of men who have inspired him, everything in its place, tidy, neat. He seemed scholarly. He placed his hands carefully flat on the desk in front of him. He said, "I have always asked my players after they left me if they felt I made any mistakes in my treatment of them. Most of them feel I have been fair, but I have learned from them. I know I have made mistakes. I do not expect all to love me. I expect respect. In getting it, I think I have gotten love from many. From a magazine article Lewis Alcindor wrote, I was distressed to learn that he felt I had held myself too far from my players. But he was a young man who would not let you get too close to him. I have found young players now prefer their coaches not get too close to them. So I respect their wishes. When one welcomes me into his life, I am only too happy to help him.

"I thought Lewis Alcindor was an outstanding young man. He was extremely coachable and cooperative on court, and he played as unselfishly as a player can play. You do not go through three years with a player without stresses, but for the most part our relationship went smoothly. Off the court I was not close to him, so I was surprised to find he had been unhappy here. However, college life far from home often is upsetting to youngsters, and, when you add the pressure his success placed on Lewis, his unhappiness is perhaps not surprising. However, he seemed happy to me. He was a young man of extremely strong convictions about life. If I did not agree with all of these, I respected them. I respected him. He says I learned from him. I surely did. I hope he learned something from me.

"As for Bill Walton, he is a most unusual young man, too. He is a young man of many varying moods. His attitudes change from day to day. He is not unlike Lewis in that he is a very private person, who does not let people get too close to him, and who has strong convictions about life. People wonder about him because he's so outspoken. When he speaks, he speaks with conviction. He lets you know where he stands at any given time. We do not stand on the same side on every issue, but that is no reason we cannot respect one another. For instance, Bill and I disagree on a number of things, but we have no disagreements. Like Lewis, he is extremely coachable and cooperative on court and a completely unselfish player."

John Wooden leaned forward. He said, "I'd rather command respect than demand it. I do not make as many demands as I used to. I am far more permissive than I once was in matters of hair and dress, for example. I tell my players I won't decide how everything should be done. I will only decide who plays and who doesn't."

11

There is a certain way he feels sweat socks should be put on and a certain way shoelaces on basketball shoes should be tied, so when the players come to him, he lectures them on this, and after that he watches to see that they have put on their socks correctly and tied their shoelaces exactly as he wants them to. John Wooden pays attention to details. He feels there are a lot of little things that play a part in winning and losing, and he tries not to overlook anything which will help his teams win instead of lose, no matter how small a matter it may be. He writes each player a letter each summer telling him exactly what will be expected of him when he reports in the fall.

Ducky Drake, the great veteran trainer of Bruin teams, says, "We rule out anything harmful to our chances of winning. We believe smoking and drinking fall into that category. It is one of John's rules. I help him enforce it. We do not do so in a negative way. We do not say if the player is caught smoking he will be dismissed from the team. He will not be. But we take a positive approach. We say these things cannot help you. They may hurt you. Almost certainly they will affect your play. So be smart and do not do it.

"We don't vary their pregame meals much. We have found what works best for them and from this we have selected what most players like best and that is what we feed them. We want them to feel comfortable in routines. We want them to come up to each game exactly as they came up to every other game. Accordingly, our meals, naps, free time, bedtime stay pretty much the same. John no longer sits in the lobbies checking out curfews, but the players know what is expected of them.

"John does not demand the impossible. As a trainer, I am different from a doctor in that my job is to not only treat the players' injuries, but keep them playing as much as possible. However, we have fine doctors who are called in whenever the injury or ailment requires it. And John would never play a player, no matter how important the player, no matter how important the game, he has been told should be sidelined. We take the best possible care of our players. They are people to us, not just players."

John Wooden's basic strategy is simple. On offense he uses the controlled fast break as much as possible. He likes a running game, but at a tempo his players can handle consistently. He varies the direction and flow of his fast break to keep the other teams spread and off balance. Within reason, he wants his players to take chances, to force the action. He does not like them to make mistakes, but believes that many times the team that commits the most turnovers will win if these come from playing aggressively. He believes it is vital to play aggressively.

His centers are instructed to get the rebound and make the fast outlet pass as fast as possible to get the fast break going. Walton is the best at this basketball has had. But, if this is not possible, Wooden wants his players to slide smoothly into a set attack. They will play off a center such as Alcindor or Walton, but, basically, Wooden wants all his players in fluid motion, all participating in the attack. Each player has places from which he shoots best, and if the ballhandler finds him free in these places he is to pass to him. "Think pass first, then think shoot," Wooden says. Every player is supposed to get his shots.

Wooden's attack is guard-oriented. He relies on his guards whenever possible, but he had won with teams without great guards. He likes one guard to be his best ballhandler and court quarterback, the other his best out-side shooter. If he has two who are great shooters, but primarily shooters, they may alternate, but they will not play together. He likes one forward who is primarily a rebounder and another who is primarily a shooter from the corner.

He prefers a high-post attack to free the area near the basket, but with an Alcindor or a Walton, who can be so dominating under the basket, he may use them at a low post and use the others primarily as perimeter shooters.

All must play defense. He has had some players who were so good on offense he had to play them despite defensive deficiencies, but he never stopped trying to develop them defensively. He is sensitive to the fact he used to be con-sidered an offensive coach and now wants to be considered as much a defensive coach. He has changed here more than anywhere else. But Indiana players and teams always were more offensive-minded than defensive-minded. He was brought up one way, but was shrewd enough to go the other way when he found it worked. Now if one player is better offensively and one defensively, he may well play the one who is better defensively.

He uses the zone press because he has come to believe it is the single best defense. It applies complete, continuous pressure on the opposition. A great defensive player might be more effective in a man-to-man defense, but the zone press covers up the weakness of a weak defensive player, so is better team-wise. Wooden does not so much ask his players to steal the ball from their foes as he wants them to force them into mistakes. With his defense he feels he can disrupt their rhythm, upset their tempo, alter their style.

"Pressure, pressure," he yells. "Force them. Force them all the time. Never let up. Never. Apply that pressure to them."

To put his tactics into practice, his players must be exceptionally well conditioned. So he stresses this from the start. While he will accept a skilled seven-footer, he has won with small teams, and he primarily tries to recruit quick players for his teams. He believes height is overrated in basketball and quickness is the greatest single asset any athlete can have. He has helped such small, but quick players as Walt Hazzard, Gail Goodrich, John Vallely, Henry Bibby, and Tommy Curtis to help him and they have become enormously effective. He believes quickness is more important than overall speed. Basketball is a game of short sprints, not long runs. Thus he does not favor the cross-country running favored by others, but the short spurts, the go-and-stop-and-go for his players. He wants 30-yard speed, not 100-yard speed. The one thing he tells his players and shouts at them, more than any other thing, is "Be quick . . . but don't rush." He wants explosions of speed, under control.

He works his players tremendously hard. Gail Goodrich says, "After some practices, I was so tired I could hardly make it back to the dressing room and then I could barely bring myself to shower and change." In some ways every practice is the same and in some ways every practice is different. He meticulously prepares the program for each practice. He covers everything he wants to cover every week, but different things different days. What they will do is broken down into 20, 15, 10, and even five-minute periods. Different players may be doing different things at different times, but every player has something to do all the time. No one stands around. When he was with the Lakers, Joe Mullaney's players complained they wasted a lot of time standing around during disorganized practices. Eventually, it cost him his job. Even good coaches sometimes are not as organized as they might be and some run poor practices. Some are excellent strategists, make good substitutions and make good adjustments in games, but do not prepare their teams properly. Wooden's practices are tremendously well-organized and his teams are prepared perfectly.

Gail Goodrich, who played under Wooden and now plays

with the Lakers under Bill Sharman, says, "I guess there
are just two different ways to win. Maybe more. Both
Wooden and Sharman know the way. Their record shows
it. I think Wooden decided that in college competition,
when your players still are learning, the simplest system
was best. He perfects his players, gets them to play
together, and outclasses the teams he plays. But in pro ball
there is not much to choose among the players and the
teams, especially at the top. The Lakers, Knicks, Bucks,
Bulls, Celtics, Warriors, and others all have almost equal
talent. One year one team wins the title, the next year
another team. The veterans are almost all fully developed
players. If the coach can get them to pull together as a
team and hold a high emotional level through the long
season, the only thing left for him is to find any little edges
he can to help his team beat a team which is almost equally
good. Sharman beleives in taking a long, hard look at the
other team and its players and trying to take what they do
best away from them. Possibly if Wooden coached pro he
would do the same. They are on different levels, so they
operate somewhat differently, but both are among the
greatest the game has seen."

While a Sharman is posing for his players the problems
their next foe will present, Wooden is telling his players
how wide to keep their feet, how to hold their hands up,
how to make the proper pass, to pass and not dribble, never
dribble fancy. Curtis Rowe says, "Wooden simplified the
game for us and taught us the fundamentals. He taught us
things like running and cutting and filling a lane on the fast
break. You'd be surprised how many pros weren't taught to
do these things in college. Basketball is basically a simple
game. You need two things to win—talent and execution. A
lot of teams have talent, but few execute the way Wooden's
teams do. It was a process of repetition. Every day, every
week, every season we went over the same things, over and
over again. Eventually, you get to where you do everything
you're supposed to do right almost every time, so you don't

even have to think about it, you just do it. Little things. No complex system. But the basics."

Before the first practice each season, Wooden tells his team, "When you walk out onto that court, you stop being an individual and you start being part of a team. You practice the way you will play. You win games in practices, you only play them in games. You help one another. I do not want to see a player make a basket without then looking to the player who passed him the ball, acknowledging the pass, perhaps patting the passer on the back."

In practices, Wooden snaps his comments. He speaks sharply, which is not his normal way. He says, "Speaking to a player privately I use a soft tone, I take a calm, comforting approach. But I believe a sharp, commanding tone of voice gets better results when you're in a practice or team situation." Practices last about two hours each. The players drill on shooting from the field and the foul line on a rotating basis. They practice rebounding. They practice passing. The emphasis is on quickness in each area of play. They do not play one-on-one. Individual play is discouraged. Nor do they often play five-on-five. This is saved for games. But they will work two-on-one and two-on-two and three-on-one and three-on-three on fast breaks on offense, for example, and on fast breaks on defense. Wooden, dressed in windbreaker and shorts and sneakers, watches intently, speaking to the players sharply in tones just short of a shout:

"Move . . . move. . . . Be quick don't rush. . . . Be sure of yourself. . . . Be in balance when you shoot. If you're not in balance, don't shoot. . . . Make sure the head follows through toward the basket. . . . Goodness, gracious sakes alive, what kind of shot was that? . . . Did you get a good view of that shot? It missed, so why weren't you in position to rebound it? Always assume every shot will miss. Always be ready for the rebound. . . . Get that pass off quick. . . . Get that loose ball. Dn't expect someone else to get it. . . .

Help out ... help out.... Don't relax.... Don't let down.... Do a job.... C'mon, move."

To stress a point, he blows his whistle and stops all for a lecture. Then play starts again. The bouncing ball and scraping feet echo in the almost empty field house with its tiers of empty seats. Wooden's voice and whistle carry eerily across the arena. The players are pushed hard. Their practice uniforms grow wet with sweat, which drips from their faces. They gasp for breath. But they go and keep going.

Shackelford says, "If Wooden has a weakness it is that he plays the players who play best in practice. Some poor practice players are great in games. But Wooden is an exceptional judge of talent. He figures out fast what every player does best and worst and works with him accordingly and fits him into the team accordingly.

"He does not play favorites on the basis of personality, but on the basis of play. For instance, he favors the player who will dive for a loose ball, who is not afraid to hurt himself, who goes all out every practice as well as every game. Well, that's the kind of player he was. But, it's all right, because that's the kind of player who wins games.

"He does not pick his five best players as starters, but the five who fit together best. It is the team concept. He also picks a backup man at each position. He prefers to stick with seven or eight men during a season. He doesn't call the backup men subs. They're players, part of his team.

"He may neglect the others a little. His job is to win, after all, to put the players on court who will win for him. He experiments during the early season, changing these players around. He wins anyway, but he's not too concerned with winning until the conference comes along. That's what counts. That's what gets you into the tournament. He points for the tournament."

Wooden says, "I think I've been a better coach every year than I was the year before. Sometimes in tactics. More often in working with people. In the long run it's getting the most out of your players and getting them to pull together as a team that counts most. It's what you learn after you know it all that counts. Every player is different. The sooner you find out as much as you can about him, the sooner you can help him. What you want to do is fit him into your team. This is a team game. An individual can win a game for you here and there, but only a team can win consistently.

"I know there is a theory that your best shooters should take most of your shots, that you should feed the man with the hot hand, and that may work at times, but you will discourage your other players so it will not work at other times. You can't have players playing as spectators. You have to make everyone feel part of a combined effort. Once the players see there is pleasure and satisfaction in that, too, you have gotten somewhere.

"I believe you first must be better conditioned than the other players. This frees you to execute. When you have confidence, you still will be performing at top speed in the last part of games when the other players are tiring, you will retain your poise even when you are behind. You will feel you will finish fast. Then, I believe in execution. That comes only from practice. I believe in simplicity. I don't care if the other teams know what we are going to do. They don't know when we are going to do it. And if we execute properly, they won't be able to prevent it. We're an easy team to scout, but a hard team to stop. Most teams don't even scout us anymore. They know us. But they don't beat us.

"I plan each practice with extreme care. I do believe that as you practice, so shall you play. I believe if you prepare properly, you will win. You have to have the talent, of course. The thing is not to waste it. I take my time picking my regulars. Once I pick them, I try to stay with them. I probably have had better talent in recent years than I did before. But I think we came very close to winning championships before. We had some good teams when Bill Russell's San Francisco teams were great teams. We had some good teams when Darrall Imhoff's California teams were great teams. They beat us, but they also beat everyone else. The year Cincinnati beat us by two points in the NCAA semifinal, we were good enough to beat anyone. After that, I made a few adjustments and they paid off. We now have won with teams that did not have the most talent. But we have a system which works and we fit our players into that system.

"At one time I stressed offense. Now I stress defense. In tournament play, a good team may be able to defense your offense for a while, but if you are playing good defense, too, you will stay close enough to win in the end. The important thing is to keep playing your game. It is important to retain your poise. We are champions. We have pride, which is passed on from team to team. Each of our teams wants to do as well as the teams which preceded it. Our players have a great tradition to uphold and this inspires them.

"I seldom mention winning. I seldom call special meetings. I say what I have to say in practice or in a few words before games. I do not want to get my players so high for one game, they will come down with a crash for the next. It is no good to beat a good team if you turn around and lose to a weak team.

"It is possible I push my players too hard in the early part of my early seasons. I do not want them worn out emotionally or physically when the conference campaign comes along. If they can win the conference, I want them to look at the overall picture. You play one game at a time. You advance one step at a time.

"We are good. We win almost all our games. But I am not upset by occasional losses as some people are. You cannot win them all. Streaks are freaks. You keep winning. Sooner or later you will lose. It should not destroy you. If you have played well, you should be able to accept it. Even winning, if you have played poorly, you should be disappointed. All any of us can hope to do is our best. In life as well as in basketball."

Wooden's life-style has altered astonishingly little all these years in the big town. He still has a small-town air about him. He and his wife lived for years in a small apartment in Santa Monica, near the ocean and not far from the campus. It is furnished in conservative style. There are prints on the walls, classics on the bookshelves. It is such a home as small-town people have lived in Indiana for years. He knows his neighbors. They accept him as a neighbor as much as a celebrity. They smile and nod when he strolls by. He has been going to the same church every Sunday for years and is a deacon of the church. Here he is just one of the congregation. But he has outgrown his house. His den overflows with the photos, plaques, and trophies he has acquired. There is little room to entertain, even his son and daughter and daughter-in-law and son-in-law and beloved grandchildren, with whom he spends almost every Sunday. In the summer of 1973, he finally purchased a larger home, in Encino, in the San Fernando Valley. He can afford it. He is entitled to it. But it is a wrench for him to leave his home of so many years, his neighborhood, his neighbors, his church. He was comfortable where he was.

When he first arrived in Westwood, he found a small luncheonette near campus much like one he might have frequented in Martinsville or South Bend. He began to go there then for lunch or a snack and he still goes there, eating perhaps a deviled-egg sandwich, a bowl of chili, a cup of custard or an ice-cream sundae. He does not pay much attention to his diet. His favorite food is his wife's baked chicken, such as she might have served on a Sunday afternoon in Martinsville or South Bend. Hollis Johnson runs the luncheonette. He and John Wooden have become fast friends. Johnson says, "Some great coaches have come in here, but John Wooden is also a great man. He is special."

He seldom parties. Although a celebrity now, he seldom attends swank affairs and he would as soon lunch at Hollis' place as at Scandia's, though he and his wife do favor Lawry's, a roast-beef place on Restaurant Row, for dinners out.

He dresses conservatively, but well, mostly in suits, and these are sent to him free from Gilbert's, a South Bend store he frequented when he lived there and for which he now does commercials. When he goes out, it usually is to a ball game, though not necessarily a basketball game. He goes to football and baseball games and still considers baseball his favorite sport. He says he has learned a lot from Notre Dame's former football coach, the late Frank Leahy and Los Angeles Dodger baseball manager, Walter Alston, who generally were cut from similar cloth. He follows baseball closely, prides himself on his knowledge of it and will argue it amiably for hours. He watches John Wayne and other Westerns on television, the volume high. He reads a lot. He has read every Zane Grey Western. He reads the Bible every day. He writes as well as reads poetry, but it is the poetry of others he carries around with him in a zippered loose-leaf notebook.

He seems so composed on and off the bench these days that it surprises you when he confesses he suffers. Normally, he is early to bed and early to rise, but he says, "I can't get to sleep after games. I'll take a walk. I won't be able to sleep."

He will deny it, but he relies as much on superstition as on strategy. He will spot a hairpin on the floor and pick it up and attach it to wood. Baseball players years ago felt it would bring them a hit. He feels it will bring him a victory. Well, he doesn't really believe it. But he's not taking any chances. He has been known to go through fortune cookies until he found a favorable one. He carries with him a small cross given him by a South Bend minister 30 years ago and he holds it in his hand during games. He keeps a lucky penny in his pocket. His pregame ritual is striking. Since the first game he coached, his wife has been at most of his games and he turns around and waves and winks at her. Once in Houston's Astrodome, he couldn't find her and there was a crisis until J. D. Morgan found her. Morgan stood up waving frantically at John, so John could wink and wave at her. She used to sit in the row right behind the bench at home games, but when he heard her shouting second guesses at him, he moved her five rows back, where she now sits with the rest of the family.

He sits down on the bench, courtside. His assistant, now Gary Cunningham, sits alongside him. Wooden does a ludicrous little drum solo on his assistant, patting him on the knee and shoulder. John then reaches down and straightens his own socks. He crosses his left leg over his right. He adjusts his glasses on his beaked nose. He rolls up his program, clasps it in his right hand, pounds it in his left fist, then reaches down and taps the court with it. He turns, waves to and winks at Nell, turns back, pulls the silver crucifix from his pocket, begins to chew gum, and is ready to go. All the details have been tended to.

Wooden, once called "the worst bench jockey in sports," now sits calmly through most games. But he admits, "I may appear calm. I strive to be calm. I strive to keep my players calm. But, inside, I am not calm. It does not matter how many games we have won. You always want to win this one, too. And no matter how confident you are, you know you may not win. And so you suffer until you have won.

"You worry you have not prepared your players properly. You wonder if you overlooked anything. Then the players go out there and make mistakes you have cautioned them against making. You cannot go into the game and do it for them. You sit on the sidelines and you suffer.

"You are very intense. You shut out everything else. It wears you out emotionally. When the game is over, there is a letdown. Even if you have won, you begin to worry about the next game. Coaching is not a comfortable profession.

You cannot take it easy during games or between games or even between seasons. You always have to stay one step ahead.

"I have been fortunate that I have had better job security than most coaches and have won more than most, but I still put pressure on myself and I still am criticized."

At a meeting of the Bruin Hoopsters, a fan club, following the UCLA loss to Elvin Hayes and Houston, Wooden was questioned so sharply by those who wondered how their team could have lost that neutrals were appalled. "It was a case of, all right, you've won 47 straight games, so how could you lose this one? All right, you've won some championships, but are you going to blow this one? Sure you've done a lot for us, but what have you done for us lately?" an observer noted. Wooden with a smile of wistful wonder, comments, "It brought me back to earth in a hurry."

For years, he resisted doing a book. When it became clear several books were being done *on him* for publication during the 1972–73 season, he did do a book *by him,* as told to Jack Tobin, *They Call Me Coach.* It is an inspirational sort of book and it has had an enormous success. However, he was bothered by the other books which were published, though all were sympathetic to him. Some writers did see flaws in him. Some gave more credit to his assistants than to him. Some unfairly offered critical comments about him from former players and others who were not identified, so the comments were suspect. Some said he wanted to lose some games. Wooden told one writer, Dwight Chapin, he hadn't read his book and didn't like it. J. D. Morgan sent him without comment a reprint from a 1915 *Saturday Evening Post,* entitled "The Penalty of Leadership," suggesting that those at the top always are subjected to criticism from those beneath him. Nell Wooden said, "Those who snipe at John are just jealous of him."

Generally, however, Morgan and Wooden took well the books done on them, even those that had criticisms of them and UCLA's basketball dynasty, did not turn away from the writers and cooperated with them all, including this writer when he was preparing this book. They did become concerned when it was reported Walton, of all people, who turns away from writers, was writing a book, but mainly because as an amateur he would jeopardize his eligibility if he took money for a book, which is unfair, of course, but which is the way it is.

Wooden, now in his sixties, no longer is a young man. He has suffered from a ruptured disc in his back, received when he fell on a concrete court playing basketball while in the Navy in the 1940s. Thirty years later it causes him the slightest sort of stoop, it causes him to walk with short steps, it causes him pain on occasion. Yet he refused to reduce his schedule and spent most of every off season lecturing at coaching clinics and teaching at boys' camps, including one he runs himself. It was profitable, but it is doubtful he did it for profit. "I owe it to the profession," he said.

Sometimes it seems he never stopped. He had just returned from such a trip to celebrate his wedding anniversary with his wife in 1967 and he was weary when he collapsed. Driving home, he got so dizzy he had to stop the car and ask his wife to take over. At home, he felt better, but that night he woke up with the world spinning and his head aching horribly. He tried to sneak out of bed, but fell on the floor. Nell called for help and he was rushed by ambulance to a hospital. He rested there 10 days and at home for three weeks, but soon he was back on his old schedule. "I felt I had just let myself get run down physically," he said. "After the initial scare, I supposed I was all right."

He was fine for five years. Then just after the new season began in the fall of 1972, Wooden was stricken a second time. Like the first time, this was at first dismissed as a mere case of exhaustion. Then it was diagnosed as a gastrointestinal problem. Finally, it was conceded he had suffered a "minor heart attack." He was taken to St. John's Hospital on Sunday early in December, and as the fourth game of the tenth season of his dynasty drew near, The Wizard of Westwood lay recovering in his bed in this place where the Marcus Welby television series often is taped.

Hearing Wooden was recovering rapidly, Bill Walton said, "He has to. The team could win without any one of us, but we won't win much without him."

12

Bill Walton: "I laugh at the people and what they do. I laugh at our fans and what they do for us. What makes a person stand in line for four hours before a game and then come and sit in the front row and go crazy? I look at the people and they're going nuts. It makes me wonder what's going on inside their brains. That's the wildest thing in the world, 12,800 people going to a game and going raving mad."

Pauley Pavilion is a palace.

When John Wooden arrived at UCLA, basketball was anything but big time in southern California. Twenty-five years ago, coast-to-coast travel was far from what it is today. There was no television. There was radio, but there was a sense of isolation from the rest of the country in Los Angeles.

College football was king among sports here, especially USC, more than UCLA. The Coliseum, built for the 1932 Olympics, was and endures more than 40 years later as home field for both. Also for the Rams, the first major-league team to move here. They came right after World War II, in 1946, and seized enormous support.

Pro baseball, minor league but popular with the Los Angeles Angels-Hollywood Stars rivalry, moved in as major league with the Dodgers in 1958 and got a grip on the local population which remains unsurpassed.

The Lakers brought major-league pro basketball to town in 1960 and struggled with small crowds for a couple of seasons in the new Sports Arena, adjacent to the Coliseum, and assorted lesser facilities, until they caught on with a championship contender.

The Lakers made basketball big in L.A., but the college version remained without support until UCLA became a champion. After all, this is a town with summer winters. People have pools and no one is far from the beach. From Disneyland on down, there are countless amusement parks. If one wants to see a sporting event, he wants to do so sitting outdoors.

When Wooden arrived at UCLA, the Bruins played in a campus gym nicknamed B.O. Barn and seating 2000 people. It seldom was filled. He was promised a fine facility from the first and repeatedly thereafter, but waited 17 seasons for it, until he had finally forced it himself. Meanwhile, after the original gym was condemned, the Bruins played in mediocre, small high-school, junior college, college, and public facilities like a gang of gypsies.

Finally, they landed in the Sports Arena, which was fine, except that they shared it with arch rival USC, it was next door to the USC campus, and it was completely across town from the UCLA campus. Only the cohosted Holiday Classic Tournament drew well. Crowds of 2000 and 3000 were not unusual other times.

Even when UCLA got into its undefeated season in 1963, the turnouts stayed small. Even today, with strong, but overshadowed teams, USC's turnouts are small.

After a second straight championship season, a new home for the Bruins, Pauley Pavilion, opened on campus in June of 1965. It was named for Edwin Pauley, who contributed $1,000,000 of the $3,250,000 cost of construction. Among the prominent fund-raising alumni was H. R. Haldeman.

The boxy, rectangular pastel-colored building sits alongside Sunset Boulevard. Inside, the twin-tiered place has 12,000 seats, which almost always are full. The Bruins play some games here when school is not in session, and then there may be extra seats available to the public, but the public, used to being shut out, often does not know it and does not take advantage of it.

UCLA has 29,000 students on campus and these get one out of six of these seats. They get around 5000 seats in the floor section directly opposite the benches. Of these, 3000 are sold for the season on the student cards, 2000 are put on sale 10 days before each game. Some the morning of a game. Another 2000 go to faculty members, who sit in the section behind the Bruin bench with alumni and friends of the university, most of whom get the rest of the seats. Presumably, the public had access to some seats, but a favored few have long since gobbled these up. There is a waiting list for season tickets of more than 5000 names.

Since Morgan pulled the Bruins out of the Los Angeles Christmas Classic at the Sports Arena, the average fan in town has little chance to see the team in person. Some considered this a slap in the face of the public.

J. D. Morgan says, "We do what we can to bring the Bruins to the public, but our basketball team is a function of our university and we wanted it on campus and available to ourselves primarily."

All games are broadcast live on radio. All home games are aired on television, on tape beginning at 11 P.M. Most L.A. fans get their Bruins through these broadcasts. Some selected road games are telecast, but, surprisingly, not all. There are some regional and national telecasts of Bruins games each season. It is easier to go out of town to see the team than to get in to games at home.

UCLA plays most of its games at home. It is the big team, Morgan wants it this way, and he gets his way. During the 1971–72 season, 17 of its 26 regular-season games were at home. Even these figures were deceptive. The Bruins have to play seven of their 14 conference contests on the road. If they did not have to, they would not. Otherwise, they played only two road games in 1971–72, in Chicago and Notre Dame. They played only these two in 1972–73, too, plus two at the Sugar Bowl Tournament in New Orleans. They play a holiday tourney on the road in alternate years.

Through the end of the 1972–73 season, the Bruins had won 102 of 104 games played at home, both losses to USC. The Bruins have an enormous edge at home. It is tough enough to play UCLA anywhere, but it is especially tough at Pauley Pavilion, where the more than 200,000 fans who turn out each season are rabid.

They raise an enormous racket. They are incredible. Spoiled by success, they are savage when a visiting club comes close to the home team. Even when the Bruins are beating their foes badly, these fans ask for blood.

From the first, every contrary call by the officials brings howling outrage from the fans. If by odd chance the contest is close, such as in the early stages, the fans physically threaten the referees. The visiting players are subjected to streams of abuse and seldom are offered applause. Even when the visiting team has begun to fall farther and farther behind, the fans do not let up. And the worst of Pauley Pavilion pressure seems to pour from that section behind the bench which holds the Wooden family, faculty, and alumni mainly. These seem to root harder than the younger fans. Little old ladies can be seen standing and shaking their fists at officials or foes and screaming obscenities. Aging and sedate professors rise to roar for the Bruins to pour it on.

Somehow, you expect more sophistication at UCLA, where the Bruins have won so much. Still, their supporters remain dissatisfied. They have been given a lot, but they want more. They have won so much they are now intolerant of even the threat of defeat, no matter how slender. Defeat, itself, would be almost intolerable.

Entering the 1972–73 season, the Bruins had lost only one regular from the preceding team, Henry Bibby, and had no outside shooter of such quality as a replacement. However, this was their one weakness. There was no other.

They were a more experienced and deeper crew than the club which had preceded it.

Returning were seniors Larry Farmer, Larry Hollyfield, and Swen Nater, and juniors, Bill Walton, Greg Lee, Tommy Curtis, Vince Carson, Keith Wilkes, Bob Webb, and Gary Franklin, while moving up were sophomores Dave Meyers, Andre McCarter, and Pete Trgovich, as well as freshmen Ralph Drollinger and Casey Corliss.

Farmer and Wilkes filled the forward slots, with Carson and Meyers behind them. At 6-11, center Walton now supported by another 6-11 player, Nater, and seven-footer Drollinger. Curtis beat out Lee to team with converted forward Hollyfield at guard. Trgovich backed them up.

Competition for playing time at guard was intense, but many considered McCarter the most gifted guard on the team. However he was an individualist with a flashy style frowned on by Wooden. He felt he would not be used much and decided to sit out the season as a redshirt.

The Bruins were out to duplicate their unbeaten 30-game season of the year before, they brought a streak of 45 straight victories into the new season in quest of the college record of 60 straight, which they could reach by midseason, and they were going for a seventh straight national title and ninth in ten years.

Victory No. 1 This Season/
No. 46 in a Row, Overall

The opener came on a late November Saturday night, just after Thanksgiving. It was warm in Los Angeles. You come off the San Diego Freeway at Sunset and drive east on the boulevard's sharply curving streets until the northwest corner of the campus and the pavilion suddenly appear on your right. The fans were moving from the outside to fill Pauley. Among them was Nell Wooden, who sat with her son Jim and his wife and her daughter Nan and her husband.

The Bruins blast Wisconsin, 94–53. The 41-point margin does not entirely satisfy the fans, who want the team to score 100.

Two/47

Bradley arrived determined to hold the Bruins in check. Their system was simple. They would hold the ball. They might not ever shoot it. They might not score, but then neither would UCLA. They did not shoot for almost six minutes. They did not score for almost eight minutes. The only trouble was they kept losing the ball and the Bruins kept scoring. After almost 14 minutes they were behind, 18–3. After 20 minutes, at intermission, they trailed, 28–9. After 40 minutes, at game's end, they trailed, 73–38.

The fans hooted and howled. At the end, they were roaring. Walton scored 16 points, collected 17 rebounds, and blocked 18 shots. Bradley coach Joe Stowell said, "He is the best I've ever seen. And this is the best team ever." Wooden, the perfectionist, was dissatisfied. "I thought our play was ragged," he said. Whatever, it brought the team even with its longest winning streak ever, 47 in a row.

Three/48

The 1000th game in the complete coaching career of John Wooden was his 804th victory and 48th in a row, the latter surpassing the previous school record. Pacific's Tigers arrived determined to carry the attack to the Bruins, ready to run with them. It was eight minutes before they scored. By then, they trailed, 12–0. After 17 minutes they trailed 36–6. At half time it was 40–15 and after the reserves came in and everyone relaxed, at game's end, 81–48. No single Bruin scored more than Wilkes's 18 points. Walton had 12, plus 15 rebounds.

Wooden said, "We have to work on our defense a little harder."

This was the first game Wooden would miss in 25 years as UCLA coach. Felled by a minor heart attack on Sunday, one week and one day after his milestone 1000th game as a coach, he might have missed more except that his team had a two-week break in its schedule. Now, on Saturday night, he lay in his hospital bed in Santa Monica while his Bruins took on the University of California at Santa Barbara in Pauley Pavilion.

For the time being, Gary Cunningham was the head coach with Frank Arnold as his assistant. After playing for UCLA, Cunningham coached high-school basketball in Manila, then returned to his alma mater to get his master's degree so he could enter the field of education. He said, "I wanted to go out and burn the world up in research. I felt I'd had enough of basketball and coaching.

"But, I began coaching the freshmen while I was getting my doctorate and got hooked. Working with Wooden, with these wonderful teams, well it was all exciting again. I could still go out and get a job in education, but I've found out there's a lot that's intellectual in coaching. I know now I can do it, too. I feel secure with it."

He looked out at the court and said, "All I have to do is win. Wooden would." And he smiled.

The team won.

Of course Santa Barbara was not the sort of foe to strike fear into the hearts of the nation's number one team. The Gauchos used the same full-court press the Bruins did, but the Gauchos' did not work and the Bruins' did. Walton scored 17 points in the first half and 30 in the game and took down 22 rebounds. He was bumped hard in the forecourt and limped off with two minutes left in the first half, but came back in the second half, until relieved late by Nater, who was relieved late by Drollinger, debuting.

Called for goal-tending in the second half, Walton turned so angrily on the official, he was called for a technical foul and he stormed away in animated anger. The

Bruins were only ahead by 25 points. They won by 31, 98–67. Tommy Curtis did not score a point, but he had 11 assists, accounting for 22 points. "I count them in my column," he smiled. Wilkes, who scored 16, said, "It was different not having coach Wooden here, but the team decided to play just like he was here.

The winning coach said, "I didn't do anything different than Wooden would have done." The losing coach, Ralph Barkey, said, "I didn't see anything different out there. This is one of Wooden's teams. He has prepared them properly. I have never seen a team employ the basic skills better than this team."

Five/50

This was Thursday afternoon, the day before Friday night's game with Pittsburgh. John Wooden, attired in a blue windbreaker, brown slacks, and basketball shoes, walked onto the court at Pauley as if it was just another day of work. The players were on court waiting to practice. Reporters and photographers were courtside in a way that was not usually permitted. The seats were empty.

He had been released from the hospital on Sunday and had been resting at home and had been given permission to return this day. Athletic director Morgan said, "He is fine and we want him to stay that way. We are cutting down on his work load. He usually answers his own mail, personally, but we are taking care of his correspondence now. We would appreciate it if he was not subjected to any lengthy interviews."

However, Wooden smiled and said he would say a few things. He said, "It was nothing serious. If it was, I would not have been allowed back so soon. Although it doesn't seem soon. I have been told to watch my diet. No more chili or banana splits after games. But I can still have plenty of fruit and I like that. I have been told to take it easy for a while, although I don't know how you can take it easy and coach. I have always told my players not to hurry. Now I have been told not to hurry."

His complexion was pale and he seemed a bit older than before. Of course, he is 62 and had just been through a bit of an ordeal. And possibly circumstances caused you to imagine added age. His manner certainly was softer than usual. Instead of standing at courtside, he sat on a chair. His players came up, one by one, and shook his hand. A smile, a pat, a few words, nothing excessive.

Before practice began, Wooden left his chair and met with his team in the middle of the floor. He spoke to them in a soft voice, saying he felt fine, he would take it slow for a few days, but all would be as before, that was about it, short and sweet, and when he finished, the players clapped. Then John resumed his seat while Cunningham and Arnold directed the practice. However, Wooden often stands off to take the overall view while his assistants run practices.

Once in a while Wooden left his seat and crossed the court to get a closer look at something. Then he would return to his seat. From time to time, he would call over one of his players and talk to him. "Larry, why did you do that?" he asked Hollyfield. "Why not do it this way, Tommy?" he told Curtis. Finally, it was finished. The players trooped off to the dressing room. Wooden stood in the almost-empty building, looking wistfully at the deserted court and said, simply, "It is good to be back."

A half hour before game time Friday night, at 7:30, John Wooden walked out onto the floor following his team, and those spectators who already were in their seats all stood up and clapped and cheered him. As the team left the court following pregame practice Wooden walked off, the people who were there stood and gave him another ovation. When he returned with his team to start the game, he got yet another ovation from a now full house. When his name was announced during the team introductions, he

got yet another ovation. When he went to midcourt at
half-time intermission to accept a Grecian urn from *Sports
Illustrated* magazine, which had named him its Sportsman
of the Year, he received yet another ovation. By then, he
had broken all records for standing ovations. He nodded
and waved his hand slightly, not ostentatiously, and hung
his head humbly and smiled slightly.

Pitt had a bad team, but a good player in Bill Knight, an
agile forward who scored 37 points. With his efforts, Pitt
did better than most do against UCLA. After falling
behind, 22–6, in the first seven minutes, Knight scored 15
of Pitt's next 17 points and the Panthers closed to within
31–23 with 5:17 left, but then the Bruins broke free and
went to 45–31 by half time, to 61–36 early in the second
half, and then coasted in, 89–73.

While the UCLA team disappeared into the dressing
room, Wooden emerged and sat down in a corner and
sipped from an orange drink and spoke to the press. "Oh, I
feel fine," he said. "It is nothing to make too much of."

The next night his team would take on Notre Dame.
The Irish were the last team to beat UCLA and they
would be hosting the Bruins in late January in what would
be the Bruin bid to set a national record for a college
basketball winning streak.

Wooden is asked about the streak and the record. He
said, "We prefer not to talk about it. I do not discuss it
with my players. I tell them to try not to think about it.
We do not want to get ahead of ourselves. We cannot get
to that point unless we get past all the games in between.
We must take these games one at a time. We can lose any
one of them."

"Can you, really?" he is asked.

"Of course, we can," he said, somewhat peevishly. "We
will lose a game one of these nights. We will not be able to
go on winning forever. No team can."

"Some say with Walton you will win 105 in a row at
least."

Wooden winced. "Well, some may say that, but they do not have to win games, we do, and I do not say any such things."

Notre Dame had won only one of six games, but had a better team than that, and in time Digger Phelps would pull his talent together and begin to win. This was not the time. Walton was triple-teamed within a zone defense and got only four shots in the first half, but this freed the others and eventually Walton worked his way free.

Walton scored only 12 points, but assisted on 12 others and had 12 rebounds, and UCLA waltzed past the Irish, 82–56, with no trouble at all. Afterward Wooden was asked about it. He said, "We played well. We could have played better. They played well. They could have played better, too. They gave us a good game" It was what he would say in almost the same words after almost all games all season.

With the press not permitted in the dressing room, one player was brought out to the area at one corner at the end of the corridor that fronted the dressing rooms to talk to the writers. This often was Tommy Curtis. He came to be called the designated talker. A bright, lively young man, good-looking with sharp features and a ski-jump nose, he sat sweaty on a table at corridor's end and said, "We just try to play our game, but we do adjust to the other team during every game. In this case, Notre Dame was slowing things down and collapsing on Bill Walton. We tried to keep the tempo up and be patient until we could penetrate. I'm the point man. That means I have to field-general the attack."

"Might you have more problems at Notre Dame?"

"It's always more problems on the road than at home."

"What about New Orleans and the Sugar Bowl Tournament?"

"We'll have problems," Curtis smiled. "We'll solve 'em."

He was very confident about this first trip which was

coming up now. Christmas was two days away. The Sugar Bowl tourney was the coming weekend, the last weekend of 1972. Wooden was confident, too. "We look forward to it. I'm sure we will do all right," the coach said, smiling thinly.

Was he in shape for a trip? "I'll be checked out this week, but I'm sure I will pass with flying colors," he said. He was wearing a blue suit, a blue tie, and a yellow shirt. He looked almost jaunty.

Seven/52

In the Deep South, in New Orleans, at Municipal Auditorium, before just under 7000 fans, UCLA started its usual team—four blacks and one white, Walton. Only when Lee replaced Curtis did the ratio lessen to three-to-two. Lee was close to Curtis and had played ahead of him the previous season, but Wooden was going with Curtis right now. Trgovich had been pressing Hollyfield in this first part of the season, but now he had begun to slump. Trgovich was more talented than Hollyfield, but less experienced and less disciplined. Wooden might have played Lee ahead of Curtis and Trgovich ahead of Hollyfield and had two black and three white starters, but he did not. He did not, I am sure, even think about it. He couldn't care less about color.

He cared about discipline. He was putting pressure on Trgovich to discipline his freewheeling style and Trgovich was starting to press and slump. Lesser sophomores were starting for good clubs all over the country. Trgovich missed his part of the country, Indiana, at the holidays. He was playing poorly and Wooden was beginning to play him less.

On the opening night of the Sugar Bowl Tournament, Drake did not give up when UCLA led by 16 points after 12 minutes. The Bulldogs battled back and outscored the Bruins by 12 points, 18–6, in the last eight minutes, and trailed by only four points, 38–34, at intermission. The

Bulldogs' 6-8 center Larry Seger was disturbing the Bruins' defense by staying outside and shooting from there and hitting from there. While Walton stayed inside, Seger sank seven baskets from the outside in the first half. Drake was within two, 38–36, and the Southern fans were hysterical, screaming for an upset.

Now, Wooden went to Wilkes to defend Seger outside. And the Bruins began to go to Walton inside. Bill hit the Bruins' first seven points of the second half and UCLA pulled away again. Larry Farmer fired in three straight baskets that demoralized Drake then, and the Bulldogs collapsed. At the end, UCLA was pulling away, 85–72. Walton would up hitting 13 of 16 shots for 29 points. Wilkes, Farmer, and Hollyfield each had 14 points and Curtis 12. Walton had 14 rebounds and Wilkes 13. Seger settled for 10 baskets in 19 shots and 21 points.

The Bruins had responded to pressure perfectly. They kept their poise and pounded away. Quick, agile, and acrobatic, they passed the ball fast, took passes on the fly, and flew through the air to convert them into baskets. You were reminded again and again what good all-around athletes they were. You were impressed with them. Wooden was not. He was almost angry. He said, "Our offense was very, very poor. Bill was open all the time inside and we should have been hitting him all night. We took too long to get the ball in to him. Our ball-handling was poor. We just didn't play well. I'm very displeased."

Eight/53

Illinois had made Temple its sixth victim in eight outings, 82–77, to qualify for the finals against UCLA on Saturday afternoon. Illinois had a good team with the Big Ten's best scorer, Nick Weatherspoon. Illinois took it to UCLA. Walton scored nine of UCLA's first 11 points, but Illinois was even at 11–11. Farmer hit a free throw to put UCLA ahead 12–11.

When Walton was called for goal-tending on a

Weatherspoon shot, Illinois went ahead, 19–18, but two free throws by Farmer put the Bruins back in front, 20–19. Illinois tied at 21–21, but Farmer hit two more free throws. Illinois tied at 23–23, but Farmer hit two more. He was flying, getting fouled, and hit nine of 10 free throws in the first half and the Bruins spurted to a 37–31 lead.

The Bruins bounced out after intermission and blitzed the Illini into a 16-point deficit after six minutes. Illinois fought back to within eight at 63–55 with six minutes left, but the Bruins pulled away again to win, 71–64, as the unfriendly fans settled back in their seats in disappointment. Walton outscored Weatherspoon, 22–18, and led all rebounders with 16. But Farmer had his season high of 19 points, they were the critical points, and he added 10 rebounds.

Afterward, Wooden seemed more composed than after the previous game. He said, "I'm not as displeased today. I think this tournament was very good for us. We were away from home for the first time this year and played against pressure in both games. It may wake us up a little. This is not an arrogant team, but it may have been a little too easy for us, and this may help them keep things in perspective. And maybe the coach will, too. I must be very careful that I don't get in the position of expecting too much from our youngsters. Our fans already do."

Walton and Curtis made the all-tourney team, Farmer did not. Walton was tourney MVP, but some felt Farmer was most valuable to his team in this tourney. Walton walked out to midcourt to get his trophy as though he was fetching some garbage he had to carry out. His left hand was in his jacket pocket. He took the trophy, paused only briefly for the pleading photographers, then strode off fast, sticking out his trophy to a teammate as though to get rid of it.

Larry Farmer and Larry Hollyfield were the only senior regulars on the UCLA team. Originally, Farmer wanted to be a football player. As a sophomore at Manual High School in Denver he was a fourth-stringer on the junior varsity basketball team. He thought he might not even go out for basketball as a junior, but he did and he had grown enough and improved enough to make the varsity. He continued to grow and improve as a senior, but was not widely recruited.

He wrote to UCLA and asked for a basketball scholarship. He was known to UCLA as a growing, improving player, a steady sort, well disciplined, a good student and a fine young man, the vice-president of the honor society and a student commander in the ROTC. He was brought to campus where Wooden asked him if he thought he was good enough to play for UCLA. Farmer said he was. Wooden said he could have a scholarship. UCLA usually recruits hard on alternate years, and this was an in-between year in which it had not landed the few top players it sought.

Farmer played behind Sidney Wicks and Curtis Rowe as a sophomore and now, almost 22, "Moose" was in his second straight year as a starter. He was not a spectacular player, but he was a steady one who played a lot of defense, did a little shooting and a little rebounding, and contributed to the team effort. He was 6-6, now weighed 215 pounds, had spent the summer running errands on a movie lot for UCLA alumnus Mike Frankovich, a prominent producer, but was majoring in sociology and hoped to work at that after a fling in pro basketball. It was not clear he would make it in pro basketball, but Wooden felt he had made it in college basketball. Wooden said, "He's one of the most likeable players we've ever had. He always has a smile. As a sophomore when he didn't play too often, he never complained. Since then he has played often and contributed considerably to us. You can count on him."

Farmer is flashy only off the court. He wears flashy clothes to games—suedes, leathers, capes, two-toned shoes, and wide-brimmed hats. He says, "I have been told I am the finest, most super-bad dresser in college basketball. Now, I don't know about that, but I taught Wicks and Rowe everything they know about clothes." In between games he wears Levi's and T-shirts.

Sundays, holidays, and blue days the Bruins often escape the crowds by visiting Sam Gilbert's handsome house overlooking the ocean in Pacific Palisades. The host always welcomes them. This Sunday morning, Farmer is munching bagels. He told a reporter, "Everything runs its course here. It has been worth it."

He says, "I'd like to think I get better each year. I'm playing better this year. I think I've got some ways to go before I reach my potential. The team is more mature and better than it was last year. If we're having closer games than last year, it may be because the teams we're playing are playing better this year. When you win as much as we have, it's hard to get yourself psyched up for every game, so we look forward to games against ranked teams. We hope to break the record for winning streaks, but we've mentioned it only once or twice around the dressing room. We're trying to take it in stride. Maybe five or six years from now, if we do it, it'll mean more to us. Right now we're just trying to win every game. We aren't hurting from pressure."

All the Bruins kept saying the same sort of thing.

9/54

Came the conference campaign. Oregon and Oregon State arrived for Friday and Saturday night games against UCLA and USC, switching foes after the first night. Each had won seven of 10 games this season. Oregon was the weaker, but Oregon State never had beaten the Bruins in Los Angeles. Although a lot is said in Los Angeles about how good are the basketball teams in the Pac-Eight, there seldom has been in 10 years a top team outside of UCLA.

On Friday night, Oregon came in cautiously. They held the ball for long stretches, boring the fans, who booed them. UCLA let them, playing patiently. Midway in the first half, the score was 6–6. With less than six minutes left, Oregon led, 12–10. UCLA scored eight of the next 10 points, however, and led, 18–14, at intermission. After Wooden prodded them, the Bruins roared out and outscored Oregon, 23–4, in the first half of the second half to finish off the Ducks. Lee helped inspire the spurt, replacing Curtis. But Wilkes hit key baskets, firing in 14 points, to star. Walton scored only six points on a night when he was listless.

Wooden said later, "I don't think this is the way to beat us. I think a team has a better chance to beat us if it plays its normal game." Coach Dick Harter of Oregon said, "I think this is the only way a team can hope to beat UCLA. You have to upset their tempo..They would run right away from us if we played our normal game."

10/5

Oregon State had good players, including a fine freshman guard, Ron Lee. The Beavers had reached the final of the Far West Classic before bowing to undefeated Minnesota by three points. But undefeated Minnesota could not be compared to undefeated UCLA. Minnesota would soon start losing, while UCLA would not.

As the Oregon State players were introduced before this nationally televised test, Wooden stood off to a side, program folded under his arm, applauding politely each of them, as he usually does for his foes. There is no need to be nasty. As each of his players was introduced, he clapped for them, too, and sent them out on court with a pat on the back. Unlike most coaches, he is more given to pats on the back than on the backside.

He did not clap when his name was given, but everyone else in the building did. The big crowd roared for the Bruins, as usual. The big Bruin band blasted away. It plays like a champion, too.

As the Bruins run out to line up one by one, they reach

out and shake hands with their nearest teammate. When Walton ran out, his nearest teammate stuck out his hand and Walton hit it with his fist and they both laughed. Clearly, they were loose, the Bruins, brilliant in blue and gold. Oregon State, clad in orange and black, seemed solemn, tense.

However, in the early going, some of the officials' calls go against the Bruins, several against Walton, and the Beavers stay close. The fans boo the contrary calls. One on Walton brings a barrage of boos. As he goes back on defense, he shakes his head and waves his arms as though in disbelief. He cannot imagine what he has done wrong. He is innocent, his actions say. A lady stands up in the section behind the Bruin bench and screams, "You're calling the wrong player, ref. Start calling number 22. Number 22 is a dirty player." Number 22 is guarding Walton.

Another foul is called on Walton. He stands as though stunned by it. The fans all over the arena rise in sympathy, screaming at the ref. Behind the Bruin bench, the comments come in outrage, from men and women alike: "Why don't you retire, ref ? . . . You stink, ref. . . . Pull your pants up. . . . Get your mind on the game. . . . You're missing a good game, ref. . . . Do you accept money? . . . Go to hell, ref, go to hell. . . . Look at number 22, ref. . . . How come you haven't called a foul on number 22, ref?" The ref calls one on number 22. A fan stands up and yells, "Hey, ref, now you're going." Another stands up and yells, "Hey, look at number 22, ref, he just insulted your mother."

Oregon State hung within five, six, seven points most of the first half, but then began to fall back. Wooden started to run in his reserves to rest his starters. Walton had three fouls and with three minutes left, Wooden sent in Nater for him. Walton started to run off, then slowed and limped off. At intermission, the Bruins led by 12, 43–31. The main-floor fans filed upstairs for food. Near the stairwell in one corner, movie star Walter Matthau stood with friends munching a hot dog and sipping a soft drink. No one bothered him. Fans are used to movie stars at UCLA games and at other games in L.A.

Early in the second half, Walton picked up another foul and said something about it sufficient to get a technical, too. Some of the fans merited technicals, too. After five minutes, Walton was relieved. The Beavers then closed in a little, but Hollyfield got hot with 12 points and the contest was tucked away when he was taken out with eight minutes to play. Wilkes wound up the top scorer with 19 points and the Bruins breezed by 26, 87–61.

Later, the writers were given a treat as both Hollyfield and Wilkes came out to talk to them. Wilkes, slender, handsome, skin the color of coffee-with-cream, said, "They were rough. I don't like it, but we have to expect it. It hurts your execution. Our play kept them close more than their play. As we went along, we got better."

Hollyfield, dark and handsome, was asked about the streak.

"What streak?" he asked, smiling.

"Your winning streak. Fifty-four straight now. You gonna beat that 60?"

"I don't know if we're gonna' get 55," he said, "We just take 'em one at a time."

Outside the air is cold, almost as if it was the north. Most of the fans have left. The parking lot is almost empty. The dark night is quiet. There is no celebration. It is just another game, another victory, taken one at a time.

The Notre Dame game in 1971, the last one UCLA lost, is the only loss Hollyfield played in since he began in basketball on a competitive level. At Compton High School, Compton Junior College, and now at UCLA, his teams otherwise never lost. If this continued through the end of the season, he would have a record of 89 victories in 90 games at UCLA and 184 victories in 185 games in his career.

With Farmer and he the only seniors among the starters, Hollyfield was the only player who had suited up for every game every year. As a sophomore, he played little, but he played a lot against Notre Dame, sent in to try to stop Austin Carr, which he could not do.

He recalled, "Farmer and I sat on the bench kidding one another that one of us was going to be sent in to stop Austin. When Wooden sent for me, I said, 'Oh, no, my God!' Here Austin was doing his stuff on Sidney Wicks and everybody and here I got to go be embarrassed. Coach said, 'Go get him.' I said, 'Wahhhh.' I couldn't stop him. No one could.

"I was so angry afterward I stormed around the corridor, afraid to enter the dressing room for fear I'd break down. When I did go in, there was Farmer sitting turned away and Wooden was talking of the loss, the only time I've had to hear him discuss defeat.

"I'm one player here who thinks about the streak and going back to Notre Dame to break the record. Farmer and I talk about it. It's like a play, setting the big game there where we lost last."

The 21-year-old Hollyfield, a sociology major, but hungry for a high-paying pro career, stands 6-5 and weighs 215 pounds. For two years as a forward he has, when permitted to play, flourished flashy moves, but he was played on in spurts and complained constantly about it. Now converted to play guard where he was needed more, he exploded only occasionally and protected his starting spot with conservative tactics. However, he remained colorful on court, flailing physically with his foes, talking to them, taunting them, talking to the fans, who saw him as a show-off.

Wooden said, "I am particularly pleased with his play. He has had problems with a knee and so hasn't been in the best of shape, but he has done what we have wanted him to do. He has worked hard. His attitude has been excellent." Hollyfield said, "I am happy to be playing. I have no complaints now. I get a lot of publicity for the things some people think I do on court, but it's not what it looks like. It's a physical game. I play hard and I'm extroverted and have some things to say. On the road, the fans get on me and it gets scary. My main thought is about getting out without getting hurt. I put up a big front. I'm really not a bad guy."

Teaming at forward with Farmer, Keith Wilkes was a soft-spoken minister's son from the soft, Spanish-traditional town of Santa Barbara, a couple of hours up the coast from Los Angeles. His father pushed his family in education. An older sister was teaching in Berkeley, while Wilkes was living in L.A. with another sister who was in law school at USC. He, himself, had advanced sufficiently fast to be a junior at UCLA at 19, which made him the youngest player among the regulars and the butt of many jokes because of it.

He was majoring in economics, a tough course, and admitted, "I'm supposed to be a student athlete, but basketball takes up most of my time. However, I'm working it out. I picked UCLA as much for academics as athletics, and I want to take advantage of my classes."

Wooden called him, "My most consistent and most underrated player." The writers wrote about him as UCLA's most underrated player so often he became the team's most overrated player. But he had become a good player, as conservative as Hollyfield was flashy, smooth, steady, and unselfish, the perfect starter in the coach's system. At times his expression on court is such some expect him to fall asleep at any moment. He sighs and says, "It's out front. I try to control myself. I haven't always had control of myself. I suppose I do now."

Called a Boy Scout sort, Wilkes insists, "I'm just plain old Keith Wilkes. I'm a person, that's all, like everyone else. There's nothing special about me. Just because I'm a minister's son and quiet, I'm no different than anyone else. I'm not very outgoing, but I like playing basketball.

"I could have gone to Harvard, but I chose UCLA because I thought it would be better for me athletically. I thought I could play for this team, but I knew it was a gamble. I've got a great deal of confidence in what I can do. I don't let the fact that I might not get a certain honor or make a certain all-star team bother me. I don't put that much importance on being recognized. I've learned to play for my own satisfaction. I'm satisfied to be in the shadow of a player like Bill Walton. He's so outstanding it would be unreal if he didn't get most of the attention. He doesn't ask for it and doesn't want it but he gets it. I'm beginning to get some attention now and actually I feel uncomfortable with it. I just want to be part of the team and have the team keep winning," he said.

11/56

The Bruins kept on winning with a trip north for a Friday night conference clash at Stanford and a Saturday afternoon league game at Cal in Berkeley. The Bruins were without Tommy Curtis, who had a severe case of the flu, and had to use Hollyfield and Wilkes despite minor cases of the ailment. With Farmer first sinking two straight shots, then Hollyfield three straight, the Bruins broke to a 10–0 lead, and with Farmer then flinging in two more, they went to 14–2 before the Cardinals got into it. Six-six Dave Frost, who scored his side's first 10 points, shot his team to within 14–10 and the home fans started to holler. The Bruins blitzed for 12 points, most of them on four straight baskets by Walton. Then, however, seven-foot Rich Kelley began to give Walton all sorts of trouble and led the Cardinals back to within 40–32 at intermission with the partisan spectators screaming wildly.

Within five minutes of the second half, however, the fans and foes were subdued. The Bruins stole three straight passes and scored with them to start a surge that shot them into a 19-point lead and they coasted in from there, 82–67. Frost led all scorers with 22 points. But balance paid off as Walton, Farmer, and Hollyfield each scored 18, Wilkes 12, and Lee, taking over for Curtis, assisted on 12 more and scored six himself to account for 18.

12/57

Cal, which had won only five of 13 games, but had a brilliant freshman in Rickey Hawthorne and a big center who could hit from outside in Carl Meier, whaled away at Walton inside while Meier whaled away from outside to take a 35–33 lead at intermission, one of the few times the Bruins would be behind after one half. Hollyfield missed his first 10 shots, Walton had only four points in the first half, and Meier had 16. The startled fans in tiny Harmon Gym were going wild. But in the calm UCLA dressing room, Walton told Wooden, "Don't worry, coach, we won't be behind when it ends and that's all that matters."

They were not. As usual, Wooden showed he is as good a game coach as he is a practice coach with the adjustments he asked of his athletes at intermission and as usual they swiftly put away a threatening foe with fury in the first part of the second half. Meier was shut off with only four more points, Walton put in 10 points and Hollyfield nine in the second 20 minutes, and the Bruins steadily pulled away to win, 69–50, silencing the fans and frustrating their foes. Walton said afterward, "We were never worried."

Now, however, came a crucial part of their season. The next game would bring them to the midpoint of the regular season and it against San Francisco and the following game against Providence would put them against the two toughest foes they would face all season. Also, following these two, they would take off for the Midwest, and if they remained undefeated they would be going against Loyola in Chicago for record-tying victory number 60 and then against Notre Dame in South Bend for record-setting victory number 61. "The last time we played Notre Dame, I felt the loss might be good for us," Wooden observed, smiling slightly. "This time I do not think a loss would be good for us."

In December, 1972, Bill Walton sat on the floor of the trainer's office, his long legs stretched out, each knee covered by a heating pad. He said, "I try really hard not to even think about them. The less I think about it, the easier it is."

He was asked about his political protest of the previous spring, his arrest, his fine and probation. "I'd really rather not talk about that," he said. "We could go on for days, and it might not come out right anyway."

How long did it take him to hitchhike across Canada? he was asked. He said, "I was in no hurry." Did he like it? "Yes, I really like nature. I like to be outside," he said. "Canada is a fantastic place."

No one bothered him there. A lot of people bother him here. He was giving one of the few interviews, perhaps the only one he would give throughout the 1972-73 season. You have to catch him just right.

He was the hottest item in sports, but during the season, not one Los Angeles area newspaper had even one real interview with him or feature on him. Still the writers and broadcasters protected him by not making a point of it.

He felt like talking to this writer one day in March, 1972. It was published, and its quotes from Bill were virtually the only ones used in national magazine and newspaper stories on UCLA basketball and Walton the following fall.

He complained privately about this. He said he had changed his mind about some things. What things? He would not say. Presumably he had decided he would not want to be gunned down by a black man.

He complained publicity had caused him to break up with his girl, though he did not explain how this could be since he had said little about her and she had said nothing to anyone.

He said he was not the same man he had been in March; he was not the same in January he had been in December. Clearly, he was a man of many changes.

He regretted the use of old quotes but did not say what the writers were supposed to use since he offered no new ones.

"I just don't like publicity," he said.

When Lew Alcindor arrived at UCLA, he and his parents met with Morgan and Wooden and asked that he be protected from the press as he had been in high school. The Bruin officials agreed to continue the practice by closing their dressing room, screening all requests for interviews and permitting only those few approved by Lew.

This policy was extended into Walton's time after Bill on his arrival asked, "Will I have to submit to interviews?" and was assured he would not have to. That this denies the other players a great deal of publicity they might want did not bother Alcindor and has not seemed to bother Walton. It has seemed to cause other players to consider the press and public intruders rather than supporters. Many Bruin basketball players treat writers and fans as foes, not friends. Larry Farmer, for example, three times agreed to an interview and failed to show up each time. Other players were seen to push aside youngsters asking for autographs.

When Woody Hayes brought his Ohio State football team to town for the Rose Bowl, he barred the media from his dressing room, and the writers and broadcasters complained publicly and privately about this as if they never had seen anthing like it, all the while it was being repeated after every UCLA basketball game in their own backyard.

They stood in the corridor outside the UCLA dressing room one night waiting for Wooden and his one designated speaker of the evening to appear, all the while howling about Hayes' tactic. When it was pointed out Wooden was following the same format, they laughed and agreed, as though realizing it for the first time.

At the same time, assistant publicist Frank Stewart was in the dressing room desperately trying to get some quotes from Walton he could give to the press. Walton was giving him a "yes" here, a "no" there and a grunt everywhere else. Finally, annoyed, he said, "Leave me alone, Frank. Write what you want and put my name on it."

Frank did not tell this story. One of Walton's teammates did. The teammate said, "Bill makes it hard on Vic Kelley and Frank Stewart. It's their job to publicize the team and keep the writers happy, and Bill makes it impossible for them to do their jobs. If he doesn't want publicity, why is he in sports? He knows he'll get it anyway. He doesn't care that the rest of us won't. He says he's all for the team, but he's all for himself, or else he'd be out there talking to the guys and spreading the credit around. He's a phony who spends all his time trying to live up to an image he's created of himself."

Some writers and broadcasters agree, and some disagree. One says, "His job is to play ball. It's his right to refuse publicity if he wants to do so." Another says, "Publicity is part of sports. Sports would die without it. It's part of his job to talk about his play and the games. If he doesn't, how can we do our jobs?"

One says, "He's a nice young man. He's just shy." Another says, "He's just not a very nice young man. He doesn't care about the writers, and he doesn't care about the fans. What he passes off as modesty is just the opposite. He has a big head and no heart. He feels he's above it all."

Vic Kelley, who has been at UCLA for 40 years and has been sports information director longer than Wooden has been coach, says, "It's my job to publicize our teams. But it's also our jobs at the university to care for the kids while they are on our campus. We take the place of their parents. And we have to respect their wishes and protect their privacies where asked.

"It has been an unusual situation since Alcindor arrived, followed a few years later by Walton. Both were fine young men who wished to be left alone. They were young, and we had to protect them from the pressure which was put on them. We took measures we have not taken with other teams."

Frank Stewart has been at UCLA 25 years and as Vic's assistant does all the detail work. He works hard and does a good job. He admits, "When a Walton doesn't want to talk to the press, it makes our job hard. We have to tell all the guys 'no.' We become the villains who get all the complaints. But that's our job, too. I like Bill. He's an extremely bright and personable young man. If he doesn't want to talk about himself, that's his right. Most of our players will talk to the writers. If you can't go into the dressing room, you can arrange interviews with them outside.

"Most of our staff in all sports are open to the press. J. D. Morgan is a marvelous interview. John Wooden always has been good to the writers. If he's not given to controversial statements, I've never seen him rude to anyone. Anyone who needs a story can go in to him and get one. If the publicists need an angle, we can go in to him and he'll help us figure one out.

"Neither Morgan nor Wooden asks a Walton not to talk to the press. But if he says he doesn't want to do so, they ask him only to be courteous with his refusals."

It was pointed out to Morgan that an Alcindor who refused to talk to the media and avoided fans had grown up into almost a recluse who was withdrawn from the public and unhappily pathetic when forced into the spotlight and seemed far worse off than an O. J. Simpson who learned to deal with the media during his starring days at USC and now was happy and comfortable in all public situations.

Morgan shrugs and says, "These are young men, now old enough to vote, certainly old enough to decide how they want to deal with the press and the public. I never have told our coaches to close their dressing room doors. I have left it up to them, what they want. Tommy Prothro and

Pepper Rodgers, our football coaches, never felt a need to shut out the media. Our Gary Beban was as big as Simpson in his football days here and as good then and now with the media.

"Wooden has had important players who preferred their privacy, and he has provided them this. I'm not sure it's wrong. The players are young and going to school as well as playing basketball. If we had let everyone who wanted to interview Alcindor or everyone who wants time with Walton, there would be no time left. I mean this. We get hundreds and hundreds of requests. There are countless small newspapers. There are countless radio stations. If we draw lines, we're playing favorites. So we let the players draw the lines."

Wooden says, "It is possible that our protections provided our players make it difficult for them to deal with the real world when thrust out into it. This is possible. However, these protections were not our ideas, but the players', and we only went along with their wishes. I'm not sure they weren't wise. Sometimes you have to protect a young man from pressure until he is old enough and experienced enough to handle it properly. Rash statements can disrupt team harmony, too, and the team comes first."

Late in the season, he said, "I see no reason to have writers and broadcasters running around our dressing room talking to our players while they are naked."

For some reason, athletes do tend to undress, then sit down and talk to interviewers in dressing rooms. The writers are used to it and think little of it, but it is a ludicrous situation. At this point, Bill Walton may be the outstanding athlete in the country who never has been interviewed naked. But then he seldom has been interviewed with all his clothes on, too.

"I'm on the basketball team, not the debating team," Walton told a writer. He was standing in a doorway on campus, a cloth sack slung over one shoulder, possibly containing his laundry.

"You're not playing with as much emotion this year as last year. You're throwing fewer temper tantrums."

"I'm trying," he said.

"Do you have the temperament to be the leader of this team?"

"We don't need a leader. We need fifteen ballplayers."

"You're playing very well, personally."

"I'm doing the same things I did last season only I'm doing them better."

"Will the team break the record?"

"I don't know."

He was itching to get away. His feet shuffled nervously.

"Thanks for your time, Bill," the writer said.

"No trouble. Come again," Bill said, showing his teeth in a sort of smile, and then his feet were moving, and he was on his way.

13/58

UCLA had been the last team to beat USF before the Dons went on to win 60 straight games before the streak was snapped in Illinois. The Bruins would be in Illinois in an effort to tie that record a week hence. UCLA had won 17 straight when the Dons beat them in the NCAA regionals that year, 1956, and the Dons went on to win their first of two straight national titles before losing after Bill Russell, K. C. Jones, Mike Farmer, and other stars of that team graduated. "Yes, indeed, we would have had trouble beating this UCLA team," Russell said. "I don't know if we could have or not. It would have been fun to try. I know the pressure of our streak was the worst I ever felt in sports." K. C. Jones said, "I feel we'd have beaten this team. They don't get that much out of their guards. I don't think we could have beaten that other UCLA team, the one with Kareem, Allen, and Warren. They were the best team I ever saw in college ball. But, this is a good team. Walton is hard to handle. Only I never played with him. I played with Russell and I got confidence in him. He was the man. We felt we could count on him. I have to feel I could count on him to take care of Walton. Of course, that's prejudiced. With Russell, we didn't feel much pressure. We just went out and won. Of course, that's what this UCLA team has been doing. Of course, there is pressure. It's a helluva thing to have to win every game."

Phil Woolpert, who coached that USF team and now has retired to a trailer in a national park in Washington, said, "We were tense going for our forty-fourth to break the old record of 43 held by Long Island University and by Seton Hall. We had to play Cal in Berkeley and it was the only time the attention affected us. There was so much hoopla we played like zombies and they led up by 10 points after 10 minutes. We got the lead and they went into what became famous as a nine-minute stall. But we went on to win. The closest we came to losing was in the 1956 NCAA regionals against Oregon State in Oregon. We won by one point, but the end of that game was like a nightmare. We went on to 60 straight and now I'm sure UCLA will surpass that and I'm not sure how far they'll go and more power to them. If a team is good enough to break a record, they deserve it. I'm proud to hold the record and I won't be ashamed when we lose it. They've made some runs at it before but this time they should go all the way. Maybe they could have beaten us, maybe not. What does it matter? Times have changed and you can't compare clubs almost 20 years apart."

Pete Newell, who coached Cal and the Darrall Imhoff clubs which went on to succeed USF at the top of the heap said, "Woolpert's teams were ahead of their time. They played a pressure defense before others did. UCLA plays it better, but Wooden has had the benefit of many years to refine the system. Russell was the first shot blocker. Walton has had the opportunity to observe this tactic while learning it. Yet Russell remains the best ever at it. It's very hard to adjust your frame of reference time-wise to compare classic clubs like these. I think it would be a great

game. Pressed, I'd have to say USF would win. They had
more good players than people remember. They had great
players on the bench. They were a team, too, as UCLA is.
This UCLA team probably would beat my championship
team at Čal. It's quicker, more versatile, and deeper. It's
the succession of championship teams that's the real
tribute to Wooden. Sure he wins with a Walton, but he
wins without him, too. Several teams account for the
streak. This team hasn't gotten it all together yet. Walton
may only have scratched the surface of his potential. Yet
UCLA wins easily against good teams."

Now, another USF team was ready to try to end
UCLA's streak before it surpassed that of the old USF
team, and this was a good team, too, winner of 13 out of 14
games, ranked in the top 10 nationally, coached by an
exceptional young coach, Bob Gaillard, and with big
players up front and quick players behind them. "It's just
another team," John Wooden said. "Just another game."
But the Bruins were roused. Finally, they had a threatening foe. Two, counting Providence, which followed. And
the record was near now. Greg Lee said, "I don't think
we've been this ready since the Long Beach game this year.
I could feel it in the dressing room. Everybody was a little
excited and nervous." Wooden admitted Walton was
ready. "I could see it in his eyes. He always seems to get up
for the good teams."

It was cold and windy outside and you went inside
Pauley where it was warm and the fans were in a festive
mood and the big band was blasting, "I Left My Heart in
San Francisco." Flags hung from the rafters. The players,
the Bruins in blue and gold, the Dons in green and gold,
were warming up. The cheerleaders, and the pompom girls,
too, were warming up. Wooden, a whimsical smile on his
face, went over to say something to them and got a cheer
from them. Obviously relaxed, he took his team to the
dressing room. When he returned with them, the players
ran through a lane formed by the girls and the fans stood

and cheered. The Dons hunched around Gaillard, getting instructions.

The Dons went out and took three shots and missed them all and the Bruins took three and hit them all and after a minute it was 6–0. The Dons came back, but with Walton working hard and performing well, the Bruins kept pulling away. Good teams come into Pauley and play bad against the Bruins. The Dons were a good team playing bad. The Bruins were a great team playing good. Walton was intimidating the Dons. They fell behind 19–10 midway in the half, then 42–25 at half time. Swiftly, they were finished.

Starting the second half, the Bruins blitzed the Dons, 14–2, and shot out to a 56–27 lead. Desperately Gaillard called time out, but when he got his team around, he had nothing to say to them. For some seconds the coach, appearing tense and nervous, simply looked at them before finally he began to speak to them. Nothing he said could have helped. Walton shook his fists at his foes after every basket. The fans chanted "Pour it on" and "We're No. 1." The Bruins lead rose to 78–40 before Wooden went to his bench mercifully. The final score was 92–64. Walton, active and awesome, had 22 points, 22 rebounds, and seven assists worth 14 more points. He also blocked seven shots, maybe worth 14 more points.

Afterward, Gaillard said, "They had Tommy Curtis out with the flu. The only way to beat them would be for the rest of them to have been out with the flu, too." Wooden said simply, "It was our best game of the season. It was Walton's best game, too." Walton said nothing. As usual, he could not speak to the press because he was in the dressing room icing his knees. Vince Carson was the speaker for the evening. With the game tucked away early, he had gotten to play some. He is a good player, but he doesn't get to play much. Sweat streaming down his handsome face, the big junior said, "I used to get down not playing last year. I'm more mature and more content with

my place this year. I guess I waited 20 years to sit on the
bench but there are good players ahead of me and I have to
keep myself ready when needed. I practice with the
regulars and I'm a part of a great team, so I can't complain.
Rebounding is my thing. If they need rebounding, they call
on me. Of course, with Walton, they don't need rebounding
too often," he said, and he laughed a little.

In the San Francisco dressing room, no one was laughing,
not the players who played and not those who didn't.

14/59

Providence had height on UCLA, but its star was a mere
6-0, Ernie DiGregorio, a cocky shooter, a remarkable
ballhandler, a demon dribbler, and a sensational passer,
perhaps the most exciting player around the college cir-
cuit. Leader of the big men was 6-8 Marvin Barnes, a good
scorer and one of the nation's best rebounders. Barnes
arrived at Pauley attired splendidly in a full-length coat
with flashy duds inside. He was followed by cool dudes in
wide-brimmed hats and wide-belled trousers with coats of
fur or leather. They walked past the preliminary game in
which the Bruins JVs were gobbling up the Anteater JVs
from UC Irvine as if it was not being played. The early
arrivals among the fans saluted them. The Friars looked at
the UCLA pompom girls and disappeared into the dressing
room. The UCLA pompom girls were practicing in the
otherwise empty corridor. Their dancing routines seemed
strange down there, cramped by concrete. The clapping of
their hands and shrill yells bounced eerily off the walls.

Providence had won 10 of 11 games, it had a good team
and this was one team which didn't tighten up against
UCLA. It played its game, a good game. It just wasn't good
enough. Barnes is a tough guy. He was in trouble on a
charge of having hit a teammate over the head with a tire
iron earlier, but Barnes still was playing, even if the
teammate was not. Barnes was the better player. And he
played Walton well and tough. Bill did not get off a shot

for nine minutes and did not hit a basket for 15 minutes. However Bill was beating Barnes off the boards. UCLA shot out to an 11-4 lead, but Providence battled back to 19-16. The Bruins bolted in front 25-16, and the crowd was stomping its feet in anticipation of the KO punch, but the Friars ralled to 29-26. Wilkes was hitting and Walton started to hit and the Bruins pulled away again at 42-28. Then Walton and Barnes went up for a rebound and Walton came crashing down, groaning and holding his left ankle. He was helped away and someone said they might have to shoot him. Rumors he had a broken ankle spread, and some Bruin supporters thought of shooting themselves. With him out, Providence surged to within 44-36 at half time. DiGregorio had not been as flashy as expected, but had popped in 14 points. However, Wilkes, hitting seven of eight, had pumped in 15.

It turned out Walton was still alive. He came out and on the first play of the second half he tipped the ball to Hollyfield, whirled around him, took a returning pass, and laid the ball in the basket. Lee fed Farmer for a basket. DiGregorio threw one in from 23 feet and Fran Costello one from 10 feet, but Wilkes countered with one from 10. DiGregorio jumped one home from 16 feet, but Lee fed Farmer for a lay-up. Costello hit a layup, but Hollyfield countered with one. Barnes hit a jumper, but Hollyfield countered with a lay-up on an assist from Walton. DiGregorio jumped one in from 15 feet and Costello another from 15, but Walton tipped in a miss and Lee stole the ball and sped in for a lay-up and suddenly you looked up at the scoreboard and UCLA led by 15. How did it happen? Providence is playing good and suddenly it is being beaten bad. The Bruins just keep coming at you and before you know it you are in retreat. The Providence players squirm in disappointment. A reserve, Al Baker, yells something from the bench and is called for a technical foul. He threatens to attack a UCLA player, Hollyfield. A fan runs from the stands and stands behind the bench and yells obscenities at the Friars and no one moves him away. Eventually he just leaves. DiGregorio is called for a technical foul. Frustrated, the Friars fall, finally, 101–77.

DiGregorio had finished high in the game with 22 points and 13 assists. Lee also had 13 assists. Farmer had 21 points, Walton and Hollyfield 18 each. Walton outscored Barnes, 18–12, outrebounded him, 24–13, and had eight assists to account for 16 more points.

Afterward, Hollyfield says, "It wasn't really too tough a game. What it was, it was a tough mouth game." And he laughs in the easy way of a winner. In the Providence dressing room, DiGregorio sat quietly looking down at his feet and peeling the tape off them. He looked up wearily and said, "I'm sorry we couldn't have played a better game. I thought we were playing pretty well, but then I guess we weren't. They deserve to be number one. Maybe if we could play them again, we could do better." Barnes stood with his back to a wall and said, "You beat those guys and you've beaten history, an institution, the gods. You're famous for life. They can be beaten. They didn't seem too tough to me. Maybe if we could play them at home, it might be different."

Out in the corridor, Providence coach Dave Gavitt said, "We can't get them to come to us. If we want to play them, we have to play them here. Maybe we're foolish for doing so, but you always feel you can pull off the upset and you want to try. Well, we tried everything and nothing worked. It's no disgrace. This is the team that next weekend will set a new record for the longest winning streak in college basketball history. Of course, they'll set it. Is there any doubt?" Down the corridor, Wooden said, "There's always doubt. We should get the record, but there's always a chance you can be upset. Yes, we can talk about the record now because it's out there for us to get in the next two games and we're certainly going to give it a good try. It will be harder away from home, but it's always better to do something like this on the road." They had won 33 at home and 26 on the road. Now, they shot for 60.

Bill Bertka, basketball's "super scout," who is chief scout for the Lakers and operates basketball's best college scouting service in Santa Barbara, said, "It doesn't matter where they play. I'd like to say Loyola or Notre Dame has a chance against them, I'd like to say Long Beach or anyone else has a chance, but I'd be lying. I don't like to scout them because I have to tell the team that pays me that it has no chance against them."

15/60

The seventh longest winning streak in NCAA college basketball books almost went unnoticed. It went from February of 1970 to March of 1971, lasted 39 games, and was put together by Marquette. LIU and Seton Hall had strings of 43. Three of the longest belonged to UCLA. The Bruins had 41 straight from January of 1968 to March of 1969, 47 straight from February of 1966 to January of 1968, and now 59 straight from January 30, 1971. On January 25, 1973, they could tie, and on January 27 top San Francisco's streak of 60 straight which ran from December of 1955 to December of 1957.

San Francisco had only one undefeated season in its streak. It lost to UCLA in the third game of its 1955-56 season and went on to finish with 26 straight victories and a 28-1 record. The next season, it went 29-0. The following season, the Dons won five more in a row before host Illinois ended this string. The first year Oregon State lost to them by only a point, but no other team came within 10 points. The second season, no team came closer than seven points. In the fourth game the third season, Elgin Baylor and Seattle came within five. In the sixth game the streak was shattered in a rout by Illinois, 69-33.

The Dons won their first championship game from a La Salle team led by Tom Gola, 77-63. Russell had 23 points and 25 rebounds, but the hero was Jones who scored 24 points and stopped Gola without a goal for 21 minutes. The Dons won their second title handily from Iowa, 83–71.

After losing to Notre Dame in the 1970–71 season's 15th game, UCLA won 15 straight to finish at 29–1, winning the national title from Villanova, 68–62. Aside from its loss, UCLA had a number of close games, winning by five points at Stanford, four at USC and Washington State, two at Washington and Oregon State, one at Oregon, and two again against Long Beach in Utah. The next season, however, it went 30–0, won the title against Florida State in L.A. by five, 81–76, and no other team all season had come closer than that. Oregon State came within six. No other club came within 12. Now, in winning its first 14 games of this season, only Illinois, which fell short by seven, had come within 12.

The Bruins flew out early Wednesday morning on TWA flight No. 24, arrived in Chicago at midafternoon, and checked into the Bismarck Hotel. Seventeen years ago at ancient Chicago Stadium, George Ireland's Loyola team became USF's 60th straight victim. Now Ireland's Ramblers returned to the old arena to become UCLA's 60th straight victim. The crowd of 15, 817 howled in hopes of an upset until well into the game, but it wasn't to be. The Bruins were so loose they committed 27 turnovers, 11 more than Loyola, but still won easily. Loyola stayed close for a while. After UCLA led, 30–19, midway in the first half, Loyola scored 10 straight points to close within 30–29 as the fans went wild. But that was the end of it. UCLA spurted away again to lead 47–39 at half time and strolled in at the end to win, 87–73.

Walton was a wonder. He hit 14 of 19 shots from the field, totaled a season-high 32 points, and took in a career-high 27 rebounds. He was so enthusiastically active he blocked five shots and was called for goal-tending five times and for basket interference three times, which produced displays of emotion. None of the other players showed any emotion. "It was a big game in the record books, but I did not try to tell my players it would be a difficult game before the game. Why should I have? It did not figure to be," Wooden said. He let some writers into the dressing room afterward, and they were surprised how silent it was. The players quietly showered and dressed. One writer wondered if it was a museum instead of a winning dressing room. Another wondered where was the celebration, the emotion. "The way we coach these young men, we don't want them to be too emotional," said John Wooden.

16/61

The Bruins rode by chartered Greyhound bus to Notre Dame, Friday, and checked into the Ramada Inn. The Irish campus resounded with pep rallies. The Irish coach, Digger Phelps, said, "We've won five out of seven games since we lost in Los Angeles. We're at home now. We're a better team and we're going to give them a better game." His star center, John Shumate, said, "We're going to beat them. I'm going to whip Walton. They're in the pressure cooker." At the motel, the Bruins were calm. Walton said, "We're cool." Lee said, "We'll win. After all, we always win." Wooden said, "I want to win, but for the players, not for myself."

There were two nationally televised games that Saturday. Early in the morning, the North Carolina-Maryland game was telecast. You were struck by how intense and exciting it was. After all, you did not know who would win. As it turned out, Maryland won, though without much of a contribution from Tom McMillen, who originally was supposed to be better than Walton. These were at the time two of the four top-rated college clubs in the country, but they were not in a class with UCLA. North Carolina State also was in the first four, also was unbeaten, and probably was not in a class with UCLA, either, although it would not get to prove it was. It was on suspension from the NCAA for recruiting violations and ineligible for post-season championship play. Long Beach was ranked fifth and saying it was ready to beat the Bruins now, its players bragging how they would do it, but you knew they would not do it even if they got the chance. No matter who played UCLA, you knew who would win. Which took most of the excitement and fun out of it.

That afternoon the television cameras turned on Indiana, the state where John Wooden was born, near the high school he had coached. The UCLA players were introduced and booed heavily. Wooden stood with a serious expression on his face. Walton jiggled from foot to foot nervously. The Notre Dame players were introduced and cheered heartily as the students came to their feet, where they would remain throughout the game. They made an enormous racket in the vast center. The Notre Dame fight song was blasted by the band and almost all in the place sang along. *They* thought their team could pull off an upset. They remembered two years earlier. Two years to the day. They remembered Austin Carr. But now he was gone. And now UCLA had Bill Walton.

The score was tied three times in the first three minutes and the noise rose and rose. At 8–8, Walton rebounded a Wilkes' miss into the basket with one hand and it was 10–8. Then it was 12–8. Then 14–8. Notre Dame made it 14–10. Then Hollyfield fed Walton a long, high pass, which he took above the basket and he dropped it in and it was 16–10. Soon, Lee was leading Walton with these long high passes and Walton went up and with perfect timing and incredible control of his body dropped them in and at half time UCLA led, 38–25, and the crowd had not been making so much noise, except when Hollyfield was busy bloodying Peter Crotty's nose and then they threatened him. He smiled at them. Later, he said, "That was fun, them wanting to kill me."

In the second half, UCLA as usual just kept pulling away. Notre Dame kept working on keeping the ball away from Walton, but he'd get it and pass off and turn around to rebound misses. Shumate in frustration was working on him so furiously Wooden went to complain to the Notre Dame coaches and the officials, and a brief rubarb ensued, but it came to nothing. The score mounted to 82–63, at which point time ran out. Hollyfield slapped Farmer's hand enthusiastically and they told each other they had gotten even for two years before, but there was no other sign of enthusiasm among the Bruins, no one even jumped in the air, and the photographers, who had pressed in, later said it was the most disappointing thing of its kind they had ever seen. There were some ceremonies. Wooden received the game ball and smiled and said, "This isn't the greatest thing that's happened on this day. It is my granddaughter's birthday. But the most important thing is that this was cease-fire day in Vietnam. That's much more important than this."

The press got into the Bruin dressing room again. Walton said, "It's an accomplishment for the team. But, remember, the team with Wicks and Rowe won the first 15, we've only been part of the last 46." He had scored 16 points, taken down 15 rebounds, and blocked 11 shots. "I played OK," he said. "It was a team triumph." Wooden had used all players on his roster and 10 had scored. Curtis remained home, recuperating from the flu. Lee had taken charge in his absence. Lee said later, "It was very nice. But when you win all the time, it's not all that much fun." He startled some by predicting the record would not last long. Then he smiled and said, "We'll break it with our next victory."

Bill Walton is at the ready on defense and directing traffic like a cop in
UCLA action at its Pauley Pavilion. (UCLA)

"The Gang" goes: *Upper left:* Larry Farmer leaps to make a two-hand pass to Larry Hollyfield. *Upper right:* Smooth as silk, Keith Wilkes jump-shoots against Wisconsin in home opener. *Lower left:* Tommy Curtis drives on Pacific's John Errecart. *Lower right:* Hollyfield defends against Wisconsin's Gary Anderson. (UCLA)

op: Greg Lee jump-shoots against rovidence as Walton watches, and riars' star Ernie DiGregorio (15) oves in widemouthed. (UCLA) *ower right:* In rare appearance, g Swen Nater hooks one over reach Badger Ken Hughes. *Lower left:* g sophomore Dave Meyers drives gainst foe from the University of alifornia at Irvine.

Walton works against archrival USC and Trojans Clint Chapman (35), Gus Williams (25), and Brian Heublein (34) in 1973. (Lower right photo by James Roark, *Los Angeles Herald-Examiner*. Other photo by UCLA.)

The expressions of John Wooden as he coaches his UCLA Bruins in action, from anxious advice offered his players in the heat of action to smiles of satisfaction as the foe is cooled off, are shown in this series of portraits. Assistant coach Gary Cunningham, possibly his eventual successor, is shown by his side in two of these photos. At *upper left,* he is shown seated at his office desk in front of his "Pyramid of Success" (photos of men who inspired him and inspirational sayings). (UCLA)

Taking a trip—to Chicago and South Bend to take on Loyola and Notre Dame in quest of their record-tying 60th and 61st consecutive college basketball triumphs—UCLA's Bruins seem relaxed. *Upper left:* Bill Walton reads while he waits to place a telephone call. *Upper right:* Coach Wooden chats with wife, Nell, who makes most of the team's trips. *Below:* Back in the bus, Larry Farmer and Vince Carson play cards. In the very back of the bus, Walton sits by buddy Greg Lee, an unseen tape spinning out acid-rock music. (UCLA)

Walton pulls down a rebound and looks for a fast pass to get a fast break going, and Lee drives in for a two-handed lay-up, in record-tying victory number 60 in a row, over Loyola at Chicago Stadium. (UCLA)

The scene in Notre Dame's Cen[ter] as UCLA ripped Irish for reco[rd]-setting victory number 61 in a r[ow] is shown above. *Left:* Walton g[oes] high to take a pass and lays the b[all] back into the basket over his he[ad]. *Right:* Walton and Farmer s[hake] hands happily as triumph is wrapp[ed] up. (UCLA)

At ancient St. Louis Arena, The Walton Gang won its second straight national title in NCAA championship tournament. Here the Bruins stave off young Indiana University team's spirited bid, as Tommy Curtis squirms up behind blocking of Walton for a jump shot while Don Noort (43), John Ritter (42), and John Laskowski (31) of Fighting Hoosiers look on. (UCLA)

Walton leaps high to lay one in over Ritter, and Quinn Buckner (21). (UCLA)

Walton reaps a rebound. (UCLA)

In final against Memphis State, Greg Lee fires a pass to Larry Farmer as Tigers Billy Buford (20), Bill Laurie (10), Wes Westfall (42), and Larry Finch (21) move in. (UCLA)

UCLA completes a decade of dynasty with its ninth national title in 10 years, in final game action against Memphis State at St. Louis. Bill Walton takes a high pass from Greg Lee and drops it in the basket. Teammate Dave Meyers (34) and Tigers' Billy Buford (20) and Ronnie Robinson (33) watch while Tiger Bill Laurie (10) moves on by. (UCLA)

Walton hauls in rebound high above ground-bound Buford and Wes Westfall. (UCLA)

Memphis star Larry Finch, a sportsman, helps Walton limp off after hurting knee near game's end.

The victory is theirs: *Above:* Larry Farmer leans in to exchange congratulations with assistant coach Gary Cunningham and Larry Hollyfield. *Below:* Hollyfield, the net cut down and draped around his neck, whoops it up with Swen Nater.

The winners: *Front row:* Senior manager Les Friedman, Larry Hollyfield leaning on title trophy, and Larry Farmer, giving the number one sign. Behind them, leaning in at left, are Casey Corliss and Tommy Curtis, and, standing at right, coach John Wooden, trainer Ducky Drake, and junior varsity and assistant varsity coach Frank Arnold. In a row behind them are Gary Franklin, Greg Lee, Bob Webb, assistant coach Gary Cunningham, Dave Meyers, and redshirt Andre McCarter. In back row are manager Ken Jaffe, Vince Carson, Keith Wilkes, with head turned, talking to Ralph Drollinger, Bill Walton and, holding up finger as symbol of being number one, number two center Swen Nater. Missing, Pete Trgovich. (UCLA)

Bill Walton.

13

The following week, Curry Kirkpatrick came out with a story in *Sports Illustrated* which rocked the Bruin boat a bit. He wrote that Walton preferred Lee in the game rather than Curtis, that Curtis' style disrupted the team, that Walton was getting at Wooden about who should be playing. He wrote that the players kidded about the situation, and that some urged Curtis to be "loud" and have "soul," and that it was a real situation.

Well, no one really laughed much about the story. Walton had spoken of the team's blacks as his brothers and had gone out of his way to speak on behalf of blacks, but he was white and his best basketball buddy Lee was white and some of the blacks decided if he favored Lee over Curtis it was a prejudiced thing. They resented the way the story described Curtis and drew away from the whites.

One white player said, "It was damned unfair. Walton could care less about color. He might prefer Lee's playing because Lee really does pass to him better, but otherwise he could care less. He's been hurt by this and is very angry about it. Now he feels he's right for not talking to writers." A black player said, "Maybe we're super-sensitive, but you always wonder about whites when you're black and this made us wonder about Bill. We didn't do anything exactly, but before he was always welcome with us and after this all of a sudden we'd be talking and he'd walk into the room and the talk would stop. The blacks and whites still got along, but we just weren't as tight."

Wooden said, "Lee and Curtis have been extremely competitive. Both are point men in our system. Lee started 29 of 30 games last season and did a splendid job. He is a superior passer to the pivot. Curtis is quicker and a better outside shooter and with Bibby gone we needed that so he moved ahead of Greg. I think Greg was upset by this and it affected his play for a while. However, Curtis has been sick and he will be awhile recovering and Lee has played very well in his place and may have won back the job. I believe Curtis can come off the bench with more snap and fire. That's a consideration. I do not believe Walton is concerned about color, nor are Curtis or Lee, and I do not believe any magazine story can create concern."

Walton would not say anything about it. Curtis said, "It doesn't bother me. I'm above such stuff. But it makes me think. I think it's probably true and that's sad. I'm sorry it has to be that way, but that's life, and it never surprises me when such feelings come out. Hey, I'm black and I'm sensitive to it. But it won't affect my relations with Bill. I'll be pleasant to him and I expect he will be pleasant to me. He always has been. We were buddies. But it won't affect my play. I want him to do well because the team needs it and he deserves it and I'll do anything I can to help. I hope to get my job back from Lee because I want to play, but I wish Lee well. I wanted the team to get the record with or without me. I didn't want them to fall flat because Tommy Curtis was out. I just want to live and play good and have the team play good and steer clear of any controversies."

Lee said, "Tommy and I play the same position so we have to compete for it. We both want to start. Our feelings don't enter into it. The coach makes the decisions. He's a rational, fair man. It's normal to be jealous of the guy playing ahead of you. We all think we can do the job better than the other guy. I'm sure Tom thinks he can do the job better than me. We both have egos. And we're probably pretty close. I'm friendly with Walton and I have a style that complements his, but I don't know who he thinks

should start and I don't think anyone else does, not a writer
and not anyone else, because it's not Bill's style to say. It's
not his choice, either. And one thing I'm sure of, whatever
his preference, it's not dictated by color. I like Tommy. I
think he likes me. We don't run together. We come from
different backgrounds and we have different personalities.
Color doesn't come into it."

Lee is 21. He stands 6-4 and weighs 190 pounds. The son
of the coach at Reseda High School in the San Fernando
Valley, Greg is a bit slower than the usual Wooden guard,
but also a bit stronger, and a brilliant floor leader of a set
attack. He has a soft touch and makes the high pass to the
jumping pivot at the basket as well as any player
anywhere. He sat in an office in the school athletic department and said, "Because of my father, I was schooled in
fundamentals. But I developed my own style. In high
school I could go one-on-one with anyone near my size and
whip him. People would say, 'This guy can really play,' and
I really could. Now, I'm not so sure anymore. If I'd gone to
any other school, I think I'd have been a star. But here only
a Walton or an Alcindor is a star. The rest sacrifice for the
team. That's fine. No player is worth anything if he's not a
team player. No matter how I'm playing, if I'm helping the
team play well I'm doing my job. But it hasn't helped me as
a player individually. You have to be able to go one-on-one
to make it as a pro and my one-on-one has deteriorated. I'm
not the shooter I was. I don't have the old confidence I had.
When I found myself sitting on the bench the first part of
the season, I almost quit. I seemed to be going backward. If
you're not playing, what's the point of taking the time? But
now I'm playing, and if I get the chance I'll probably play
pro just to see if I can cut it.

"The thing is," he said, "I've found there are other things
besides basketball in life. Growing up, you play games
every night the year around. But when you get grown up,
there are other things you want to do with your nights.
Girls?" he grinned. "Sure, why not? But more than that,

other things that interest you besides sports." A 4.0 student
in high school, he was described as a person with an almost
photographic memory and a flair for mathematics.
However, he dropped his first college course in math and
was quoted as saying he "couldn't get psyched up for com-
peting with a bunch of kids with two-inch glasses studying
their heads off." He switched to history, but reportedly
remained dissatisfied, saying sometimes he was inspired
and sometimes he was not and, "mostly, school is a joke." A
handsome lad with a quick and open mind, he told us, "I
like to take history courses, but I don't know how I'd use it.
I don't know if I want to teach. The only thing I've really
found I like in life is working with kids, so I might become a
social worker. I don't know what my scholastic average is
now. I get mostly A's and B's. I don't worry about grades. I
want to learn, but I don't think school is the only way."

He had become a vegetarian and was into health foods,
which are plentiful in his room in the Phi Kappa Psi house.
The walls are covered with posters warning of the dangers
of drugs and carrying quotes from Thoreau. Message songs
spin on the record player. He said, "I like basketball.
Players usually are able to relate to one another better
than in the society outside. I enjoy the fraternity of my
teammates. But I don't enjoy the games much anymore.
There is no way any intelligent person can play in 60
straight victories and feel threatened by defeat. You play
your best, but without competition you can't be inspired.
It's no fun to win when you always win. It's no fun when
the fans not only want you to win; but want blood. It's fun
when you go to a game wondering if you can win and play
your guts out and win just enough of the time to be on top.
The thrill is winning a game you weren't supposed to win,
not one you figured to win. The way it is, I'd just as soon lie
on my back in the sunshine, swim in the ocean, play
volleyball on the sand, share a hot dog with a young lady.
That's fun."

Another time, another place, Tommy Curtis conceded it was no longer fun for him, either. "It's just no fun to win easy all the time. You don't feel any satisfaction afterward," he said. "Last year when Florida State took it to us, it was beautiful. We both came to play, it was tough, and we won. I freaked out it was so much fun. But let's face it, we all want to win. The cat who says he wants to lose once in a while isn't telling it as it is. Let him lose a few and he'll be having a lot less fun than he is now. There is a lot of satisfaction in being the best, in blowing into Chicago and saying, 'Hey, man, I'm here, and I'm going to whip you.'

"Wooden wouldn't let us become complacent. He gets you on a level and holds you there. He pushes you to perfection. But we're men, not machines, and we need to make some mistakes to remember it. I've bent to his way. Everyone does. You do or you don't play and we all want to play. I have moves I haven't used yet, but he won't let me use them. I passed behind my back one game and he pulled me right out of the game. It came natural to me, but I have to concentrate on stifling it. If I get carried away and make some moves, the last move I make is one in which my head spins back over my shoulder so I can see if the coach saw. If he did, the move after that is to the bench.

"Wooden inhibits the individual. We're all different, but he punches out copies. My game is inhibited now and I'm not the player I was. But I'm the player he wants. He wants to win. So do I. He knows the best way. He's proven it. So I have to go his way. But it's no fun to play as a machine instead of as a person. I'm small, but I hope to play pro ball just to see if I can still play my old way.

"Basketball is a business with the old man. He stays, while the players come and go. He can't let the players fly off in all directions. He has to discipline them to his style. The style stays. He's a great coach. The proof is in the winning. I've learned a lot from him. He's forgotten things I'll never know. But maybe it means more to him than it does to me. Other things mean more to me. He's a good man, I guess, but we see goodness from different sides of a fence. We have different lifestyles. Away from the court, he doesn't get to me."

Curtis is a 21-year-old from an unusual background. His grandfather founded one of the first black insurance companies and one of the first black funeral homes in the South. His mother researches vocational rehabilitation with the retarded at Florida State. He says, "She is my idol. Ours was a broken home, but she kept it together. We had no father, but she was strong and gave us strength. She sent my two older sisters to college. She started me on the right road. She taught me what life is all about. She told me you have no control over the situations which will develop in your life, but you have control how you will react to them. She said you're gonna have setbacks in life, but you gotta keep taking those big steps. Do what you know is right. Inner peace is what matters."

A member of The Fellowship of Christian Athletes, Curtis says, "To me, God isn't just a picture on the wall you worship. He's the one who makes the trees grow and the birds fly. He's a feeling, not a figurehead. But I never want to shove the way I feel about God down anyone's throat. I'm a strong believer in different strokes for different folks."

Curtis was the first black to play basketball at Leon High in Tallahassee. He says, "Compared to Tallahassee, Los Angeles has no ghettos. Hell, Watts has paved streets. I was fortunate. We were wealthier than most blacks. I had opportunities others didn't have. Some didn't like the idea of my playing for the team. Some didn't like me helping to beat the other teams. One man said, 'Nigger, you score 30 points tonight, you're a dead man.' He had a gun. I scored 28. But things are getting better there. I blazed a trail others have followed. It's beautiful."

Curtis, 5-11 and 170 pounds, but cat-quick and clever, was all-American in high school and received more than 300 scholarship offers. He says, "I figured I was the best, I wanted to play with the best, so I went to UCLA. It's an ego trip. You can't tell a high-school all-American he's going to have trouble making a team. He just won't believe you. But a high-school all-American like Andre McCarter is sitting out this season because he knew he wouldn't play. Look, I know I'm good. But Andre is better. He's the best. He's got moves I'll never make. But as long as he makes them, he won't play. He has to play it straight to play here. He'll learn as I learned. It's an experience. All of life is an experience. What counts is what you make of it."

A lovely guy, brilliant and lively, "T.C." is making the most of his life at UCLA. He is majoring in sociology. He shrugs off what he calls the subtle racism on the campus. "These people don't even know how to be prejudiced," he laughs. "Down South, you know where a man stands. I can respect any man who is honest. I can respect George Wallace, even if I can't agree with him, because he's out in the open. I can't respect the cat on campus who says, 'Hey, T.C., basketball star, wait a minute, let's be friends!' I don't need false friends." Wary of his situation on the UCLA team, he intended to make the best of it. He said, "I'm a self-motivator. I'm doing this thing, I'll do it right. I've thrown tantrums, but I don't want to do that. I'll take the bad with the good. I have my personality. I can't change. I'm lively. I like to have fun. I like to walk into a dead dressing room and give the lads a lift. I'm a talker. I keep things perking. I prod people. I'm not going to let up now."

17/62

"Now that you've got the record, might you have a letdown in your next game?" Bill Walton was asked.

"Against USC? No way," Walton said.

USC had won 13 of 17 games and had soared to third in the national rankings. Bob Boyd's Trojans had dealt the Bruins their only two defeats at Pauley Pavilion, which was twice as many victories as any other coach had scored over Wooden in recent seasons. UCLA had won 33 consecutive conference contests since last losing to USC.

And this one was at the Sports Arena, USC's home court. Inside, the noise was awesome. USC players were so excited that on the way out two of them tripped and fell flat in the channel leading to the court, unseen by the audience, fortunately. The Trojans poured on court and the band struck up, "Fight on for USC." The beat of the big drums sent a pulse pounding through the place. Coolly, Hollyfield clapped and danced to the USC music just before the tip-off.

Boyd had a game plan. On offense, USC would hold the ball until it could set up a good shot. The Trojans took a minute to take their first shot, four minutes to take their second. At first, they hit their shots. On defense, the Trojans tried to shut off Walton by fronting him with 6-10 Mike Westra and cornering him with 6-9 Clint Champman. For a while, it worked. Walton didn't get his first shot until almost 11 minutes were gone. At the time, the score was 12-12 and the Trojan rooters were roaring. But Walton hit his first shot and the Bruins reeled off 12 straight points and, suddenly, it was 24-12, and the game was over, although they kept playing until it was 79–56.

Walton left with 20 points and 17 rebounds. Hollyfield stood and laughed at the fan who had been shouting all along, "Hollyfield, shut your mouth, you mother." In an alcove of his dressing room, Boyd was laughing, too. Not happily, but with acceptance of the inevitable. He sipped from a can of soft drink. He said, "Well, we tried some things. They didn't work. We lost our poise. But they do that to you. I think the strategy was all right. I don't know if there is a strategy sufficient to beat them. They have too many good players. And Wooden never lets them get screwed up, which is the real tribute to him."

18/63

It was February now and the Bruins went into the cold Pacific Northwest to pick off two more. In Washington State's matchbox Bohler Gym, the Cougars were crushed,

88-50. George Ravelling, the Cougar coach, has been considered one of the country's premier recruiters. After this game, he said, "I don't know where to go to get the kind of players it takes to beat the Bruins. They already have them."

19/64

In Seattle, where Washington waited, Marv Harshman, a good coach with a bad team, decided to give a tall freshman his first start. Lars Hansen got to go against Bill Walton, man-to-man. In the first half, Walton outrebounded Hansen, 12-1. By then, the Bruins had spurted from 24–19 to 44–26 and the game was locked up. Walton scored 29 points and picked off 21 rebounds before Wooden ran in the reserves and UCLA coasted to a 76–67 victory that wasn't as close as the score might make it seem.

20/65

The Bruins returned home the following weekend to host the same two foes. This time they took on Washington first. Ahead only 21-15 after 12 minutes, the Bruins blitzed to 42-22 at the 20-minute mark and rolled in, 93-62. His knees aching, Walton had practiced only one day all week, but he scored 26 points and got 17 rebounds off luckless Lars Hansen. Lee lobbed perfect passes to him and fed others for 11 assists. Subs sparkled here. Curtis, back in action, but behind Lee now, came in and hit five straight shots. "Spider" Meyers, now the third man up front, picked off loose balls, grabbed rebounds, and covered the court in his awkward, but awesome way.

21/66

Washington State again. After 2-2, it wasn't close. At 18-6, the Bruins had put another away. It was boring, really, as they went on to win, 96-64. Walton got 29 points, but the only interest one could find in the game was the opportunity to see the subs perform. Wooden flanked the 6-11 Walton with 6-9 Meyers and 7-0 Nater at forwards at one point. Meyers scored 12 points and Nater 14. Wooden probably had the second-best team in the country on his bench. Nater probably was the second-best center in the country and would be a first-round draft choice of the pros. Meyers was a sophomore good enough to start for any other team in the country. And he had barely beaten out Vince Carson as the top reserve up front. Curtis was good enough to start for this team. Pete Trgovich, who would start for most teams, now seldom played. As a freshman, the seven-foot Drollinger would start for many teams. "There were years," Wooden said, "he'd have started for me." He seldom dressed for games. Redshirting, McCarter, maybe the best young guard in the country, never dressed.

Morgan said, "You have to protect yourself. You have to recruit the best players you can. You never know which ones will work out. Some may quit. We've had quitters. USC was hit hard with quitters they counted on this year." Some of UCLA's super-subs seemed content to accept their lot. Carson, the 6-5 junior, said, "I just have to wait my chance. It's better to be part of a winner than a starter with a loser." Meyers, the 6-7 sophomore, one of 11 children, said, "It was my dream to play for UCLA. I wasn't one of these guys 300 schools came after. It was more like 20. I'm not fancy. I just work at it. I didn't know if I could make it at UCLA. I wanted to try. I waited for a call. When it came, I was so surprised I could hardly speak. Just making the team was a thrill. Now I know I may start next season. Hey, I've got stars in my eyes."

Nater, a 6-11, 250-pound senior, was born in Holland, came to this country when he was nine, did not play high-school ball in Long Beach, but developed fast in two years in junior college. He was picked up to back up Walton. He didn't develop much interest in his studies, switching

majors for German to sociology, geology, music, and back
to German again, did not have the credits to graduate, but
was by now only interested in playing basketball for a
living, anyway. When Walton passed up the Olympic trials,
Nater was invited, led the candidates in scoring, and made
the team, but quit it before it ever left the country because
the workouts were too much and the food too little. "I lost
25 pounds. My health was in jeopardy," he said. Back on
campus, he stoked up on hamburgers and resumed his seat
on the bench.

He said, "It's tough sitting it out. I need the exposure to
get the good money from the pros. But, I figured I learned
more practicing against Walton than I would have playing
regularly against the rest." I suggested that if Milwaukee
drafted him, he'd learn so much practicing against Jabbar
he'd be the smartest sub in the country by the time he was
30. He just laughed. Sure, enough, Milwaukee later drafted
him. No longer laughing, Swen swiftly signed with Virginia
of the other league.

Meanwhile, Ralph Drollinger was ready to replace Nater
as Walton's sub. The towering youngster said, "Walton has
one more year. Then it'll be my turn. I can wait." He didn't
know Wooden was about to acquire six-nine Richard
Washington, the most-sought-after high-school center in
the country. Wooden said, "Drollinger is bigger than
Washington, but not as maneuverable. Washington is good
enough to move in as a starter as a freshman. He won't take
Walton's place, but Walton's last year Washington could
play forward. That would put him ahead of Meyers."

Meyers had moved ahead of Vince Carson. All season
Carson kept saying it was all right, he could wait his turn,
he did not feel bad about it. But after the season Carson
would change his song. After the season he would an-
nounce he was transferring to Cal State of San Diego and
say, "Wooden has his favorites, and I'm not one of them, I
guess. Wooden told me I was making a mistake, but I don't
think I am. I had more than one hundred offers, but I came

here, and that was my mistake. Wooden decides what each man will do, and it,doesn't matter what the man thinks he can do. Most of the other guys not playing are upset about not getting a fair chance, too, and some of them talk about leaving, but I don't know if they are serious or not."

Pete Trgovich sat in a hallway in the athletic department, waiting to be counseled by Frank Arnold. As a senior at East Chicago's Washington High School, he led his team to the Indiana championship, he was acclaimed the outstanding player in the state, and he was likened to Pistol Pete Maravich. At 6-5, he was agile and quick enough to play guard or forward and he could shoot from anywhere. He could have gone anywhere he wanted in college ball. He chose to go to UCLA. "They were the big team and they had the big coach, Wooden. At first, it was fine. Now I'm no longer playing. It never occurred to me I might not make it. I guess it's my style which doesn't suit the coach. I've tried to change, but now I'm so confused I no longer play well. The coach has to pick the team he feels will do the job for him. If I thought my time would come, I could wait. But now I'm not sure it will. If I transfer, I lose a year's eligibility. I guess I'll just have to keep trying and keep waiting and hope for the best. I feel like I'm a long way from home," he sighed.

Between halves of a varsity game, Andre McCarter, the sought-after player from Philadelphia, stood in civvies unnoticed in a corridor. They say the 6-2 sophomore guard is the greatest thing since sliced bread, but Wooden doesn't say it. McCarter said, "I've thought of transferring, but I doubt that I will. It's really unfair that a student can switch schools without losing a year academically, but a player loses a season athletically. I was wanted everywhere. I know I would be playing anywhere else. I wanted to play for Wooden. I feel I should be playing now. I know I'm one of his two or three best guards. It's not an ego trip. A player knows. The others will tell you. But the coach decided I didn't fit in as well as some others. Once he set his seven or eight, which is all he ever really plays, I knew I wouldn't play, so I said I was going to sit the season out. Wooden stalled a few days before he gave in. He wanted me to be on the bench in case he needed me, but I couldn't see wasting a season.

"It's a difficult situation where he rounds up all the standouts in sight and then can use only a few. We all think we're so good we'll be the ones to play, but we don't understand the system until we get here and then it's too late. A youngster makes a decision without being informed and then he's stuck with it. Well, it's no problem. I can handle it. I'm not emotional. I suppose I'll have to tone my style down. I'll make the adjustments that have to be made. I practice with the team. I think he feels now I could have played for him this season. He asked to activate me recently so I could be available for the playoffs, but I'm not going to use up a season by playing a few games at the end. If I can start playing for the man next season, it'll be all right. He's a great coach. He turns out great teams. I'd like to be part of it. I don't even want to think of what will happen to me if I don't get to play."

After the game, I asked Wooden if he did not feel bad about the outstanding players he recruits who do not get to play. He drew back in anger. Sparks glinted from his eyes. He said, "Of course, I feel very bad. Do you think I'm without compassion? But I don't decide who plays. They do, by their play, especially in practice."

"But you recruit more outstanding players than you can possibly use."

Sourly, Wooden said, "They want to come here. Should we turn them away? We really don't know which ones are going to be good."

"You have some who are good who are not playing."

"You can't play them all. I play them when I can. I've found out that it is best to stick to seven or eight, rotating them in practice, to develop the teamwork that is necessary to win in tournaments. If a forward is hurt, we have a forward who fits in smoothly with the other four. Some players don't fit in as well as others. Some require discipline. If you play them all, no one gets enough time for us to develop properly as a team."

"Some of your subs would be stars elsewhere."

"Possibly. Possibly it is better for them to play with the best. They develop faster practicing against the best. We give fewer scholarships than most schools. We give four or five or six a season. We're very selective. Would you have us pick poor players? Some we pick are not widely sought, but we feel they will fit in with us. Others we know will not fit in right away but have so much ability we feel we can train them."

"Some players say your team style stifles their individual styles and inhibits their natural talents and may have hurt them as pro prospects."

Wooden peered at me over his glasses. Flatly, he said, "I would say in a team game the object is to play as a team and win as a team and we have done all right on that account. And I would say that learning to discipline their talents and play unselfishly for a team will help their pro careers, not hurt them. We have by far more graduates in professional ranks than any other school. I would have those who say this ask Walter Hazzard or Gail Goodrich or Sidney Wicks or any of many others to see what they have to say about my coaching hurting their pro prospects."

And with that, he had nothing more to say.

22/67

Back to the Northwest and Eugene, Oregon, to tackle Oregon. Dick Harter's Oregon team did the tackling, really. It did everything but beat on the Bruins with brooms as the fans taunted them and threw debris on them. Walton was kicked in the leg by a fan when he fell by the basket, he was elbowed by a foe, he warned Doug (Cowboy) Little about it, and he spent a lot of time cursing the opposition. Hollyfield was involved in several incidents and wound up punching a foe in the face. "You can only take so much," shrugged Wooden later. By then the Bruins had put away the foe, 72-61, despite 31 points by Oregon freshman Ron Lee. Oregon coach Harter said, "We played hard, but clean." Wooden said, "It was the roughest game I've ever been involved in. I'm glad to escape with my life and with no injured players."

23/68

At Corvallis, Oregon State played it straight. The Beavers shot extremely well and trailed only 42-35 at half time, but reserves Meyers, Nater, and Curtis provided inspiration, and the Bruins pulled away, then eased in 73-67. The following Monday, Wooden gave his players the day off. He said, "Even winning, it has been a long, hard season. My players are tired and some are not sharp. Everyone is carrying on a crusade against us. My players' tempers are getting frayed. So is my temper." He sighed and said, "It only looks easy."

24/69

It was easy against Cal, 90-65 at Pauley, which clinched the conference championship the following Friday. Nater, Meyers, and Curtis subbed brilliantly. There was no sign of celebration later. Wooden insisted, "It's never old hat. Winning the conference championship is our goal every season and it's always exciting." He did not seem excited. His teams had won 41 straight conference contests.

25/70

It was not easy against Stanford. The league title clinched, playing the next-to-last game of the regular season, waiting now for the tourney, the Bruins let down badly. Seven-foot Rich Kelly and 6-11 Tim Patterson worked on Walton, who was weary and uninspired. The Cardinals shot well, while UCLA shot poorly. Aggressive on defense, deliberate on offense, the Cardinals became the second team to lead the Bruins at half time all season, and they led by seven, 25–18. Wooden offered words of encouragement to his team at intermission. It took them the first five minutes of the second half to catch up, and then the Bruins pulled away and eased in again, 51–45.

"We just weren't worked up," Wooden said. "This is a dangerous time for us. The streak is all we have at stake. I'd like to end the season with a good game against USC going into the tournament, however."

26/71

He got a good game if not a great one. The Trojan rivalry was just enough to get the Bruins going. On the second Saturday afternoon in March, concluding The Walton Gang's second straight undefeated regular season, the Bruins pulled away from a 32-25 half-time edge to an easy 76-56 margin at the final buzzer, its forty-third straight league victory, forty-seventh straight victory at Pauley and 71st straight overall. All that was left was four more games to the ninth tournament title in 10 years to conclude the Decade of Dynasty.

"I think we'll win," Bill Walton said, shrugging.

14

John Wooden: "The only thing worse than winning all the time is losing all the time."

Sports spin in cycles of domination. Professional major leagues often are dominated by one team for a long time. In baseball, the New York Yankees won 16 pennants and 11 World Series championships in 18 years from the middle 1940s to the middle 1960s. In football, the Green Bay Packers won six pennants and five playoff titles in eight years in the 1960s. In hockey, the Detroit Red Wings won seven straight pennants and eight out of nine, though only four Stanley Cup playoffs, from the late 1940s to the late 1950s, and the Montreal Canadiens won five straight pennants and eight out of 10, plus five Cup crowns from the middle 1950s to the middle 1960s. In basketball, the Boston Celtics won nine pennants and 11 playoffs, eight in a row, in 13 years from the middle 1950s to the late 1960s.

However, the pros cannot be compared to the collegians. The Yankees had a Mickey Mantle and a Yogi Berra, the Packers a Bart Starr and a Paul Hornung, the Red Wings a Gordie Howe and a Red Kelly, the Canadiens a Doug Harvey and a Jean Beliveau, the Celtics a Bill Russell and a Sam Jones for eight, 10, 12, 14 years or more at a stretch during these dynasties, while a John Wooden had a Kareem Abdul-Jabbar or a Bill Walton three years at the most. The pros could keep their nucleus of stars, while a college club could not. Thus, the coach and his system are the continuing factors in college dynasties. And there have been some in college that extended a decade or more. There is no national title tournament in football, but the Notre Dame teams of Knute Rockne and Frank Leahy, the Minnesota teams of Bernie Bierman, the Oklahoma clubs of Bud Wilkinson, and a few others were at the top for 10 years or more, though none consistently classed as number one nearly as often as John Wooden's UCLA basketball teams have been. Adolph Rupp's Kentucky basketball teams won three national championship tournaments in four years and four in 11 years and were the dominant dynasty of the college court until Wooden took possession of the crown, but now Wooden is far beyond Rupp.

No team, professional or college, has so dominated its competition in a major sport for a decade as has John Wooden's UCLA basketball teams from the early 1960s through the early 1970s. Through and including the end of the 1972–73 season, the Bruins have won nine national titles in 10 years. They have won 75 straight games, 93 of their last 94 games, have had other winning streaks of 47, and 41 games, and have won 281 of 296 games. Throw out one bad year and they have won 263 out of 270. The "bad year" was 18-8. Otherwise they have had four years with perfect 30-0 records, three with 29-1 marks, and two with 28-2 marks. They have won 36 straight NCAA tournament contests.

How do you sustain such a dynasty with differing players over a prolonged period? J. D. Morgan says, "It is an excellence of our overall program and especially an excellence of coaching. With our coach, our campus, our facilities, and our record, we attract the highest type of young person and player, they are prepared properly, and a pride has been built up which continues from year to year. Even we are astonished by it. It could not be deliberately done, planned, or anything like that, but we have worked at it and it has happened."

John Wooden says, "The most difficult thing in life is to sustain success. Once a person has reached the top and reaped the rewards, he tends to slack off. He no longer is as hungry as he once was. However, none of my players ever has participated in more than three championship seasons, and each season we have new players who have not taken part in any. The new players provide a lot of drive, while the older men provide confidence and stability. I tell each team at the beginning of each season they are a new team, this is a new season, and they must make their own destiny. I tell them the past is past. I won't let them sit back and be content with what they've done. I constantly remind them it is only what they do now that counts.

"The past doesn't help us, except that our players inherit a tradition they find themselves pressed to uphold and it inspires them to extra effort, in practice as well as games. Suddenly, they realize they are with the best and they wish to remain the best. You may say our reputation intimidates the opposition, but I believe it also inspires them. Everyone wants to beat us, everyone wants to see us beat. This is the penalty of such success as we have had. Everyone is on a crusade to see our reign ended. Few stop to think what tremendous pressure this puts us under. I would never want to be a coach whose teams lose a lot, but somewhere in between there is an easier way of life than to be part of a team which almost always wins.

"Of course, we get talented players. The best players tend to want to play with the best team, so we get our share of the good ones. Others are afraid of the pressure or the competition or want to play for teams which might beat us, and we lose these. We give fewer scholarships than most schools and we give nothing extra. Those who are jealous of us hint we do, but we do not. We do not have to. And we do not take some talented players we feel will not fit in or are not the type of person we want here. We strive for balance, a blend of talents, much more than to get the five most talented youngsters on court. We recruit primarily from southern California. A player from out of state must contact us first.

"Many coaches say they could win with our talent. But I believe many would not have won with the talent we had on some of our championship teams. And I have seen many teams which did not win which I believe I could have won with. If this is immodest, I am sorry, but I am trying to tell it as I have seen it. There have been several teams with outstanding talent which were supposed to win three straight national titles which did not, such as the Cincinnati team with Jerry Lucas, John Havlicek, and others. Even the San Francisco team with Bill Russell and K. C. Jones did not win three straight. We have had talent and are proud to have sustained a series of titles with it.

"I believe my strength as a coach has been primarily in getting my players mentally ready. They hold a level, do not peak too soon, and sustain their strength through the tournament and the end of the long season. They take their games one at a time. They are never so complacent they will not go after the loose ball harder than the next player. If they do not, they do not play. They are properly prepared and sure of themselves, so they sustain their poise under pressure better than most of their opponents. We have no secrets. Everything we do is well-known and out in the open. But we practice harder and prepare ourselves more carefully than the next team.

"Some say we play soft schedules. Some say we do not risk our record on the road enough. But we schedule the prominent teams years in advance and have no control over their destinies and we wind up playing the top teams and beating them on the road in the championship tournament every year. Some say we have won so much we are bad for basketball, and some of our players say it is no fun to win all the time, but I believe it is less fun to lose, I believe one always should strive to be the best, I believe we have set a high standard for basketball and for sports, and should be an inspiration to others, who instead of criticiz-

ing us, should look to themselves and strive to build themselves up to us."

Bill Walton sighs and says, "It's not up to us to lose, but
it's up to others to win, to beat us."

When a UCLA is the glamor club of its sport, it attracts
the best talent. Wooden says he detests recruiting, it is the
one thing he dislikes in college coaching, he seldom will
travel to recruit anyone, and is content to leave it to his
assistants, but he has selected as his assistants personable
salesmen who have a big edge in bagging the big prospects.
Everyone wanted Lew Alcindor. Almost everyone wanted
Bill Walton. Almost everyone wanted Richard Washington. And, Wooden traveled far to visit each personally.
Over-recruiting helps sustain success at UCLA. Following
a season in which an Andre McCarter red-shirts and most
of UCLA's best players were underclassmen, the UCLA net
has snared not only the heralded Washington, but four
other high-school superstars—6-7 Wilbert Olinde from San
Diego, 6-6 Gavin Smith from Van Nuys, 6-6 Marques
Johnson, and 5-11 Jimmy Spillane from the L. A. area. An
annual survey of schoolboy talent, which has an astonishing record of success in predicting the coming college
all-Americans, reveals that UCLA again recruited more
top prospects than any college in the country. At UCLA
they stress most of their stars were "home-grown," but
Alcindor came from New York, Bibby from North
Carolina, the early Washington from South Carolina,
Farmer from Colorado, Curtis from Florida, Slaughter and
Allen from Kansas, Warren and Trgovich from Indiana,
Hazzard and McCarter from Philadelphia, the new
Washington from Portland, Walton from San Diego, and
so forth.

Morgan says, "We are not going to turn away a top
player from out of town who wishes to enroll here. We
do not offer them extra inducements. Our youngsters get
what is permissible under the NCAA rules governing
scholarships and nothing more. They get tuition, all com-

pulsory fees, board and room, and a few incidentals. Residence rates run to $1200 a year. Alcindor lived in a basement janitor's·apartment for $25 a month when he first arrived here. The NCAA was pressed to investigate us because so many were so sure we could not land an Alcindor without giving him something under the table, but we do not operate that way and he was not the type to even ask for anything extra. Later, he did move into a cottage. He drove an old car. Walton drives an old car. He lives in a small apartment. Actually, it would be permissible for us to give our scholarship players more than we do under NCAA rules. We give them what we feel is fair and we give every player the same."

During the 1971–72 season, Doug Krikorian, of the *Los Angeles Herald-Examiner,* wrote a story critical of the Bruins' schedule. Following a 56-point rout of The Citadel, the writer wrote they would have been short-enders against a local high-school team and quoted Greg Lee as calling them "like a real good junior college team." At the weekly basketball writers' luncheon, Wooden compared Krikorian critically to a Grantland Rice, "who had a positive influence on athletics," and called such criticisms "belittling and demeaning." He said it was unfortunate that when a team wins it must automatically be attacked.

However, Wooden, himself, once said of a weak team, "You'll have to ask Mr. Morgan why they're on our schedule," and reportedly was much more willing than was Morgan to schedule difficult foes on the road early in the season, risking losses to toughen his team for the big tests which were to follow. Many say Morgan puts a higher premium on always winning than does Wooden. Clearly, the schedules have been easier than they should have been. More bad teams are faced than good teams should face, and many more games are played at home than any team should be permitted to play. *The Basketball Weekly* analysis of college basketball schedules for the 1972–73 season showed No. 1-ranked UCLA played only the 47thtoughest schedule in the country. But, then, No. 2-ranked North Carolina State played only the 43rd-toughest schedule, and when the opportunity came up for these two unbeatens to meet in a nationally televised game on a neutral court in St. Louis early in the 1973–74 season, it was so scheduled by Morgan.

Morgan speaks bluntly about it: "UCLA supports more sports teams, 16, than perhaps any other school in the country. Football supports the sports program at most schools. Football and basketball share the support of our program. We have to make the most of it. Yes, John would like some stronger foes and more road games, but we cannot get all the best teams to come here, and we want to play most of our games at home simply because we make more money from home games than from road games. We attract good teams here because we offer attractive guarantees. We do not have to be restricted to home-and-home arrangements in basketball, so we are not. If a team will play us only on a home-and-home basis, we will not play them. Why take our players away from school and their classrooms when it is not necessary? We are fortunate that for us it is not necessary.

"We go to different holiday tournaments every year. We go to Notre Dame every year because we have a good national television contract for that game. We have been going to Chicago every year, but I doubt that we will continue to do so in the future because we do not benefit that much from it. People ask why we do not go to New York every year, but we do not because Madison Square Garden offers an astonishingly small return. They feel it is honor enough just to play there. Well, we have honors enough without playing there. They have upped their offer now, but we have not been able to work them into our schedule yet. Our schedules are drawn up years in advance. Many of our games have been scheduled with teams which were at the top when the schedules were drawn up, but which have fallen since. We cannot control that.

"It is my job to operate our basketball program on a businesslike basis and it is John's job to run it athletically. The proof that my methods have not hurt him lies in his success. His teams have been tough enough to win on the road, especially in tournaments, against the best teams, whenever necessary. We do not make much money, really. Students get tickets for 25 cents each. The faculty pays only a little more. Most seats are only $3. But travel costs have skyrocketed and we simply show more profit by staying home. And, after all, college athletic teams are for the benefit of the students at their school and should be kept on campus as much as possible. We cooperate in extensive radio and television scheduling which shows our team off to its supporters in our home area. I do not believe we should have to apologize for our system or its success."

UCLA's success remains controversial. Before the Bruins began their dynasty, college basketball was not big in L.A. Now they sell out almost every game, home and away. Bob Speck, director of sports programming at KTLA-TV in Los Angeles, points out, "I can't believe the criticism of UCLA's dominance. Before its era of success, college basketball on television was rare. There were no national telecasts, not even of the championships. UCLA and USC had maybe four games on television a season between them. They played doubleheaders for fear one school wouldn't draw enough. Now, our Channel Five had 70 telecasts last season, 26 with UCLA and 10 national specials, and some said it wasn't enough. NBC now is paying $1,000,000 for the championship tournament. Teams get $25,000 an appearance. This year they moved the title game into prime time and drew a record audience. We had 2,600,000 viewers in our area, alone. UCLA has done for college basketball what Notre Dame did for college football."

The day the 1974 NCAA finals tickets were put on sale, a year in advance of the two-day show in North Carolina, all 20,000-some seats were sold. There were 30,000 letters with money received, most of which had to be returned. Still, there are those who insist the Bruin dynasty is harmful, a monster. Bob Boyd at USC and Jerry Tarkanian at Long Beach admitted they were deeply discouraged when they developed national contenders in the UCLA area, but were so overshadowed by UCLA they did not draw fans or attract much attention. Spectacular players like Ray Lewis at Cal State Los Angeles and Bill "The Bird" Averitt at Pepperdine went unnoticed. Nationally, teams shot for conference championships and tournament berths as their ultimate aim, with little hope of taking the national title from UCLA. Some top teams skip the NCAA tourney to go into New York's NIT, which a team could win. Some coaches feel real incentive has disappeared from their programs. Some fans feel real interest has disappeared from the sport. After all, the same team wins every year. And don't be misled by a close game—the same team is going to win it.

Glenn Dickey wrote in the *San Francisco Chronicle,* "It's a sad thing what has happened to college basketball. UCLA makes everybody else play for second place." Georg Meyers wrote in the *Seattle Times,* "What Wooden has done to college basketball is to wreck it. What used to be a tingling spectacle has become like feeding time at the zoo." L. H. Gregory wrote in the *Portland Oregonian,* "Gets rather monotonous, don't it? UCLA, week after week, month after month, season after season, winning every basketball game it plays." Frank Dolson in the *Philadelphia Inquirer* wrote, "Is winning the end that justifies the means or can it become a cancer that eats away at the fun in sports?"

Oklahoma City coach Abe Lemons said, "What a horrifying subject. It's like having to think about buying a cemetery plot." Washington coach Marv Harshman said, "It's like watching a hanging." Washington State coach George Ravelling said, "UCLA is like an IBM computer. You just punch out W-I-N and that's what they do."

In his *Los Angeles Times* column, John Hall described an act put on over drinks by Dick Enberg and Rod Hundley after they had telecast another Bruin triumph:

"This is old Doc Enberg," creaked Dick. "And this is Cold Rod Hundley," creaked Rod. "By cracky, there was a time I was known as Hot Rod, but that was years ago when old Doc and I first started covering the Bruin winning streak. Back to you, Doc. . . . We've just brought you UCLA's 573rd straight triumph. It's obvious now the streak will never end. And back to you Cold Rod for a word with the coach. . . . Thanks, Doc. Coach Wooden, it must be gratifying to you to win your 573rd on your 115th birthday. Quite a milestone. Tell me, coach, were you satisfied with the team performance? And how does your new nine-foot freshman center compare to those Bruin greats of past decades, such as Bill Walton? . . . Well, you just don't make comparisons. It's a different game in 2033 than it was in 1973, said Hundley, imitating Wooden. I like to think we keep improving. Yes, I was satisfied with the overall team play. I was disappointed with our shooting for 30 seconds there at the start and our defense lost its intensity momentarily when we got that 60-point lead. My concern now is next week's Oregon game. We lost to Oregon once 47 years ago. . . ."

Well, Hall received letters that were beyond belief. He was called "a pinko pig, a nationalist dog, a slob," and so forth. He was portrayed as a man without respect for achievement in life and in sports. Enberg and Hundley, brilliant broadcasters, were castigated for their few moments of irreverent fun, after hours and out of sight of the public, but then reported. Hall shrugs and says, "I suppose you're not supposed to look at the other side of the coin." John Wooden says, "I don't think we've created a monster by winning so much. Rather than calling what we've achieved a dynasty, I prefer to think of it as a cycle. And I believe all cycles come to an end."

27/72

The Bruin cycle still was spinning and apparently far
from ready to run down. Wooden had won with guards,
then a center, then forwards, now he would win with a
center again. And none of the brave talk put forth by
others as the championship tournament opened meant
much because no one believed it; everyone knew UCLA
would win again. For the regionals it had the advantage of
the home court. The games were scheduled at Pauley,
where the Bruins had won 117 of 119 games. Soon it would
be 119 of 121. It was inevitable. Its foes, Arizona State and
San Francisco, were the last teams to beat UCLA in
tourney play, but that was 1963 and this was 1973. Of all
its streaks, UCLA's 32 straight in tourney play, which soon
would be 36, may be the most remarkable. NCAA tournament play is sudden death; one loss and you're out.
UCLA could not have afforded the losses the Celtics or
other teams suffered in their best-of-seven series that took
them to their titles. They could not have afforded even one
loss any one season and still have won nine of 10. One year
it did not get into the tourney. The other years, it passed
perfectly through them.

Jerry Tarkanian's Long Beach team, which pressed the
Bruins in the 1971 regionals, failed to press them in the
1972 regionals, felt it would put them away in the 1973
regionals. "We've been waiting and we're ready for them,"
said Ed Ratleff. Commented coach Tarkanian, "From our
first day of practice, the call in town has been, 'Beat the
Bruins.' We've beaten 25 teams in 27 games and we're
rated right behind the Bruins, but all the kids care about is
beating the Bruins. I've told them again and again we're
good enough to do it, but we'll never get the chance if we
don't go one game at a time. If we don't beat the other
teams, we'll never get a chance to beat the Bruins." They
never did.

With Ratleff injured and playing poorly, the Long
Beach team played poorly and was upset by San Francis-

co, 77-67, in Thursday night's first game. An upset? Maybe. San Francisco had beaten 22 of 26 teams and it was good, despite having been beaten by 28 points by the Bruins earlier. Ratleff said, "I'm very disappointed." Tarkanian said, "We all are." Tommy Curtis said, "We've been hearing that jive about how they were going to whip us and we wanted to put them in their place, but someone got to 'em and buried 'em before we could."

As UCLA ran out on the court to take on its first foe, Arizona State, Jerry Tarkanian stood alone in the corridor looking as though he had just lost his best friend. His bid to beat the Bruins had ended for the time being. He was leaving Long Beach and the shadow of UCLA and would attack the national title from the University of Nevada at Las Vegas, which was a gamble, of course.

Arizona State coach Ned Wulk said, "UCLA has to lose sometime. We may surprise some people." The only surprise was that they tried to run with the Bruins, but then they were strictly a running team. And that they stayed with the Bruins as long as they did. In the first few minutes, Walton blocked a shot, was knocked down, complained with one of his looks, got up, and made an underhand pass to Hollyfield that was fantastic, and Hollyfield hit and it looked like no contest. A hot-and-cold shooter, Hollyfield was hot and hit 18 points in the first half. But Mike Contreras hit 10 points in the first half of the first half, and until Curtis came in to cut him cold with demon defensive work, the Sun Devils stayed in it. They even led at 21-16. Then, UCLA scored 10 straight points. Arizona State called a time out. Shortly, UCLA went on a 15-2 spree. The Bruins led, 51-37, after one half.

In the first five minutes of the second half, they stretched the score to 63-41 and it was all over. At the finish it was 98-81. Walton had 28 points and 14 rebounds. Hollyfield had a career-high 20 points. Arizona State had heavy hearts and disappointed faces. Wulk said, "We played well. I don't know what happened." Wooden said,

"The turning point was when we put in Curtis. For some reason, we're a slow-starting team. We'd start faster if we'd start Tommy, but he gives us such a lift when he comes in for Lee I'm inclined to leave it this way. I think he's most effective this way." A grin split Tommy's pixie face. "I'm a starter," he said. "I just start later than the rest."

28/73

Late in the Arizona State game, Hollyfield's hands got sweaty and he coolly asked an official if he could wipe his wet hands on the ref's pants. The official looked at him in astonishment and said he supposed he could. Hollyfield did. And laughed. Everyone laughed. It was a laugher. Hollyfield was asked if USF would be a laugher. "I suspect we'll be laughing at the finish and they'll be crying," he smiled. Wooden was asked if there was anyone he was worried about on the USF roster. He thought a moment, then said, "No, no one I can think of."

USF coach Bob Gaillard said, "We've got a better team than we did the first time we played them. We'll play them differently, but not so different as to make them mad."

It was a cool Saturday afternoon for the televised contest. More than 12,000 fans filled Pauley, most of them Bruin rooters. The hosts have charge of ticket distribution and they decided to distribute most of the tickets to their fans and only a few to the followers of the other teams. USF moved out to quiet support from a few followers. UCLA bounced out to bedlam. Gaillard's way of play was a slowdown. His side stalled to a 16-9 lead. Wooden sent in Curtis for Lee and Meyers for Hollyfield. Curtis hit two from Florida and one from merely around Texas in a hurry, and right away the gutty little guy had brought the Bruins back. Meyers hit the boards, hit a jump shot, missed one, but Walton tipped it in, then hit another, and the Bruins were rolling. But the Dons got things slowed down again and crawled to win in 33-22 at the half-time buzzer.

Eight minutes into the second half, with Phil Smith firing away, San Francisco remained within 31-28. Walton went to work. In the next few minutes he blocked shots, scrambled for loose balls, rebounded missed shots, hit on a hook and a tip-in, and suddenly UCLA had nine straight points and a 40-28 edge and the Dons were doomed. The fans taunted them hysterically. At the end it was 54-39, and with 14 rebounds Walton had surpassed the one-season school record of 466 he had shared with Alcindor/-Jabbar. Jerry West said, "I don't think UCLA could beat a pro team. Not even Philadelphia." And he never even cracked a smile.

Gaillard, his face flushed with disappointment, said, "They play like pros. We played them the only way we could and hoped to stay close. We were close a long time. We were not close at the end. No one ever is."

They gave the tournament Most Valuable Player trophy to Walton, of course, but it was not unanimous; some said this was Curtis' tourney. Tommy sat sweaty outside the dressing room and smiled and said, "I respond to pressure. The bigger the challenge, the more I put out. The bigger the game, the better I play. But it was a team triumph. I'm only a substitute. I sit on the bench until the man calls for me. When he calls, I respond." He is tough. You could see it. You said it. "Life is tough," he said.

Behind him, unnoticed, McCarter, in civvies, went into the dressing room to congratulate his "teammates." Walton came out and slipped out a side door. Wooden came out and sat down, sipping his orange drink, and the writers and broadcasters surrounded him and poked microphones at him and he said, "I was never worried. The turning point came when we put in Tommy." Someone asked what his main concern was going into the finals in St. Louis. He thought a second and said, "I don't believe I have one."

Outside, courtside, he sat for an hour patiently signing autographs for kids.

Some of the top-rated teams which were supposed to threaten UCLA in the finals—Marquette, Minnesota, Maryland ("The UCLA of the East," supposedly), Kentucky, Southwest Louisiana—had been buried in the regionals. Indiana would be there. And Memphis State. And Providence. UCLA supposedly played a soft schedule, but teams it had met during the regular season were among the leaders at the end of the season. Such as San Francisco, which reached the regional final. And Providence, which reached the national final. And Notre Dame, which would reach the NIT final. And USC, which made the NIT and narrowly lost to Notre Dame in the nationally televised tourney opener, which the Bruins could watch before going out to wrap up another NCAA Western Regional title.

28/74

On the next to last Friday in March, the UCLA basketball team met for breakfast on campus, then convened outside the Student Union building to catch the bus to the airport. They were loose and cutting up. They were teasing Vince Carson, a conservative, usually, who came mod with leather purse and a healthy helping of cologne offering enticing aromas. John Wooden, a conservative always, smiled at all the stuff, but he seemed a bit out of place among them. One of the players later said, "Hey, we were really loose. We were going to the finals, but we'd been there before. We weren't afraid of it. We knew we'd win, which was going to be fun. Hey, we weren't going just to the finals, we were going to the championship."

The flight left at 8:30 in the morning. It was full, not only with players, but with fans, many of whom had made previous flights with the team and were able to chat amiably with the players. The players paired off as usual—Walton with Lee, Hollyfield with Bob Webb, Curtis with Gary Franklin, and so forth. On buses or wherever permitted, a couple of players break out tapes, Walton plays acid rock, Webb plays soul music, they sit far apart, and the others sit with the music they prefer, and no one seems to notice the clash of sounds, while Wooden winces and tries to shut himself off from it. They are young men, the oldest of them not far from his teens, some of them still in their teens, they have been pulled together as a team only temporarily, and they try to ignore the importance of what they are doing as a team, they try to push away the pressure which is pressed in on them by writers and other people.

They bused from the airport in St. Louis to Stauffer's Hotel, where they were quartered, away from the tournament headquarters at the Chase Park Plaza. Here, the lobby was filled with coaches, conventioning as usual at the finals, swapping trade secrets and tall stories about tall prospects. Here and at other hotels, fans were full of fun and full of hope, for, after all, their teams had not lost yet. An Indiana fan said, "We have to have fun now. After we lose to UCLA it won't be any fun anymore." Some fans came without tickets, hoping to get a ticket, risking being shut out by being here because there was a television blackout for 120 miles around. Gary Finn, an Indiana student, stood in the lobby of the Chase Plaza for four hours holding a sign which said, "Need one ticket," and he didn't get one. Some were available, but for $50 to $100, five to 10 times their face value per game. One scalper said, "It's supply and demand. If I can get it, I'll take it."

Outside, there was a suggestion of spring in the air in this riverfront town. The streets streamed with out-of-towners. The shops were crowded. People waited to get into restaurants. Stan Musial's and Biggie's, a prestige place, was packed with the prominent. Biggie grinned and said, "We could use one of these things every week." Hotels and motels were full up. The NCAA had filled 700 rooms in the

Chase. The manager of the Chase called it, "one of our better conventions." NCAA publicist Jerry Miles was under pressure trying to accommodate writers who wanted rooms and press seats.

The tournament is big business. In St. Louis it was estimated it was worth $1,300,000 in extra trade in town. In 1972, the entire tourney grossed $1,741,442 and netted $1,382,000. The NCAA and the participating teams split the net down the middle. In 1972, this was $693,000 each. The NCAA pays expenses for 20 persons per team per round out of its end, however. The participants' share is divided into units. Each team gets two units per game until the semifinals and finals, when it gets three units per game. However, clubs playing consolation contests revert to two units. Thus, the further a team goes, the more games it plays, the more it gets. Independents play an earlier round and one which reaches the final may make more money than a conference club taking the title. In 1972, of the four in the final two sessions, Florida State received $64,000, UCLA $59,000, North Carolina $53,000, and Louisville $53,000. In 1973 UCLA, Memphis State and Providence each would collect $81,961, while a fourth finalist, Indiana, would get $74,510. The players received nothing, of course. They were amateurs, playing not for pay but for fun.

The teams practiced in turn for the following afternoon's first semifinal games. Each had an hour. The Bruin workout was low key. Wooden told the players he expected a slowdown game from Indiana. He told the players, "This is a fine team with a fine coach and they will not give you the game, but if you play your game you will win it." He told the writers, "Everyone is conceding this to us except the right ones." The UCLA players were looser than the other players. They weren't telling anyone how they were going to beat the other teams. They didn't have to. Providence players passed right over Memphis State and told everyone how they were going to beat UCLA this time, in the final, when it counted. UCLA players sat around their hotel talking about how miserable the long season had been and how happy they were to be finishing it off now. One player pointed out, "The external pressures put on us and the internal problems caused by the magazine piece had made it miserable, but when we win, it will have been worth it."

Saturday morning they waited away the last minutes watching Notre Dame carry Virginia Tech to the last minute of overtime in the championship game of the NIT before bowing on television. In the lobby, a UCLA graduate, I. R. Schlossberg of Chicago, was saying, "I stayed at UCLA for six years just to watch the basketball team. I never got tired of winning." Newlyweds from Memphis, Ben and Janet Crossnoe, who had spent their honeymoon in St. Louis looking for tickets to see their Tigers, finally got a pair at the last minute from a sympathetic sports editor, Roy Edwards of the *Memphis Commercial Appeal,* who bought them from SMU coach Bob Prewitt. "It's great, fabulous, fantastic, and beautiful," observed Mrs. Crossnoe.

Parking space outside the ancient arena, a bubble-domed antique of Turkish style, handsomely refurbished to be the hockey home of the Blues, had been filling up for hours with trailers and campers. Now cars started to pour in. Taxicabs did a big business shuttling customers from the hotels and motels to the arena. Inside, it was flag-draped, festive, and noisy. There were a lot of college-age youngsters cutting up, of course. Everyone was turned on. The television cameras were turned on. An estimated 42,000,000 viewers would watch this session. More would watch Monday night's prime-time final.

The opener of the double-header pitted Providence against Memphis State. Providence had won 17 straight and was looking past the Tigers to the Bruins. At first, it seemed they were safe. Little DiGregorio gave one of the greatest ball-handling displays ever seen as he prodded his side to a 13-point lead. Time and again he whipped half-court, behind-the-back passes to teammates who were open under the basket. They were flashy and they were long, but they were the right passes because they were right on target. He also shot with a sure touch. In the first half he had 17 points and seven assists and was sensational. However, the rebounder Barnes came off the boards badly in the eighth minute and injured his right knee badly and had to be benched and the Friars started to struggle.

With "Dr. K.," Larry Kenon, who scored 18 points in the first half, hitting from inside and little "Tubby" Finch from outside, the Tigers closed in. They got the lead with 12 straight points to go from 43-53 to 55-53 five minutes into the second half. The Friars got it back. But DiGregorio began to miss with his shots and passes, and, without Barnes against them, the big Tiger front line of 6-9 Kenon, 6-8 Wes Westfall, and 6-8 Ron Robinson began to bang away on the boards and the Tigers put together another run of 13 straight points to go from 82-84 to 95-84 and the Friars were finished. Barnes returned for the last six minutes, but he hobbled helplessly and the final was 98-85.

Afterward, there was as big a crush in the losers' dressing room as in the winners'. Reporters crowded around the bereaved Barnes. One in back, who couldn't hear, asked Barnes to stand on a table so everyone could hear him. A player, Al Baker, asked, "Stand on a table? The man has a bad leg and you want him to stand on a table. You must be insane." The reporter said, "No, I'm not. Really, I'm not." Baker said simply, "You must be." Another reporter asked coach Dave Gavitt, "Did you want to get Barnes back into the game?" Barnes looked at him in astonishment. "What the hell do you mean, did I want him in there? The leading rebounder in the country, did I want him in? Of course, I wanted him in."

DiGregorio sat sadly in his sweat-soaked uniform and said, "With him, we would have won. Now we'll never know if we could have beaten the Bruins." Nothing bothers the Bruins, but it seems like something always happens to teams touted to upset the Bruins. An undefeated Marquette has its big center jump to the pros at midseason, an undefeated North Carolina State or a powerful Florida State team with Dave Cowens is ineligible. St. Bonaventure loses Bob Lanier and bows out. A powerful Providence loses its big man and bows out. Memphis State's coach, "Clean Gene" Bartow, said, "Losing their big man had to hurt them. We were fortunate. But they had a shot at UCLA and lost and now it's our turn. I've read Wooden's book and I believe in his approach of positive thinking. I'm thinking positively. I think we will beat the Bruins. I hope we will. Of course, it would help," he smiled, "if they played poorly or got lost and didn't get to the game."

The Bruins did get lost on their way to their dressing room midway in the first game. They wandered around different corridors for a while until one of the players said, "What a story this will make. Not only didn't we win, but we were never found." Finally, they found their way and dressed and sat and waited. Wooden went in front of them and said, "I've prepared you as well as I can, now it's up to you. They have a fine team but if you play your game you will win. Keep the pressure on them. Be quick, but don't hurry. No matter what happens, hold your poise. No matter what happens, keep your head up and your chin up." It was what he always said. Tommy Curtis says, "If he didn't say it, I wouldn't go out there." This time, considering the circumstances, he said one more thing. He slapped a rolled-up program in his fist and said, "This is it, this is what we've been waiting for." This was his pep talk, what he always said in these circumstances.

The Bruins ran out. They always run out in the same order. Before that, in the dressing room, they always get their ankles taped in the same order. They always locker by the same players. Like Wooden, they have a lot of superstitions they will not admit. Walton always puts a piece of gum in a jockstrap hanging in his locker, and he takes it out and starts to chew it while he dresses. While Wooden talks, Walton tries, softly, to say the words with the coach. He knows them by heart. But Wooden knows what Walton is doing, and he always says something just a little different, a word here or there, to throw him off. Everyone smiles. And then they run out in order and savage their victims.

Bobby "The General" Knight really did not, as they said he did, worship at The Shrine of Saint John, but he attended Wooden's coaching clinic over the summer and says he learned a lot, though he coaches a different style. At 34, he was the youngest coach in the finals, and most felt the best young coach in the country. He had been sixth man on that super team at Ohio State, which starred Lucas and Havlicek, he had coached at West Point, had come to Indiana, and had just turned down an offer to coach the Phoenix pros to remain at Indiana. He was temperamental and explosive courtside, but close to his players and a shrewd strategist. He coached a deliberate, defense-oriented style and worked wonders with it. USF had tried it on the Bruins, but Indiana would have a better chance with it because it was their game and they worked it better. They had the youngest team in the finals, but it was a good team. With George McGinnis, who quit two years before, after his sophomore season, to become an instant star as a pro, it might have been a great team. But with big Steve Downing, who had played in McGinnis' shadow in high school and college before, coming into his own, it remained a good team with maybe a great future.

With Downing scoring 12 of Indiana's first 16 points, including eight straight at one point, the Hoosiers worked their way to a 20-17 lead midway in the first half with the 19,200 fans, most of them rooting against the Bruins, roaring. It was the sixth straight game UCLA had trailed after 10 minutes. But Downing picked up his third foul and had to be taken out. And Wooden had brought in Curtis for Lee fast and the chatterbox clutch player prodded his side. Wilkes hit three in a row, Curtis hit a couple, and they sparked a run of 18 unanswered points. Indiana went more than five minutes without a basket. The Hoosiers were outscored 23-2 in the last part of the half, and with Curtis, of course, connecting, at the buzzer UCLA led, 40-22.

Like those that fell before them, Indiana appeared doomed. But these Hoosiers were unlike others. At half time, Knight told them, "We're down to a 20-minute game. Play it like you can and you never know what might happen." They did. After UCLA scored the first four points of the second half, the Hoosiers began to battle back with incredible calm. When Walton picked up his fourth foul with 12:27 left and was replaced by Nater, the Hoosiers went on a spree. In the next 3½ minutes, they scored 17 straight points, even though Walton was returned to action in a rush. They closed to 67-55 with almost six minutes to go, and all was bedlam in that building. "I never thought a team could do that to us, and I was scared," Wooden said later.

He called a time-out and told his team, "You've still got the lead. Don't let it get away from you. Keep your poise. Play your game." Curtis, who scored 22 points, came through, connecting from a corner, following with two free throws, and the Bruins began to breathe again. The key play had come when Walton grabbed a rebound off the offensive board, whirled around to put it back up, collided with Downing, and Downing went crashing into the end seats. If it had been called offensively on Walton, he would have been finished. But the referee ruled it was a defensive foul on Downing, it was his fourth, he almost immediately picked up his fifth, disqualifying him, and without him, the Hoosiers could not keep up. The Bruins pulled away to win, 70-59.

Downing had outscored Walton, 26-14, but fell short of him in rebounds, 5-17, and assists, 2-9. "He is super," said Downing, "but I believe the foul was his, not mine." Knight said, "It was a close call. I don't want to complain. Without Downing, we were hurt. Without Walton, they might have been beat. But maybe we gave away too much too early. We came a long way back, but we didn't come far enough." Walton said nothing because no one was permitted to get to him in the dressing room. Outside, Wooden drew back when asked about the controversial call. "You saw it," he snapped. "Wasn't it a foul? I certainly thought so. What part of the country are you from?" He said Indiana would have been beat even with Downing and UCLA would have won even without Walton. Many did not agree, but UCLA usually wins no matter what happens.

Many writers were here from all over the country, and they viewed Wooden in a different light from his hometown press, and they were far more critical of the closed dressing room and the reluctance of the star, Walton, to talk, than were his journalists from southern California. A reporter from the *Indianapolis News* cornered the center and said, "Bill, I'd like to ask you a few questions." Bill said, "I don't think I'm supposed to talk to the press." The reporter said, "I just want to ask your impression of Steve Downing." Walton said, "You're with the press, aren't you? Whatever I say, you're going to turn it around." The reporter asked, "Why do you say that?" Walton replied, "Because it happens every time." The reporter asked, "How can I turn around something you would say about Downing?" Walton said, "OK, he's a nice guy." And then he walked away. By NCAA rule, Wooden had to open the doors after the finals, but he waited 25 minutes until his players had showered, dressed, and were ready to depart fast. Writers were outraged and wondered why they had come from all across the country.

Walton stirred up a storm Sunday when he checked out of the team hotel and into the Chase. He could not be reached, but Sam Gilbert said, "It got too noisy where he was." Which was strange, since the Chase, the headquarters hotel, was worse. However, Wooden said, "He wasn't happy with the beds," and Morgan confirmed this. Morgan had taken a room at the Chase, then moved in with the team at Stauffer's, and let Bill use his unused room. Morgan said, "It is not the first time we've moved a player who was unhappy with a hotel or a room. We did it with Alcindor and now with Walton." Someone suggested the move was made so Walton could be near pro representatives who wished to negotiate with him, and Morgan said, "That's the biggest bunch of garbage I've ever heard."

It was clear Bill could be considered a "hardship case" because of his bad knees and uncertain future and could be signed now with a college season left, and now the Philadelphia 76ers of the NBA were prepared to pay him a tax-free $2,000,000 to sign for five years and his hometown San Diego Conquistadors of the ABA said they would go to $3,000,000 for a similar length of time. A teammate was asked what it would do to the team if Walton left, and he said, "We probably wouldn't win as much, but it's only a game, so who cares?" Another said, "It might be more fun to play without him." A third said, "We all like him personally and respect the unselfish way he plays and consider him a great player and know he is far more responsible than any of us for our success, but it is hard to play in the shadow of such a superstar, he does shut us out from driving around the basket, and we selfishly feel it might be more fun to play on our own."

Wooden said, "I do not believe it is wise for a young man to forgo his college education to play professional a year or two sooner than he ordinarily would, but in the case of a player like Walton he might be crazy to refuse. If he has been offered what he supposedly has been offered, and refused, I personally would escort Bill straight to the nearest psychiatrist and have him examined." However, Walton did not see it that way. Sam Gilbert, negotiating for Walton, said, "I recommend to a player that he continue until he completes his college education, but I could not tell Bill Walton to turn down an enormous amount of money. This has to be up to him. Money does not mean much to him and he will not turn professional now."

After the final game, when Walton went with Wooden to Louisville in mid-April to receive the Adolph Rupp Trophy as the nation's top collegiate basketball player for the second straight year, Charles O. Finley, owner of the ABA's Memphis Tams, among other teams, asked for and received a breakfast meeting at a hotel with Bill in which in front of then ABA president Robert Carlson and Tams president Rupp he offered Bill more than $2,000,000 to join the Tams. Walton talked to them for an hour but turned them down.

His father said, "It wasn't peanuts, but Bill wasn't writing anything down. He met the man to be courteous, but he wasn't interested." Finley said, "It was a fabulous offer. He was very receptive. He didn't seem surprised. He said he prefers to stay in school and hopes the same offer will be available when he finishes his senior year. He is one of the finest young men I ever had the pleasure of talking with."

Afterward Finley turned rights to Walton back to San Diego and tried to shift or sell the Tams. Rupp left the Tams. But everyone leaves Finley's teams. Carlson even left the ABA. Failing to get Walton, San Diego settled for Wilt Chamberlain for $600,000 a season.

Walton emerged from the shadows briefly to confirm his stand. "I will not turn pro now," he said.

"The money wasn't enough?"

"Money was not a factor."

"You would say no, no matter what?"

"It could be five million and it wouldn't matter."

"They say every man has his price."

"Not true. If so, the price is not always money. I'm happy playing for UCLA. I like the school, my teammates, and the coach."

"But you will play pro eventually?"

"I will decide that later. Right now I am only concerned with playing the final game here."

30/75

Before the final game Monday night, John Wooden told his players, "I've prepared you as well as I can, now it's up to you. They have a fine team, but if you play your game, you will win. Keep the pressure up. Be quick, but don't hurry. No matter what happens, keep your chins up, your heads up. No matter what happens, keep your poise. If you win, be gracious." Walton tried to keep up with him, but couldn't quite do it. Wooden waved his rolled-up program and said, "This is it, this is what we've been waiting for." Chewing gum, Walton went out with the rest of them. He seemed especially intense. His eyes were hot and he was less animated than usual. A teammate says, "He was burning."

This season, Hollyfield averaged 10 points a game, Farmer 12, Wilkes 15, and Walton 20. Walton shot 63 percent from the field. Walton also averaged 17 rebounds a game. And about five blocked shots a game. He saved his best for last. Primarily on perfect passes lobbed high near the basket by Lee, Bill hit an incredible 21 of 22 shots from the field, two of five from the foul line, and totaled 44 points, breaking the previous NCAA championship game record of 42 set by Gail Goodrich in the Bruins' second title victory. Walton also took down 13 rebounds, blocked seven shots, and fed off flawlessly. Lee had 14 assists. Wilkes had 16 points. But this was Bill's game, perhaps the greatest ever played by a collegian, and with it, Memphis State was stunned by 21 points, 87-66.

The Tigers were tough. Finch fired in 29 points and Kenon, 20. They carried their club on a crusade against the favored foe that had the crowd of 19,301 in this ancient arena standing and screaming while maybe 50,000,000 watching on television across the country were aroused.

With Walton hitting 11 of 12 shots in the first half,

UCLA shot 60 percent. Still, the Tigers hung tight, and, when Walton went to the bench with three fouls, the Tigers caught up and were tied at half time, 39-39. Clean Gene Bartow told his troops, "We have a real shot at it now." But Saint John Wooden told his side, "Just keep playing your game and you will win." And they did. At the start of the second half, Finch was fouled and sank two free throws and Memphis led, 41-39, and the customers were going crazy. But then Walton rolled in for a reverse lay-up to tie it, and the Bruins were not behind again. He hit all 10 shots he took in the second half, and his side started to pull away and just kept pulling away.

The fans grew quiet. The foes grew depressed. The champions got cocky. Curtis ran past the Tiger bench and yelled, "Back to Memphis." Hollyfield stood in front of Wes Westfall and laughed at him. Curtis later explained, "It was beautiful. We don't like to taunt nice people, but those dudes had taunted us for days. Westfall kept saying, 'We're gonna' get you cats.' So when we got them, we breezed on by and laughed because we were so happy. The long season was over and we were winners again. It was enough to make a man blow his mind."

All season Walton had played with agility, sometimes pausing to suffer with his sore knees. Now, as the season's last game reached its last minutes, Walton, without being hit, collapsed in a pile of pain. His knees? No, thank goodness, only a mere ankle. Helped to his feet, he struggled off to an ovation, supported by a sympathetic rival. At the bench he paused to look back at the scoreboard, reassuring himself his foe was frustrated and he had his 129th consecutive victory, personally, UCLA's 75th in a row, the Walton Gang's second straight 30-0 campaign, an unprecedented second straight undefeated season, a second straight national title, and the school's ninth in 10 years. His freckled face disfigured by his agony, he looked at the television cameras, but did not seem to notice the crowd's cheers.

They took off his shoe and he sat there with his foot extended, a heroic figure with legs of clay as his teammates wrapped it up and then came together in hoots of triumph, and he never smiled that we saw, not even once. A fan pushed a program at him for him to autograph, but he brushed it away. The fan said, "Great game, Bill." Bill said, "It was just a game." In the dressing room, after the writers finally got in, his excited teammates expressed their pleasure, but Bill would not even look at the writers, he looked at the floor in front of him, and when they asked him what he had to say, he said, "I have nothing to say, nothing to say, man."

Greg Lee said, "He played for you. He paid his dues. He doesn't have to talk about it, too." Tommy Curtis said, "The big thing is, he'll be back. I've counted it up and it comes to 105 in a row for my team. And with the cats they've got coming in to follow our act, there's no telling where it'll all end." Wooden said, "It will end, perhaps before I leave, perhaps not. No, I don't know when I'll leave. Maybe after next season, maybe not. I have made commitments to the parents of some of my players who will be seniors next season, such as Walton's parents, that I would continue coaching throughout their college careers, but I have made no such commitments to any new players. Your first championship has to be your most exciting, but each one after that, including this one, is equally satisfying. I'd have to say this was my best team." The Walton Gang had brought Wooden's Decade of Dynasty to a triumphant conclusion, but perhaps the past was only prologue.

Wooden went to Walton and tousled his long hair. Bill stood up then and left, going first to the other dressing room to console the losers. As he left the emptying arena with its eerie echoes and scattered debris, members of the press tried to reach him, but he brushed them off, saying, "I have to see some friends." Obviously, the press was not among them. Others later found him with some Memphis

State people, whom he called "real people." Still later, the UCLA players, going from party to party, wound up at a "wonderful party" in Bill's room. It lasted until the next day. Then Bill Walton hurried home. And then he went on to the mountains where he could forget about basketball between championship seasons.

On the opening day of practice for the 1974 season, John Wooden thought Bill Walton's hair was too long, and he sent him to have it cut.

Appendix

1963-64

Won—30, Lost—0
Conference: 15-0

* * * *

LETTERMEN: Keith Erickson, Gail Goodrich, Walt Hazzard, Jack Hirsch, Mike Huggins, Doug McIntosh, Fred Slaughter, Kim Stewart, Kenny Washington

* * * *

Captains: Walt Hazzard
Jack Hirsch
Assistant Coaches: Jerry Norman
Frosh Coach: John Kalin

GAME BY GAME

113	BYU	71
80	Butler	65
78	Kansas State at Lawrence	75
74	Kansas at Manhattan	54
112	Baylor at Long Beach	61
95	Creighton at Long Beach	79
95	Yale	65
98	Michigan	80
83	Illinois	79
88	at Washington State	83
121	at Washington State	77
79	USC	59
78	USC	71
84	Stanford	71
80	Stanford at Santa Monica	61
107	at UCSB	76
87	UCSB at Santa Monica	59
87	at California	67
58	at California	56
73	Washington	58
88	Washington	66
100	at Stanford	88
78	at Washington	64
93	Washington State	56
87	California	57
91	USC	81

TOURNEY

95	Seattle at Corvallis	90
76	USF at Corvallis	72
90	Kansas State at Kansas City	84
98	Duke at Kansas City	83

TITLE GAME

DUKE

	FG-A	FT-A	R	P	T
Ferguson	2-6	0-1	1	3	4
Buckley	5-8	8-12	9	4	18
Tison	3-8	1-1	1	2	7
Harrison	1-1	0-0	1	2	2
Mullins	9-21	4-4	4	5	22
Marin	8-16	0-1	10	3	16
Vacendak	2-7	3-3	6	4	7
Herbster	1-4	0-2	0	0	2
Kitching	1-1	0-0	1	0	2
Mann	0-0	3-4	2	1	3
Harscher	0-0	0-0	0	0	0
Cox	0-0	0-0	0	0	0
Team			9		
Totals	32-72	19-28	44	24	83

Shooting: Field Goals, 44.4%
Free Throws, 67.9%

UCLA

	FG-A	FT-A	R	P	T
Erickson	2-7	4-4	5	5	8
Hirsch	5-9	3-5	6	3	13
Slaughter	0-1	0-0	1	0	0
Hazzard	4-10	3-5	3	5	11
Goodrich	9-18	9-9	3	1	27
McIntosh	4-9	0-0	11	2	8
Washington	11-16	4-4	12	4	26
Darrow	0-1	3-4	1	2	3
Stewart	0-1	0-0	0	1	0
Huggins	0-1	0-1	1	2	0
Hoffman	1-2	0-0	1	0	2
Levin	0-1	0-0	0	0	0
Team			8		
Totals	36-76	26-32	51	25	98

Shooting: Field Goals, 47.4%;
Free Throws, 81.3%

SCORE BY HALVES

Duke	38	45—83
UCLA	50	48—98

Attendance: 10,864. Date: 3/21/64.
Site: Municipal Aud., Kansas City, Mo.

277

1964-65

Won—28, Lost—2
Conference: 14-0

* * * *

LETTERMEN: Brice Chambers, Keith Erickson,
Gail Goodrich, Fred Goss, Vaughn Hoffman,
Edgar Lacey, Richard Levin, Mike Lynn, Doug
McIntosh, Kenny Washington
Captains: Gail Goodrich
        Keith Erickson
Assistant Coach: Jerry Norman
Frosh Coach: John Kalin

GAME BY GAME

83	at Illinois	110
112	at Indiana State	76
107	Arizona State	76
61	Marquette at Milwaukee	52
115	Boston College at Milwaukee	93
84	USC	75
99	Arizona	79
93	Minnesota	77
104	Utah	74
91	at Oregon	74
83	at Oregon State	53
76	California	54
80	Stanford	66
82	**Iowa at Chicago**	**87**
85	Loyola at Chicago	72
93	Washington State	41
78	Washington	75
83	at Washington	73
70	at Washington State	68
73	Oregon State	55
74	Oregon	64
83	at Stanford	67
83	at California	68
77	USC	71
52	USC	50

TOURNEY

100	BYU at Provo	76
101	USF at Provo	93
108	Wichita St. at Portland	89
91	Michigan at Portland	80

TITLE GAME

MICHIGAN

	FG-A	FT-A	R	P	T
Darden	8-10	1-1	4	5	17
Pomey	2-5	0-0	2	0	4
Buntin	6-14	2-4	6	5	14
Russell	10-16	8-9	5	1	28
Tregoning	2-7	1-1	5	5	5
Myers	0-4	0-0	3	2	0
Brown	0-0	0-0	0	0	0
Ludwig	1-2	0-0	0	0	2
Thompson	0-0	0-0	0	0	0
Clawson	3-4	0-0	0	2	6
Dill	1-2	2-2	1	1	4
Team			7		
Totals	33-64	14-17	33	24	80

Shooting: Field Goals, 51.6%;
    Free Throws, 82.4%

UCLA

	FG-A	FT-A	R	P	T
Erickson	1-1	1-2	1	1	3
Lacey	5-7	1-2	7	3	11
McIntosh	1-2	1-2	0	2	3
Goodrich	12-22	18-20	4	4	42
Goss	4-12	0-0	3	1	8
Washington	7-9	3-4	5	2	17
Lynn	2-3	1-2	6	1	5
Lyons	0-0	0-0	0	1	0
Galbraith	0-0	0-0	0	0	0
Hoffman	1-1	0-0	1	0	2
Levin	0-1	0-0	1	0	0
Chambers	0-0	0-1	0	0	0
Team			6		
Totals	33-58	25-33	34	15	91

Shooting: Field Goals, 56.9%;
    Free Throws, 75.8%

SCORE BY HALVES

Michigan		34	46—80
UCLA		47	44—91

Attendance: 13,204. Date: 3/20/65.
Site: Memorial Coliseum, Portland, Ore.

1965-66

Won—18, Lost—8
Conference: 10-4
* * * *

LETTERMEN: Brice Chambers, Joe Chrisman,
Fred Goss, Vaughn Hoffman, Randy Judd, Ed-
gar Lacey, Mike Lynn, Doug McIntosh, Don
Saffer, Mike Warren, Kenny Washington
Captain: Fred Goss
Assistant Coach: Jerry Norman
Frosh Coach: Gary Cunningham

GAME BY GAME

92	Ohio State	66
97	Illinois	79
66	**Duke at Durham.....................**	**82**
75	**Duke at Charlotte....................**	**94**
78	Kansas	71
76	**Cincinnati at Sports Arena ....**	**82**
86	USC at Sports Arena................	67
95	LSU at Sports Arena................	89
82	Purdue at Sports Arena	70
94	USC at Sports Arena................	76
79	Oregon State.......................	35
97	Oregon............................	65
75	at California........................	66
69	**at Stanford.........................**	**74**
96	**Loyola at Chicago ....**	**102**
84	Arizona............................	67
83	**at Washington State ....**	**84**
89	at Washington......................	67
88	Washington State...................	61
100	Washington.........................	71
51	**at Oregon State ....**	**64**
72	**at Oregon..........................**	**79**
95	California..........................	79
70	Stanford...........................	58
94	USC...............................	79
99	USC at Sports Arena................	62

(NO TITLE GAME)

1966-67

Won—30, Lost—0
Conference: 14-0
* * * *
LETTERMEN: Lew Alcindor, Lucius Allen, Joe
Chrisman, Ken Heitz, Jim Nielsen, Dick Lynn,
Don Saffer, Neville Saner, Lynn Shackelford,
Gene Sutherland, Bill Sweek, Mike Warren

Captain: Mike Warren
Assistant Coach: Jerry Norman
Frosh Coach: Gary Cunningham

GAME BY GAME

105	USC...............................	90
88	Duke	54
107	Duke	87
84	Colorado State	74
96	Notre Dame	67
100	Wisconsin	56
91	Georgia Tech	72
107	USC...............................	83
76	at Washington State................	67
83	at Washington......................	68
96	California	78
116	Stanford	78
122	Portland	57
119	UCSB	75
82	Loyola at Chicago	67

120	Illinois at Chicago..................	82
40	USC at Sports Arena................	35
76	Oregon State.......................	44
100	Oregon............................	66
34	at Oregon..........................	25
72	at Oregon State	50
71	Washington........................	43
100	Washington State	78
75	at Stanford........................	47
103	at California	66
83	USC...............................	55

TOURNEY

109	Wyoming at Corvallis	60
80	UOP at Corvallis....................	64
73	Houston at Louisville................	58
79	Dayton at Louisville.................	64

TITLE GAME

DAYTON

	FG-A	FT-A	R	P	T
May..............	9-23	3-4	17	4	21
Sadlier...........	2-5	1-2	7	5	5
Obrovac.........	0-2	0-0	2	1	0
Klaus	4-7	0-0	0	1	8
Hooper...........	2-7	2-4	5	2	6
Torain	3-14	0-0	4	3	6
Waterman	4-11	2-3	1	3	10
Sharpenter	2-5	4-5	5	1	8
Samanich	0-2	0-0	2	0	0
Heckman.........	0-0	0-0	0	0	0
Inderrieden.......	0-0	0-0	0	0	0
Wannemacher	0-0	0-0	0	0	0
Team			8		
Totals...........	26-76	12-18	51	20	64

Shooting: Field Goals, 34.2%;
Free Throws, 66.7%

UCLA

	FG-A	FT-A	R	P	T
Heitz.............	2-7	0-0	6	2	4
Shackelford	5-10	0-2	3	1	10
Alcindor.........	8-12	4-11	18	0	20
Allen.............	7-15	5-8	9	2	19
Warren..........	8-16	1-1	7	1	17
Nielsen..........	0-1	0-1	1	3	0
Sweek	1-1	0-0	0	1	2
Saffer............	2-5	0-0	0	1	4
Saner...........	1-1	0-0	2	2	2
Chrisman........	0-0	1-2	1	2	1
Sutherland	0-0	0-0	0	0	0
Lynn............	0-1	0-0	0	0	0
Team			7		
Totals...........	34-69	11-25	54	15	79

Shooting: Field Goals, 49.3%;
Free Throws, 44.0%
SCORE BY HALVES
Dayton........................... 20 44—64
UCLA .... 38 41—79
Attendance: 18,892. Date: 3/25/67.
Site: Freedom Hall, Louisville, Ky.

1967-68

Won—29, Lost—1
Conference: 14-0
* * * *

LETTERMEN: Lew Alcindor, Lucius Allen, Ken Heitz, Mike Lynn, Jim Nielsen, Neville Saner, Lynn Shackelford, Gene Sutherland, Bill Sweek, Mike Warren

Captain: Mike Warren
Assistant Coach: Jerry Norman
Frosh Coach: Gary Cunningham

GAME BY GAME

73	at Purdue	71
120	Wichita State	86
109	Bradley	73
114	Notre Dame	63
95	Minnesota at Sports Arena	55
121	Iowa State	80
108	St. Louis at Sports Arena	67
104	Wyoming at Sports Arena	71
97	Washington State	69
93	Washington	65
94	at California	64
75	at Stanford	63
93	Portland	69
69	**Houston at Astrodome**	**71**
90	Holy Cross at New York	67
84	Boston College at New York	77
101	USC	67
55	at Oregon State	52
104	at Oregon	63
119	Oregon	78
88	Oregon State	71
84	at Washington	64
101	at Washington State	70
100	Stanford	62
115	California	71
72	USC at Sports Arena	64

TOURNEY

58	New Mexico State at Albuquerque	49
87	Santa Clara at Albuquerque	66
101	Houston at Sports Arena	69
78	No. Carolina at Sports Arena	55

TITLE GAME

NORTH CAROLINA

	FG-A	FT-A	R	P	T
Miller	5-13	4-6	6	3	14
Bunting	1-3	1-2	2	5	3
Clark	4-12	1-3	8	3	9
Scott	6-17	0-1	3	3	12
Grubar	2-5	1-2	0	2	5
Fogler	1-4	2-2	0	0	4
Brown	2-5	2-2	5	1	6
Tuttle	0-0	0-0	0	0	0
Frye	1-2	0-1	1	0	2
Whitehead	0-0	0-0	0	0	0
Delany	0-1	0-0	0	0	0
Fletcher	0-1	0-0	0	0	0
Team			10		
Totals	22-63	11-19	35	17	55

Shooting: Field Goals, 34.9%;
Free Throws, 57.9%

UCLA

	FG-A	FT-A	R	P	T
Shackelford	3-5	0-1	2	0	6
Lynn	1-7	5-7	6	3	7
Alcindor	15-21	4-4	16	3	34
Warren	3-7	1-1	3	2	7
Allen	3-7	5-7	5	0	11
Nielsen	1-1	0-0	1	1	2
Heitz	3-6	1-1	2	3	7
Sutherland	1-2	0-0	2	1	2
Sweek	0-1	0-0	0	1	0
Saner	1-3	0-0	2	2	2
Team			9		
Totals	31-60	16-21	48	16	78

Shooting: Field Goals, 51.7%;
Free Throws, 76.2%

SCORE BY HALVES
North Carolina .... 22 33—55
UCLA .... 32 46—78
Attendance: 14,438. Date: 3/23/68.
Site: Sports Arena, Los Angeles.

1968-69

Won—29, Lost—1
Conference: 13-1
* * * *

LETTERMEN: Lew Alcindor, John Ecker, Ken Heitz, Steve Patterson, Curtis Rowe, Bill Seibert, Terry Schofield, Lynn Shackelford, Bill Sweek, John Vallely, Sidney Wicks

Captains: Lew Alcindor
Lynn Shackelford
Assistant Coaches: Denny Crum
Gary Cunningham

GAME BY GAME

94	Purdue	82
84	at Ohio State	73
88	at Notre Dame	75
90	Minnesota	51
95	West Virginia	56
98	Providence at New York	81
83	Princeton at New York	67
74	St. John's at New York	56
96	Tulane	64
93	at Oregon	64
83	at Oregon State	64
100	Houston	64
81	Northwestern at Chicago	67
84	Loyola at Chicago	64
109	California	74
98	Stanford	61
62	Washington	51
108	Washington State	80
83	at Washington State	59
53	at Washington	44
91	Oregon State	66
103	Oregon	69
81	at Stanford	60
84	at California	77
61	USC at Sports Arena	55
44	**USC**	**46**

TOURNEY

53	New Mexico at UCLA	38
90	Santa Clara at UCLA	52
85	Drake at Louisville	82
92	Purdue at Louisville	72

TITLE GAME

PURDUE

	FG-A	FT-A	R	P	T
Gilliam	2-14	3-3	11	2	7
Faerber	1-2	0-0	3	5	2
Johnson	4-9	3-4	9	2	11
Mount	12-36	4-5	1	3	28
Keller	4-17	3-4	4	5	11
Kaufman	0-0	2-2	5	5	2
Bedford	3-8	1-3	8	3	7
Weatherford	1-5	2-2	1	3	4
Reasoner	0-1	0-1	1	2	0
Taylor	0-0	0-0	0	0	0
Team			5		
Totals	27-92	18-24	48	30	72

Shooting: Field Goals, 29.3%;
Free Throws, 75.0%

UCLA

	FG-A	FT-A	R	P	T
Shackelford	3-8	5-8	9	3	11
Rowe	4-10	4-4	12	2	12
Alcindor	15-20	7-9	20	2	37
Heitz	0-3	0-1	3	4	0
Vallely	4-9	7-10	4	3	15
Sweek	3-3	0-1	1	3	6
Wicks	0-1	3-6	4	1	3
Schofield	1-2	0-0	0	0	2
Patterson	1-1	2-2	2	0	4
Seibert	0-0	0-0	1	0	0
Farmer	0-0	0-0	0	1	0
Ecker	1-1	0-0	0	0	2
Team			5		
Totals	32-58	28-41	61	19	92

Shooting: Field Goals, 55.2%;
Free Throws, 68.3%

SCORE BY HALVES

Purdue	31	41—72
UCLA	42	50—92

Attendance: 18, 669. Date 3/22/69.
Site: Freedom Hall, Louisville, Ky.

1969-70

Won—28, Lost—2
Conference: 12-2

* * * *

LETTERMEN: Rick Betchley, Henry Bibby, Kenny Booker, Jon Chapman, John Ecker, Andy Hill, Steve Patterson, Curtis Rowe, Terry Schofield, Bill Seibert, John Vallely, Sidney Wicks.

* * * *

Captain: John Vallely
Head Manager: George Morgan
Assistant Coaches: Denny Crum
Gary Cunningham

GAME BY GAME

90	Arizona	65
72	at Minnesota	71
127	Miami	69
133	LSU	84
99	Texas	54
121	Georgia Tech	90
76	Princeton	75
108	Notre Dame	77
75	Oregon	58
72	Oregon State	71
61	Bradley at Chicago	58
94	Loyola at Chicago	72
89	UCSB	80
115	Wyoming	77
87	at California	72

102	at Stanford............................ 84
66	at Washington....................... 56
72	at Washington State 70
95	Washington State.................... 61
101	Washington.......................... 85
71	at Oregon State 56
65	**at Oregon............................ 78**
120	Stanford 90
109	California 95
86	**USC................................. 87**
91	USC at Sports Arena................ 78

TOURNEY

88	CSLB at Seattle 65
101	Utah State at Seattle................ 79
93	New Mexico St. at Col. Pk 77
80	Jacksonville at College Park................................. 69

TITLE GAME

JACKSONVILLE

	FG-A	FT-A	R	P	T
Wedeking	6-11	0-0	2	2	12
Blevins...........	1-2	1-2	0	1	3
Morgan...........	5-11	0-0	4	5	10
Burrows..........	6-9	0-0	6	1	12
Gilmore	9-29	1-1	16	5	19
Nelson	3-9	2-2	5	1	8
Dublin	0-5	2-2	1	4	2
Baldwin	0-0	0-0	0	0	0
McIntyre	1-3	0-0	3	4	2
Hawkins..........	0-1	1-1	1	1	1
Selke	0-0	0-0	0	0	0
Team			2		
Totals............	31-81	7-8	40	24	69

Shooting: Field Goals, 37.8%;
Free Throws, 87.5%

UCLA

	FG-A	FT-A	R	P	T
Rowe	7-15	5-5	8	4	19
Wicks............	5-9	7-10	18	3	17
Patterson.........	8-15	1-4	11	1	17
Valleiy	5-10	5-7	7	2	15
Bibby	2-11	4-4	4	1	8
Booker...........	0-0	2-3	0	0	2
Seibert...........	0-1	0-0	1	1	0
Ecker	1-1	0-0	0	0	2
Betchley	0-0	0-0	0	0	0
Chapman.........	0-1	0-0	1	0	0
Hill...............	0-0	0-1	0	0	0
Schofield.........	0-0	0-0	0	0	0
Team			3		
Totals............	28-63	24-35	53	12	80

Shooting: Field Goals, 44.4%;
Free Throws, 68.6%

SCORE BY HALVES

Jacksonville	36	33—69
UCLA	41	39—80

Attendance: 14,380. Date: 3/21/70.
Site: Cᵒle Field House, College Park, Md.

1970-71

Won—29, Lost—1
Conference: 14-0
* * * *

LETTERMEN: Rick Betchley, Henry Bibby, Kenny Booker, Jon Chapman, John Ecker, Larry Farmer, Andy Hill, Larry Hollyfield, Steve Patterson, Curtis Rowe, Terry Schofield, Sidney Wicks.

Captains: Curtis Rowe
Sidney Wicks
Assistant Coaches: Denny Crum
Gary Cunningham

GAME BY GAME

108	Baylor.............................	77
124	Rice...............................	78
100	Pacific.............................	88
95	Tulsa..............................	75
94	Missouri...........................	75
79	St. Louis...........................	65
90	William & Mary at Pitts..............	71
77	Pittsburgh at Pittsburgh	65
107	Dayton	82
78	Washington........................	69
95	Washington State....................	71
58	at Stanford.........................	53
94	California..........................	76
82	**at Notre Dame ....**	**89**
74	UC Santa Barbara	61
64	USC at Sports Arena................	60
69	at Oregon..........................	68
67	at Oregon State	65
94	Oregon State.......................	64
74	Oregon............................	67
57	at Washington State	53
71	at Washington......................	69
103	California..........................	69
107	Stanford...........................	72
73	USC...............................	62

TOURNEY

91	BYU at Utah........................	73
57	CSLB at Utah	55
68	Kansas at Houston	60
68	Villanova at Houston................	62

TITLE GAME

VILLANOVA

	FG-A	FT-A	R	P	T
Smith	4-11	1-1	2	4	9
Porter	10-21	5-6	8	1	25
Siemiont-kowski	9-16	1-2	6	3	19
Inglesby	3-9	1-1	4	2	7
Ford	0-4	2-3	5	4	2
McDowell	0-1	0-0	2	0	0
Fox	0-0	0-0	0	0	0
Team			4		
Totals	26-62	10-13	31	14	62

Shooting: Field Goals, 41.9%;
Free Throws, 76.9%

UCLA

	FG-A	FT-A	R	P	T
Rowe	2-3	4-5	8	0	8
Wicks	3-7	1-1	9	2	7
Patterson	13-18	3-5	8	1	29
Bibby	6-12	5-5	2	1	17
Booker	0-0	0-0	0	0	0
Schofield	3-9	0-0	1	4	6
Betchley	0-0	1-2	1	1	1
Team			5		
Totals	27-49	14-18	34	9	68

Shooting: Field Goals, 55.1%;
Free Throws, 77.8%

SCORE BY HALVES

Villanova	37	25—62
UCLA	45	23—68

Attendance: 31,765. Date: 3/27/71.
Site: Astrodome, Houston, Tex.

1971-72

Won—30, Lost—0
Conference: 14-0
* * * *

LETTERMEN: Henry Bibby, Vince Carson, Jon Chapman, Tommy Curtis, Larry Farmer, Gary Franklin, Andy Hill, Larry Hollyfield, Greg Lee, Swen Nater, Bill Walton, Keith Wilkes.

Captain: Henry Bibby
Assistant Coaches: Gary Cunningham
Frank Arnold

GAME BY GAME

105	The Citadel	49
106	Iowa	72
110	Iowa State	81
117	Texas A&M	53
114	Notre Dame	56
119	TCU	81
115	Texas	65

79	Ohio State	53
78	at Oregon State	72
93	at Oregon	68
118	Stanford	79
82	California	43
92	Santa Clara	57
108	Denver	61
92	Loyola at Chicago	64
57	at Notre Dame	32
81	USC	56
89	Washington State	58
109	Washington	70
100	at Washington	83
85	at Washington State	55
92	Oregon	70
91	Oregon State	72
85	at California	71
102	at Stanford	73
79	USC at Sports Arena	66

TOURNEY

90	Weber State at Provo	58
73	CSLB at Provo	57
96	Louisville at Sports Arena	77
81	Florida St. at Sports Arena	76

TITLE GAME

FLORIDA STATE

	FG-A	FT-A	R	P	T
Garrett	1-9	1-1	5	1	3
King	12-20	3-3	6	1	27
Royals	5-7	5-6	10	5	15
McCray	3-6	2-5	6	4	8
Samuel	3-10	0-0	1	1	6
Harris	7-13	2-3	6	1	16
Petty	0-0	1-1	0	1	1
Cole	0-2	0-0	2	1	0
Team			6		
Totals	31-67	14-19	42	15	76

Shooting: Field Goals, 46.3%;
Free Throws, 73.7%

UCLA

	FG-A	FT-A	R	P	T
Wilkes	11-16	1-2	10	4	23
Farmer	2-6	0-0	6	2	4
Walton	9-17	6-11	20	4	24
Lee	0-0	0-0	2	0	0
Bibby	8-17	2-3	3	2	18
Curtis	4-14	0-1	4	1	8
Hollyfield	1-6	0-0	2	2	2
Nater	1-2	0-1	1	0	2
Team			2		
Totals	36-78	9-18	50	15	81

Shooting: Field Goals, 46.2%;
Free Throws, 50.0%

SCORE BY HALVES

Florida State	39	37—76
UCLA	50	31—81

Attendance: 15,063. Date: 3/25/72.
Site: Sports Arena, Los Angeles

1972-73

Won—30, Lost—0
Conference: 14—0
* * * *

LETTERMEN: Vince Carson, Tommy Curtis,
Mike Farmer, Larry Hollyfield, Greg Lee, Dave
Meyers, Swen Nater, Pete Trgovich, Bill Walton,
Bob Webb, Keith Wilkes.

Captain: Larry Farmer
Assistant Coaches: Gary Cunningham
Frank Arnold

GAME BY GAME

94 Wisconsin	53
73 Bardley	38
81 Pacific	48
98 UC Santa Barbara	67
89 Pittsburgh	73
82 Notre Dame	56
85 Drake at New Orleans	72
71 Illinois at New New Orleans	64
64 Oregon	38
87 Oregon State	61
82 at Stanford	67
69 at California	50
92 USF	64
101 Providence	77
87 Loyola at Chicago	73
82 at Notre Dame	63
79 at USC	56
88 at Washington State	50
76 at Washington	67
93 Washington	62
96 Washington State	64
72 at Oregon	61
73 at Oregon State	67
90 California	65
51 Stanford	45
76 USC	56

TOURNEY

98 Arizona State at Pauley Pavilion	81
54 USF at Pauley Pavilion	39
70 Indiana at St. Louis	59
87 Memphis State at St. Louis	66

TITLE GAME

UCLA

	FG-A	FT-A	R	P	T
Wilkes	8-14	0-0	7	2	16
Farmer	1-4	0-0	2	2	2
Walton	21-22	2-5	13	4	44
Lee	1-1	3-3	3	2	5
Hollyfield	4-7	0-0	3	4	8
Curtis	1-4	2-2	3	1	4
Meyers	2-7	0-0	3	1	4
Nater	1-1	0-0	3	2	2
Franklin	1-2	0-1	1	0	2
Carson	0-0	0-0	0	0	0
Webb	0-0	0-0	0	0	0
Team			2		
Totals	40-62	7-11	40	18	87

Shooting: Field Goals, 64.5%;
Free Throws, 63.6%

MEMPHIS STATE

	FG-A	FT-A	R	P	T
Buford	3-7	1-2	3	1	7
Kenon	8-16	4-4	8	3	20
Robinson	3-6	0-1	7	4	6
Laurie	0-1	0-0	0	0	0
Finch	9-21	11-13	1	2	29
Westfall	0-1	0-0	0	5	0
Cook	1-4	2-2	0	1	4
M'Kinney	0-0	0-0	0	0	0
Jones	0-0	0-0	0	0	0
Tetzlaff	0-0	0-2	0	1	0
Liss	0-1	0-0	0	0	0
Andres	0-0	0-0	0	0	0
Team			24-57	18-24	21	17	66

Shooting: Field Goals, 42.1%;
Free Throws, 66.7%

SCORE BY HALVES
UCLA .... 39 48—87
Memphis State .... 39 27—66
Attendance: 19,301. Date: 3/26/73
Site: St. Louis Arena, St. Louis

60th STRAIGHT

LOYOLA

	FG-A	FT-A	R	P	T
Lewis	1-9	3-4	1	4	5
Haurs	5-15	3-4	7	0	13
Cohen	5-12	0-2	5	4	10
Willey	7-14	0-0	4	5	14
Sanders	12-24	0-0	1	2	24
Compobasso	2-3	3-4	3	1	7
Hayden	0-3	0-0	2	2	0
Walker	0-1	0-0	1	0	0
Totals	32-81	9-14	14	34	18

Shooting: Field Goals, 39.5%;
Free Throws, 64.2%

UCLA

	FG-A	FT-A	R	P	T
Wilkes	8-16	0-0	15	3	16
Farmer	3-10	0-0	3	3	6
Walton	14-19	4-6	27	3	32
Lee	3-5	3-6	1	1	9
Hollyfield	5-7	4-6	4	2	14
Trgovich	1-2	0-0	0	0	2
Meyers	3-6	7-2	1	3	8
Carson	0-0	0-0	1	1	0
Nater	0-0	0-0	1	0	0
Totals	37-65	13-70	53	16	87

Shooting: Field Goals, 56.9%;
  Free Throws, 65.0%

SCORE BY HALVES

Loyola	39	34—73
UCLA	47	40—87

Attendance: 15,827.

61st STRAIGHT

UCLA

	FG-A	FT-A	R	P	T
Wilkes	10-16	0-0	9	1	20
Farmer	8-19	0-1	7	0	16
Walton	8-12	0-0	15	2	16
Lee	2-7	3-3	1	0	7
Hollyfield	4-10	0-0	4	2	8
Trgovich	1-4	1-2	3	0	3
Meyers	3-3	0-0	3	2	6
Webb	0-1	0-0	0	0	0
Nater	1-3	0-0	3	0	2
Carson	1-1	0-0	0	1	2
Franklin	0-0	2-2	0	0	2
Team		6			
Totals	38-76	6-8	51	8	82

Shooting: Field Goals, 50.0%;
  Free Throws, 75.0%

NOTRE DAME

	FG-A	FT-A	R	P	T
Shumate	8-20	5-5	12	3	21
Novak	0-4	0-0	1	1	0
Crotty	3-6	1-4	5	1	7
Brokaw	8-18	0-0	6	3	16
Clay	5-17	0-0	3	2	10
Silinski	2-3	1-1	0	0	5
W. Townsend	1-2	0-0	1	1	2
Stevens	0-2	0-0	0	1	0
Hansen	0-0	0-0	0	1	0
M. Townsend	0-0	0-0	1	0	0
Wolbeck	1-3	0-0	2	0	2
Team			8		
Totals	28-75	7-10	39	13	63

Shooting: Field Goals, 37.3%;
  Free Throws, 70.0%

SCORE BY HALVES

UCLA	38	44—82
Notre Dame	25	38—63

Attendance: 11,343.

TOP PLAYERS

	Reb.	Avg.	Pts.	Avg.
1963-64				
Gail Goodrich	156	5.2	646	21.0
Walt Hazzard	142	4.7	548	18.6
Jack Hirsch	227	7.5	421	14.0
Keith Erickson	272	9.0	320	10.7
1964-65				
Gail Goodrich	158	5.2	744	24.8
Keith Erickson	255	8.7	373	12.9
Fred Goss	99	3.3	365	12.2
Edgar Lacey	305	10.1	347	11.6
1966-67				
Lew Alcindor	466	15.5	870	29.0
Lucius Allen	175	5.8	466	15.5
Mike Warren	134	4.4	382	12.7
Lynn Shackelford	177	5.8	341	11.4
1967-68				
Lew Alcindor	461	16.4	734	26.2
Lucius Allen	181	6.0	452	15.3
Mike Warren	111	3.7	362	12.1
Edgar Lacey	110	7.8	166	11.9
(14 games)				
Lynn Shackelford	151	5.0	320	10.7
Mike Lynn	156	5.2	310	10.3
1968-69				
Lew Alcindor	440	14.6	721	24.0
Curtis Rowe	237	7.9	387	12.9
John Vallely	91	3.0	309	11.0
1969-70				
Sidney Wicks	357	11.9	559	18.6
John Vallely	111	3.7	490	16.3
Henry Bibby	105	3.5	468	15.6
Curtis Rowe	260	8.6	459	15.3
Steve Patterson	300	10.0	375	12.5
1970-71				
Sidney Wicks	384	12.8	638	21.3
Curtis Rowe	299	9.9	525	17.5
Steve Patterson	294	9.8	389	12.9
Henry Bibby	105	3.5	355	11.8
1971-72				
Bill Walton	466	15.8	633	21.1
Henry Bibby	106	3.5	460	15.7
Keith Wilkes	245	8.1	406	13.5
Larry Farmer	164	5.4	321	10.7
Greg Lee	252	8.4	252	8.7

1972-73

Bill Walton	506	16.9	612	20.4
Keith Wilkes	220	7.3	443	14.8
Larry Farmer	150	5.0	367	12.2
L. Hollyfield	88	2.9	321	10.7
Tommy Curtis	41	1.7	154	6.4
Dave Meyers	82	2.9	138	4.9
Greg Lee	38	1.3	137	4.6

CAREER

Games	Reb.	Avg.	Pts.	Avg.	Team	Rec-ord
Lew Alcindor	88	1515	15.5	2325	26.4	88-2
Bill Walton	60	972	16.2	1245	20.7	60-0
Gail Goodrich	89	512	5.7	1691	19.0	78-11
Walt Hazzard	87	475	5.4	1401	16.1	69-19
Sidney Wicks	90	894	9.9	1423	15.8	76-4
Lucius Allen	60	356	5.9	918	15.3	59-1
Curtis Rowe	90	756	8.8	1371	15.2	76-4

NCAA CHAMPIONS

SEASON RECORDS

Year	Team	W.	L.	Pct.
1939	Oregon	29	5	.853
1940	Indiana	21	3	.875
1941	Wisconsin	20	3	.870
1942	Stanford	27	4	.871
1943	Wyomong	31	2	.939
1944	Utah	22	4	.846
1945	Oklahoma State	27	4	.871
1946	Oklahoma State	31	2	.939
1947	Holy Cross	27	3	.900
1948	Kentucky	36	3	.923
1949	Kentucky	32	2	.941
1950	CCNY	24	5	.828
1951	Kentucky	32	2	.941
1952	Kansas	26	2	.929
1953	Indiana	23	3	.885
1954	La Salle	26	4	.867
1955	San Francisco	28	1	.966
1956	San Francisco	29	0	1.000
1957	North Carolina	32	0	1.000
1958	Kentucky	23	6	.793
1959	California	25	4	.862
1960	Ohio State	25	3	.893
1961	Cincinnati	27	3	.900
1962	Cincinnati	29	2	.935
1963	Loyola (Ill.)	29	2	.935
1964	UCLA	30	0	1.000
1965	UCLA	28	2	.933
1966	Texas-El Paso	28	1	.966
1967	UCLA	30	0	1.000
1968	UCLA	29	1	.967
1969	UCLA	29	1	.967
1970	UCLA	28	2	.933
1971	UCLA	29	1	.967
1972	UCLA	30	0	1.000
1973	UCLA	30	0	1.000